Father Cutbert

The Mirror of Faith

Your likeness in it

Father Cutbert

The Mirror of Faith
Your likeness in it

ISBN/EAN: 9783742834270

Manufactured in Europe, USA, Canada, Australia, Japa

Cover: Foto ©ninafisch / pixelio.de

Manufactured and distributed by brebook publishing software (www.brebook.com)

Father Cutbert

The Mirror of Faith

THE MIRROR OF FAITH:

YOUR LIKENESS IN IT.

BY

FATHER CUTHBERT (HOOKER),
Passionist.

"Whosoever, therefore, shall humble himself as this little child, he is the greater in the kingdom of heaven."—MATT. xviii. 4.

"I, therefore, a prisoner in the Lord, beseech you that you walk worthy of the vocation in which you are called."—EPH. iv. 1.

D. LANE & SON, PRINTERS AND PUBLISHERS,
310, STRAND, W.C.
1875.

TO
JESUS CHRIST,
THE SON OF THE LIVING GOD MADE MAN,
AND TO
MARY, HIS IMMACULATE MOTHER,
The Mirror of Faith
IS HUMBLY DEDICATED,
HOPING
THAT HE WHO, TO RAISE UP OUR FALLEN NATURE,
BECAME
THE FIRST BORN AMONGST MANY BRETHREN,
AND
SHE, THE IMMACULATE SOURCE
FROM WHICH HE TOOK
THE FLESH AND BLOOD OF OUR RESTORATION,
MAY GIVE A UNITED BLESSING
TO THIS HUMBLE AND IMPERFECT ATTEMPT
TO BRING BEFORE
THE MINDS OF GOD'S CHILDREN
THE GLORIOUS DIGNITY OF THEIR RESTORED NATURE
IN A DEGRADED AND UNBELIEVING AGE.

Nihil Obstat.

EUGENIUS A ST. ANTONIO,
Pass. Prov.,
Censor Deputatus.

IMPRIMATUR.

✠ HENRICUS EDUARDUS,
Card. Archiep. Westmonast.

Die 8 Oct., 1875.

CONTENTS.

PART FIRST.
GOD MADE YOU.

	PAGE
STRANGE NEWS — OUR PRESENT PLATFORM (introductory)	1
1. What it comes to	1
2. The child's new power—its dangers—the key of knowledge	4
3. Holy Mother the Church and the new platform	6
4. "The Mirror of Faith"	9

CHAPTER I.—OUT OF NOTHING . . 10

    1. Almost a gloomy thought . . 10
    2. A pleasure to which it gives birth . 11
    3. Love and confidence more than filial 12
    4. The duties of a child . . . 13

CHAPTER II.—YOUR BODY . . . 13

    1. A caution to those who would learn 13
    2. Your body wonderful in its construction 14
    3. The most learned acknowledge they know little about it . . . 16

		PAGE
4.	He who made it tells us to leave the care of it to Him—natural guides	17
5.	Your body a sacred charge—your duties concerning it	19

Chapter III.—YOUR SENSES . . 19

1.	The anatomy of your senses not our present business	19
2.	How your senses serve you	20
3.	Likes and dislikes	20
4.	The sense of touch—pain a defender against harm	23
5.	Another providential arrangement	24
6.	Cleanliness is next to godliness	25

Chapter IV.—YOUR SENSES (contd.)—Sight and hearing . . 27

1.	Sight and hearing blessings not fully appreciated.	27
2.	Your sight gives knowledge to your soul	27
3.	Your hearing extends that knowledge—how far?	28
4.	The first fruits of these senses—what you must do with them	28
5.	Sight, hearing and the will—a word about the deaf and dumb	29
6.	The senses instruments of the soul	30
7.	The senses good servants, but bad masters—a little lecture	31

Chapter V.—GOD'S IMAGE AND LIKENESS 34

1.	Revelation and exact knowledge about the soul	34

		PAGE
2.	Those fall into absurdities who reject revelation . . .	35
3.	A second absurdity . . .	37
4.	The privilege faith gives you . .	38
5.	Faith—wisdom—and the Catechism	39
6.	The Catechism on our present subject—the end attained by philosophy without its trouble . .	39
7.	And what no human philosophy can tell, over and above . . .	41
8.	One answer in the Catechism contains more than we need at present	41
9.	We know more of what a spirit is not than what it is—why so? .	41
10.	Your soul is a spirit—a contrast, yet a likeness	42

CHAPTER VI.—GOD'S IMAGE AND LIKENESS (continued)— UNDERSTANDING AND WILL 43

1.	A spirit known by its powers—the understanding	43
2.	Various uses of your understanding —the superiority it imparts .	44
3.	Free will—does it make man like God?—a question . . .	45
4.	Why God gave you free will—God's will—your liberty and the end for which God gave it . .	46
5.	Something in which your will is still like to God . . .	48
6.	Lessons to be drawn from this .	49
7.	Summing up	50

	PAGE
CHAPTER VII.—GOD'S IMAGE AND LIKENESS (continued)—immortality	50
1. Immortality a free gift—the doctrine of preservation	50
2. Gives new features to your whole being	51
3. No picture a likeness without it—the saxon warrior's parable	52
4. The significance this gift gives to life—it makes time precious	53
5. The value of your actions for immortality is in proportion to the amount of love they contain	54
6. The effect of this gift on the joys and sorrows of life	55
7. It renders eternal all other gifts—it gives us God	55
8. It makes life the beginning of eternity	57
9. Your growing debt of gratitude	58
CHAPTER VIII.—YOURSELVES	59
1. "And he became a living soul"—God's description of man	59
2. The union of many separate things—nearly all soul	60
3. Mutual dependence between soul and body	60
4. A link between the soul and the visible world—mutual good offices	61
5. Sympathy between body and soul	61
6. Your will a power of the soul—an ascetical maxim explained	62
7. Summing up of our first part	63

8. Love—conformity to God's will—
our Blessed Lady your model
and teacher 64

PART SECOND.

WHAT SIN DID TO YOU.

CHAPTER I.—YOUR PROSPECTS . . 65

1. Life an accumulated joy—our conclusions so far from "The Mirror of Faith" 65
2. An impulse to be cherished . . 66
3. The effect of obeying this impulse 67
4. A game rendered earnest by opposition 68
5. A great mistake 69
6. An uncalled for proceeding—a storm that has come and gone—a warfare in which you have more strength with than against you 69

CHAPTER II.—THE STORM . . . 71

1. A sin and a mistake—the preliminary error of Lucifer . . 71
2. The first rebel and his followers . 72
3. St. Michael—true nobility—first act of humility . . . 74
4. The Christian's watchword . . 76
5. God determines to create man—an humble inquiry . . . 76
6. The devil meditates mischief . 77
7. How he goes about it—Eve's mistake 77

		PAGE
8.	A few lessons for us	78

Chapter III.—ITS EFFECTS . . 80

1.	An unenviable acquaintance	80
2.	A concert-room turned into a Bedlam—a double parable . .	80
3.	Man—what he was—and what he still may be—explanations .	81
4.	Our first parents' eyes opened to a great uproar	83
5.	How many make themselves subject to the same misery—second part of parable explained . .	84

Chapter IV.—THE SUN OF JUSTICE 85

1.	A picture of what happened to you	85
2.	A storm in the night—a bright morning—a gentle shower .	86
3.	God's compassion—the promise .	86
4.	The sun of justice—the traces of the storm—the way—the truth and the life	87

Chapter V.—HE IS WELL CARED WHOM GOD TAKES CARE OF 88

1.	A glance at our loss and gain .	88
2.	Man at best little able to take care of himself	89
3.	Sin's traces and the remedies .	89
4.	The refreshing shower—our position altered, hardly for the worse	90

Chapter VI.—THE BLINDED UNDERSTANDING AND FAITH 90

		PAGE
1.	A well proved fact—idolatry a creation of the passions	90
2.	A curious way of satisfying a desire to be like God	92
3.	More folly—manufactured gods— devilry and roguery	92
4.	A lesson paganism should teach	93
5.	We need not, however, go so far to learn it	93
6.	The worst form of blindness	94
7.	The flood-gates of extravagance opened	95
8.	Quarrelling Christianity	96
9.	A happy family	96
10.	Faith God's remedy for our blindness	98
11.	Jesus Christ points out the relation evidence bears to faith	100
12.	Why, in spite of evidence, men refuse to believe God's word	100
13.	A sense in which it is necessary to become as little children	101
14.	The spirit of childhood the spirit of faith	102
15.	Faith the safeguard and the guide	102
16.	The greatest of all certainties	103
17.	Practical remarks	103
18.	The blessings of a living faith	103

CHAPTER VII.—THE WEAK WILL AND THE GOSPEL . . . 104

1.	Twofold weakness of the will	104
2.	How the passions draw the will by blinding the understanding	105
3.	Two remedies for a double weakness	105
4.	Reason for describing absurdities	106

		PAGE
5.	Evils it is a misfortune to know much of	106
6.	The inaction of an engine without fire	106
7.	An opportunity worse than wasted	107
8.	A mistake with two bad effects	108
9.	An advice to the wise	109
10.	Innocence without love, a doomed beauty	110
11.	A reason for what we see	111
12.	Is the devil's a pleasant yoke?	111
13.	The remedy—Gospel influence	112
14.	Awe	112
15.	The first spark of love	113
16.	The first prayer	113
17.	The true love-story of redemption, etc.	113
18.	Something to be deplored	114
19.	Gospel warnings	114
20.	Gospel promises	116
21.	A Gospel reminder	116
22.	A guide for every circumstance in life	116
23.	The Gospel is yours—use it	117

CHAPTER VIII.—THE POWER THAT RULES THE STORM . 118

1.	Why absurdities must not be treated seriously	118
2.	Religions made by passion, *versus* common sense	118
3.	Calvinism — degradation—blasphemy—false humility and cant	119
4.	A new rendering of Scripture required	122
5.	Canting literature wide-spread	122

		PAGE
6.	Calvinism and the Church, contraries	123
7.	How the children of the Church become the slaves of passion	123
8.	About grace	124
9.	A conqueror or a slave—an important epoch	126
10.	A time to become strong or weak in	126
11.	The importance of the involved question, etc.	127
12.	Your case stated	127
13.	The start, half the battle, etc.	128
14.	Grace to be had for the asking—intercession	129
15.	Practical conclusions	130

CHAPTER IX.—YOUR LEADER IN SUFFERING AND DEATH . 130

1.	The best path through this vale of tears	130
2.	Subjection to God, the truest freedom	131
3.	A narrow path—a bridge over a precipice	131
4.	A rough place after all for enjoyment	132
5.	The ardour of childhood joined to the courage of a soldier	132
6.	What makes the world a vale of tears	132
7.	The image which banishes complaint	133
8.	The sufferings of God's children small compared with those of others	134

		PAGE
9.	Hardly sufficient to make you like Jesus Christ	134
10.	Sufferings rendered glorious	134
11.	Death sweet to those who have served God	134
12.	Sufferings almost a joy	135
13.	Your leader—His imitation	135
14.	What is your cross after all?—necessary self-denial	135

Chapter X.—DIVINE COMPASSION . . 136

1.	Feelings suggested by this subject—the inheritance of fallen man	136
2.	Compassion immediately succeeds the fall, etc.	137
3.	Jonas and Nineva—compassion and petulance	138
4.	Our inheritance—it has given faith to our blindness—the Gospel to our weakness—grace to the passions	139
5.	A stretch of divine compassion	140
6.	Danger of venial sin	140
7.	Conversion of the sinner — the Sacrament of compassion	141
8.	Small requirements for receiving God	141
9.	Patience—the holy sacrifice—refuge of sinners—saint's prayers—power of God's word, etc.	141
10.	The obvious effect of the study of divine compassion	141

PART THIRD.
REDEEMING LOVE.

	PAGE
CHAPTER I.—AT THE RIGHT HAND OF GOD	142
1. In what sense we understand redeeming love	142
2. A coincidence	143
3. The virtuous pride which comes from its contemplation — the second throne near Jesus	144
4. Jesus and Mary representatives of restored nature in heaven	145
5. The reason for bringing this prominently before you	145
6. No new theory	146
7. God's method of silencing the voice of man's degradation	147
8. Jesus sanctifies each stage of life	147
9. To be like Jesus no unattainable desire, etc.	148
10. A pride which truly humbles—its value	149
CHAPTER II.—THE ETERNAL FATHER'S GIFT	150
1. What simplicity really means	150
2. An unreasonable use of reason	150
3. Ground on which simplicity is wisdom	151
4. The eternal Father's gift	152
5. A childlike inquiry—wisdom and goodness	152

		PAGE
6.	Providence	153
7.	Justice and mercy reconciled by this gift	154
8.	The only place in which God's justice does not get its due . .	155
9.	Prayer for the conversion of sinners therefore acceptable . . .	156
10.	Practical lessons	156
11.	The love of the Giver measured by the greatness of His gift . .	157
12.	Conversion only the beginning of sanctification	158
13.	Forgetfulness of this turns the life of many upside down . .	159
14.	A Scripture parable . . .	160
15.	The sum of the effects of the eternal Father's gifts	162

CHAPTER III.—BOUGHT BY JESUS' BLOOD 163

1.	The language of faith . . .	163
2.	Its different effect on different people, etc.	163
3.	In what sense Jesus' blood bought you	164
4.	A subject, not for speculation, but for meditation	164
5.	Jesus accepts His office of Redeemer	165
6.	His eagerness to shed His blood for you	165
7.	Jesus gives, to purchase your love, what was not necessary to buy your redemption . . .	166
8.	The effects of this familiar truth .	167

CHAPTER IV.—YOUR ELDEST BROTHER 168

		PAGE
1.	A preliminary remark	168
2.	Adoption	168
3.	Your family likeness—St. Paul again	170
4.	Your acquired nobility—Christ's merits	171
5.	His kindness for you	171
6.	His compassion—His sufferings—His protection	172
7.	Practical conclusions	172
8.	A dangerous power—the effect it should have	173

CHAPTER V.—YOUR DIVINE GUEST . 174

1.	A necessary explanation	174
2.	An incontestable fact	174
3.	"The Mirror of Faith," a corrective	175
4.	More than a relationship—a power within	175
5.	St. Paul on this subject	176
6.	An important question, etc.	176
7.	The conditions of the Holy Ghost's indwelling	177
8.	How you should treat your Divine Guest	178
9.	A lamentable fact—who is to blame?	180
10.	Why I put the remedy in your own hands	181
11.	A Scripture symbol explained	182
12.	The necessity of listening to the voice of the Holy Ghost—inspirations, etc.	184
13.	Begin at the beginning—effects of this devotion	185

CHAPTER VI.—GOD'S FRIENDS . . . 186

1. "As familiar as household words" . . . 186
2. No matter of chance—cause and effect . . . 187
3. Catechism . . . 188
4. God's condescension . . . 188
5. How low God puts the requirements of this friendship, etc. . . . 190
6. The effect this knowledge should have . . . 191
7. Tepidity—a warning . . . 191
8. Indeliberate frailties not tepidity . 193
9. How indulgent God is to those who love Him . . . 194
10. The main object of God's friendship—perfection . . . 194
11. The method of its increase . . . 195
12. Correspondence with grace . . . 196
13. Why you should do your best . . . 196
14. Your teacher and helper . . . 197

CHAPTER VII.—YOUR DIVINE FOOD . 198

1. Reasons for my selection . . . 198
2. Why the Blessed Sacrament necessarily comes in here . . . 199
3. The Christian's sacrifice, companion and food—the sacrifice . . . 199
4. A truth which should make you anxious to hear Mass . . . 200
5. An apology . . . 201
6. The Christian's food—an argument against exaggeration . . . 202
7. A natural inference—a parable, etc. . . . 202
8. A pause to consider the holiness of your vocation . . . 204

		PAGE
9.	God's great condescension again—the parable of the marriage feast	205
10.	Why so many keep from this divine banquet	206
11.	The invitation of Jesus to His children	207

Chapter VIII. — HEAVENLY COMPANIONS 207

1.	An old adage reversed	207
2.	Familiarity between the saints and God's friends	208
3.	A household practice akin "to the language of faith"	208
4.	Doctrine of the communion of saints	208
5.	The Blessed Virgin—patron saints, etc.	209
6.	The power this heavenly society gives us	210
7.	Other effects — encouragement in good	210
8.	The memory of saints we have known and conversed with	211
9.	Your angel guardian—a tradition—his watchfulness	212
10.	His patient concern for your salvation	213
11.	A word about spiritualism	214
12.	In conclusion	215

Chapter IX.—THE HAPPY CHOICE . 215

1.	A Scriptural illustration of our course in this third part	215

		PAGE
2.	A course the more allowable by reason of infant Baptism	216
3.	A fact which makes early choice imperative	217
4.	A warning voice needed	217
5.	Children the best choosers—childhood the best time to make the choice	218
6.	The way of the commandments—the way of sin and self-will	218
7.	An universal intention — a road easily kept on, with much difficulty regained	218
8.	The real question—a choice you have no right to make	219
9.	How men come to choose the wrong road—the effect of ignorance	220
10.	Phantom giants in the way	220
11.	First and second giant	220
12.	The attack on the two giants	221
13.	The slaughter of the second giant—the death of the soul	222
14.	God's sacrament of compassion—an apparent difficulty becomes a proof	223
15.	Your case stated—the difference between the two roads	224
16.	The benefit of remembering these things	226
17.	A consideration more powerful than self-interest	226

PART FOURTH.
BAPTISM.

	PAGE
CHAPTER I.—COMING HOME TO OUR SUBJECT	227
1. An artist's lay figure, etc.	227
2. Assistance in an artist's task, etc.	227
3. A description of you worse than useless	228
4. Creation lost sight of in the blaze of redeeming love	229
5. Hence my course	230
6. In the second and third part the same	231
CHAPTER II.—THE AVERTED DOOM	232
1. Home from our rambles	232
2. An undecided question	232
3. The real question, etc.	233
4. What the doom might have been, and is not	233
5. A sad dilemma—on one side despair	234
6. On the other ignorance and false hope, etc.	235
7. An argument from what is which shows what might have been	235
8. A proof of what ignorance can do	236
9. A third source of evil averted	237
10. A double reason for speaking of the tyranny of passion	237
11. Something more important even than ignorance of evil	238

c

		PAGE
12.	The lesson of passion read aright	238
13.	What that lesson has always been	239
14.	An objection answered	240
15.	The averted doom again	242

Chapter III.—DIVINE HASTE . . 243

1.	Shadow throws out the beauty of our picture	243
2.	A sublime sacrament bestowed upon an unconscious infant	244
3.	Some of its accompanying graces	244
4.	God's reasons for this haste	245
5.	Lay Baptism	245
6.	Anxious provisions against dangers	246
7.	A prerogative of want of confidence	246

Chapter IV.—ON THE THRESHOLD OF THE CHURCH . . 247

1.	Ceremonies the groundwork of an instruction—sponsors, etc.	247
2.	The first question, etc.	249
3.	A common fallacy explained, etc.	249
4.	The second question, answer, etc.	252
5.	The first hint to the devil to be gone	252
6.	The sign of the cross on the forehead and breast	253
7.	A word about the sign of the cross	253
8.	The two following prayers explained, etc.	254
9.	The humiliation of the devil, etc.	256
10.	A prayer for the gift of knowledge, etc.	256

CONTENTS.

CHAPTER V.—WITHIN THE DOORS . 257

		PAGE
1.	A resumè—admission into the Church	257
2.	Baptism a contract—the invitation, and what it contains . .	258
3.	A relationship we have scarcely mentioned	259
4.	The profession of faith, etc. . .	260
5.	The obligation of faith incurred .	260
6.	The child's first prayer . . .	260
7.	Approaching the font—second exorcism	261
8.	The ceremony of the Gospel miracle, etc.	262
9.	The declaration of war, etc. . .	262
10.	The devil's agents more to be feared than the devil himself—in what sense the flesh is an enemy	263
11.	Distorted ideas—one-sided quotation of St. Paul . . .	263
12.	In what sense the flesh is renounced	264
13.	Where the real evil lies . . .	267
14.	How God's children rule themselves	268
15.	A few words of advice . . .	268
16.	About the affections . . .	269
17.	Something requiring caution . .	271
18.	A truly happy omen—why I give the world a chapter to itself .	271

CHAPTER VI.—GOD'S GREAT ENEMY 272

1.	The advantages of warfare . .	272
2.	An enemy more to be feared than war	273

		PAGE
3.	The world a moral pestilence, etc.	273
4.	Important question—Does the world exist?	275
5.	Jesus Christ and the world	275
6.	The world which God hates	276
7.	Condemnations from the Gospel	276
8.	From the epistles—St. Paul—St. James—St. John	277
9.	Symptoms the only proof of the existence of a pestilence—St. John's definition	278
10.	Impiety its first ingredient	281
11.	Impenitence a quality of the world	281
12.	Pride of life	282
13.	Concupiscence of the eyes—a self-seeking world	283
14.	A test of true unworldliness—vocations	284
15.	A smothered fire	286
16.	The enemy of "The Mirror of Faith"	286
17.	The only antidote	287

CHAPTER VII.—BAPTISM . . . 288

1.	New proofs of a sacred consecration	288
2.	Anointed with holy oil, etc.	288
3.	What the changing of the stole means	290
4.	Baptism a choice to be ratified	290
5.	The solemn sacramental act	290
6.	The Blessed Trinity and the baptized child—a family picture	291
7.	This picture not an imaginary one	292
8.	The Holy Ghost and the baptized child, etc.	293

		PAGE
9.	The anointing with chrism	294
10.	The two concluding ceremonies—the light and the white garment	294
11.	The pax	295

Chapter VIII.—YOUR FINISHED PICTURE 296

1.	Lights and shades	296
2.	Its component parts—creation	297
3.	Your body—its senses	297
4.	Your soul, its powers—immortality, etc.	298
5.	The shadow—lessons and conclusions	298
6.	Our tour into the promised land, etc.	299
7.	The averted doom—ceremonies—engagements—enemies—the great sacrament	300
8.	Two questions and their answers	301

Chapter IX.—GROWN-UP CHILDREN AND PARENTS . . . 303

1.	A providential arrangement	303
2.	A propensity with an object—a proposal	304
3.	Example of St. Paul—a chasm to be bridged over	304
4.	Objections answered	305
5.	A personal benefit to be derived from this proposal	306
6.	A word about the special subject chosen	307

		PAGE
7.	Address to parents—Blanche of Castile the type of a class—the peculiarities of the times, etc.	308

APPENDIX.

The ceremonies of Holy Baptism, according to the Roman Ritual   309

THE MIRROR OF FAITH.

PART FIRST.

GOD MADE YOU.

INTRODUCTORY.

Strange News.—Our Present Platform.

1. EDUCATION (in the only true sense of the word) having been abolished by law and by the magical power of an Act of Parliament, we have in fact arrived at this ridiculous position: Children must be their own schoolmasters and schoolmistresses! They cannot indeed exactly raise the joyful cry "Away with the cane, away with angry teachers, away with dry books," for the routine work of schools is not only more laborious than it was, but is even rendered compulsory; and every child must at any rate be taught to read! Yet are his would-be friends so anxious not to interfere with his liberty, that they will not even oblige him to believe in the God who made him; and, for fear they should do so, they reduce education to a mere reading lesson—instead of making it what it should be, guidance for the youthful mind and heart "in the way in which they should go."

Every one wishes to be happy, and it is probable that all would like to go to heaven. Suppose, then, the question asked of one of these kind friends—"How am I so to act as to obtain happiness and get to heaven?" What will be his reply? If he be logical, it will be something like this: "I am your friend, and love you so much that, rather than interfere with the liberty you have of making yourself miserable, even under a mistake, I will tell you nothing at all, not if by so doing I could prevent you from going to hell!"

But to give children the power of reading whatever they like, and to call that training, is so manifestly absurd, that even very young readers must perceive such a course to be ridiculous; and should they ask how those who pretend to wisdom can be so foolish, the answer is ready: Those who have brought things to this pass are, more through their misfortune than their fault, utterly ignorant of the way to true happiness and of the road to heaven; and they know it. Indeed it is perhaps better on the whole that they should not attempt to teach, because, not knowing the truth, their instructions could but lead their pupils astray. And if it should seem strange that the blind should have become so powerful as to have gained the victory over those who see, and have been able to neutralize all efforts to establish a scheme of sound education, let it be remembered that there is in this world a war continually going on between good and evil—darkness and light—and that, in this war, the devil, the enemy of mankind, uses man's forgetfulness and ignorance of the things of God as tools wherewith to do all the mischief he can. What he aims at, my young friends, is your destruction; but he is not likely to get his own way altogether, because your holy mother the Church stands by you firm as a rock, and declares that she will teach you the way to heaven, no matter what any Parliament or body of men may say. Unfortunately, however, she stands almost alone. It is true that there are some persons who pretend to have your interests at heart, and who talk loudly of their devotion to the cause of Christianity; yet when the time of trial comes they show what this devotion means by joining with those who, in order to insure your freedom, persist in turning Christianity out of the school! A strange idea! It sounds like blasphemy when put into words! Almighty God must stand outside the door during school hours whilst His children are being taught to read and write, lest they should, against their inclinations, be taught to know and to love Him! And men who believe themselves to be Christians advocate a system like this.

Thus it is that your Mother the Church is outnumbered in the battle, and has to take all she can get and make the best of it.

Ah! thank God, this is just her strong point. By making the most of what she can get she can overcome all her enemies. If they prevent her from educating her children as she likes—if they force her to teach them religion out of school hours—they are at least going to teach every child to read; and if, instead of educating the young, they give them the power of teaching themselves, they had better take care. We have heard of a master who has sent a child to cut a rod for its own back, but we never knew of one who gave his pupil the means of beating his teacher. Does the devil himself know the power which, by means of misguided men, he is handing over to the whole rising generation in having them taught to read? Why the power of self instruction is unlimited, as much so as is the number of books which the world contains.

2. What is this gift which children are to receive? Only a little key. But this key opens libraries, unlocks books without number, feeds curiosity, and provides without measure or stint for the attainment of knowledge. The possession of it is nothing less than the possession of power to turn your masters and mistresses out of school and to teach yourselves just what you may choose to learn. It is a grand gift, this little key; and, were everything that is written only true and good, those who bestow it upon you need not repent of having saved themselves the trouble of giving you instruction. But it is not so, and when they make readers of you they at once enable you to read all sorts of books—books full of lies—books full of poison—books full of both ingredients nicely blended together!

Never mind. There are plenty of good books also—books containing Divine Wisdom, as well as books of human science, written by those who, having themselves the faith, are competent to teach others. And there are also books of human science, in which the mistakes in the matter of religious truth can be easily seen and accounted for by young persons well grounded in the first teachings of the Catechism. But this key of the sciences has its dangers, and these may be fatal to you, if, being misguided in your choice of books, you should happen to swallow lies instead of truth—poison instead of bread—and plenty of nicely-flavoured poison is provided for you by the very persons who, after crying out to have you taught to read without being guided as to your choice of reading, employ more than one printing establishment in supplying you with such a selection of books as will so spoil your eyesight as to make you in a short time as blind to the truth as are the very writers themselves.

But, after all, dangerous as the art of reading may be, it cannot be much more dangerous than ignorance. Ignorance is an unmitigated evil, certain in its bad effects; whereas reading is at least as powerful for good as for evil; and if it be a key which opens to you the knowledge of a quantity of perhaps poisonous trash, no one can deny that it also opens to you immense treasures of knowledge of better things wherewith you can inform your minds. So that, by making you readers, a *certain* evil has been changed into a great good, but that good is attended with an unavoidable danger.

The question is, what is to be done with the danger?

It is useless to lament over the inevitable; lamentations will not prevent the imagination from being intoxicated by poisonous vapours or surfeited by trash. And if to waste time in lamentation be useless—to label printed matter, like bottles in a doctor's shop, would be impossible, on account of the great masses of it which are constantly issuing from the press; and, could we even do it, where would be the use unless at the same time we could endow our young people with judgment to discern truth from falsehood, wisdom from folly?

3. But since children are at any rate to be put in possession of the key of knowledge, we may at least write books which will enable them to see through the folly of the day which would otherwise do them harm. Out of anxiety lest Catholic youths and maidens should be taught to love their holy faith too well, blind men have conspired to exclude religion from the school, and yet would have every child taught to read. What, then, is the action of our holy mother the Church? Never in want of a resource, she accepts what she cannot prevent, and outside the school, where she need submit to no interference, she turns this power which has been given to her children into a coat of armour to preserve them from danger—or, to use another simile, into a pair of spectacles by the use of which they can discern truth from falsehood.

In other words, she says to them: "Since, in spite of all I could say to the contrary, your would-be friends have made you your own schoolmasters, I will not interfere with your supposed promotion; but, on the contrary, will give to it a real value by supplying you with works which, if you make them your own, will render you wise indeed, teaching you to recognize literary rubbish, and making your power of reading a real key of knowledge. Who knows, indeed, but that this strait into which necessity has driven me may not even, by the designs of Providence, be the means of showing how utterly ridiculous it is to try to separate religion from education, whilst at the same time it enables me to appeal to the good sense of those young persons with whose career, according to human judgment, I have no right to interfere."

May this little book, then, be one of those which shall do good service in our holy mother's cause. Pray, my dear young friends, that God may make it the means of reaping for Him a rich harvest of those hearts the possession of which He condescends so strongly to desire.

The malice of the devil, and the blindness of foolish men, do so much meddling in this lower world—they hinder, spoil and blunder to such an extent, making so much noise withal, that it might be thought that men as well as devils were the sworn enemies of God, so given up are they to mischief. Talk of the mischievousness of children, it is as nothing in comparison. If any one watches, however, the movements of these workers of evil, he will perceive that, although they have it in their power to destroy a great deal, they can build up nothing. And not only are they powerless save for destruction, but when they have done their worst Almighty God still rules the world just as He did before, by means far above the reach of their little storms. With education on their lips, they may do their best, my young friends, to forbid your being trained for another world, even at the risk of your growing up unfit to live in this; but God loves you, and in His love has clothed you with grace, beauty, and wisdom, which they cannot destroy, because they can neither see nor reach them. These persons may teach you to read, they may amuse you with stories, recreate you with fairy tales, and teach you to count the stars; they may exhaust their brains to interest you in a thousand ways, but they can compose nothing that will compete for beauty and interest with the true story of your Catholic Catechism, teeming as it is with the message of the love of God for you.

Let them search the universe for something worthy of admiration, and is not a baptized child, its own Christian self, an object of such ravishing beauty that the whole material universe is as nothing compared to one of Christ's little ones clothed in its baptismal robe? In the Catechism, by the light of faith, you can see yourselves clothed with all those beautiful things which the love of God has heaped upon you. Yes, in that light of faith, of which your mother the Church is the keeper, you are taught to see a great deal which eyes cannot reach, but which has as much to do with making you what you are, as that body and soul which form your personal identity and individuality, making you yourself and not another.

All your greatness springs from your baptism, yet we shall have to search heaven as well as earth, go where faith alone can penetrate, and far beyond all human science, to find out all the beautiful things which go to make up your wonderful selves. My intention is to make you familiar with your own beauty, by describing it. This familiarity will make you wise and choice in your reading. It will give you the habit of regarding yourselves as clothed in the robes which your Catechism tells you are yours. It will make you fear to contaminate them by that which may sully their whiteness, just as when you are clothed in a new and beautiful dress you are careful to avoid whatever may stain or soil it.

4. Taking the Catechism, then, as a text-book, there is room for a whole library of books, each contributing its quota towards describing in the light of faith that wonderful being, the Christian child. The whole of this description is like a vast field of beautiful flowers, wherein like butterflies we may disport ourselves in the sunshine of our Saviour's love, passing from flower to flower, examining the beauty of each, or rather, like bees, drawing from them the honey of the knowledge of our Christian dignity, and of the love of God who has made us what we are.

If you, my dear young friends, will take to such an occupation as this, there is little fear that you will spend much of your time in the perusal of worthless books, which, although possessed of a sort of false attraction, can in no wise approach in interest to that which your mother the Church provides. I have said enough to make you understand what I ask you to do, when I propose to you to join with me in looking into the mirror of faith in which, by the help of just three or four truths of the Catechism, we can examine together what constitutes the beauty and the blessedness of the baptized child.

CHAPTER I.

Out of Nothing.

1. As I sit down to pen this chapter, I hope with the special blessing of our Blessed Lady, I am struck with the thought of a wonderful event which happened on this very day, long before you and I came into existence.

On the 25th of March, more than eighteen hundred years ago, the great archangel, Gabriel, went on a message from God to a humble house in Nazareth, revealed to our Blessed Lady that the Son of the living God was about to become man according to His promise, and announcing to her the wonderful tidings that the Blessed Trinity had chosen her to be His mother, asks her consent. No sooner is this consent given than the event of which I speak takes place.

By the power of the Holy Ghost, a body of surpassing beauty is formed out of the most pure flesh and blood of this purest of creatures—for it, God creates the most perfect of souls; and, instead of this body and soul being a mere human child, they are taken and made His own by the Eternal Son of God, the second Person of the Most Holy Trinity, who, being from all Eternity God, becomes in time God-man—*Incarnate*—for the love of you and of me.

With the light of this mystery shining upon us we may begin to examine the beautiful things that are involved in the truth—God made us.

The kitten which plays with a cotton ball, and the lamb which gambols in the meadow, have each within them a conscious life, and by their playfulness show that they enjoy it. But they know not whence comes the life of which they are so full—they know not what is that sun which shines upon them and by its brightness gives them enjoyment—they know not the God who made them. They only feel the life within them, and the light and warmth which comfort them, and they rejoice in their way, as it were in thankfulness.

Before God made you, my dear young friends, you were less than these creatures; you were simply nothing. Not merely to be without the comprehension of what surrounds us, but to be actually unconscious of existence, is a state of things the very thought of which fills one with gloom.

2. But this feeling changes into intense pleasure when we reflect that we possess a being full of conscious life and happiness—not such a one as that of the playful kitten and the sporting lamb, but a being which contains within it the delight of understanding all that by which we are surrounded, and that we owe all these blessings to the good God who made us out of nothing. Yes, so great is the joy of owing everything to our Creator, that it changes a gloomy thought into a source of rejoicing.

There is a great deal in this; more, indeed, than is often thought upon. For if the relationship between parent and child is one of tender reciprocal love, because the child owes to a certain extent his existence to his parent, what more than filial love should we not feel towards God, knowing as we do that we owe to Him our creation out of nothing; and what joy cannot but be ours when we consider His more than parental love, whose power and goodness made us what we are and gave us all we have!

8. What results, then, from our creation out of nothing? Simply this: First, that as our whole being is a present from Almighty God, this gift from its very nature makes us the object of our Creator's tenderest love—a love of which that of a parent is but a shadow; whilst, on our part, our creation out of nothing should give us a love for Him, of which the love of a child for its mother is a mere picture, although one of touching beauty. This love which God has for us is called creative love.

Secondly, it follows naturally, from the feeling that God must regard with affection the being which comes from Him, that we should have a natural confidence in Him; filial confidence is a figure of this.

Yes, that feeling so often the refuge of a naughty child—that, in spite of its faults, there is still a soft place for it in its mother's heart, simply because she is its mother, so faith influences us as regards the great God as to soothe down that awe which might otherwise render us too fearful. Whence proceeds this feeling save from a voice within us which seems to whisper, "He made us after all"?

4. Thirdly, it follows, as another consequence of being created by God out of nothing, that it is our duty to love Him and obey Him as children.

Who, then, should chide the playfulness of childhood, which has for its source so many joys? Neither should the light-heartedness of youth be blamed, but rather cherished, seeing that the conscious possession of the love of a dear Father should indeed make His children happy. The confidence, my dear young friends, which you must feel in Him from whom your being comes is the very thing to make you happy. Rejoicing then in more than a Father's love, and filled to overflowing with filial confidence, offer your whole heart as a tribute to that dear good God who has so lovingly and wonderfully created you out of nothing.

CHAPTER II.

Your Body.

1. As I am writing for young persons, who, by the force of circumstances, are reduced to become their own teachers, I may as well impress upon you that it is necessary, if you wish to learn well, not only to keep always to your subject, but also only to look at so much of that subject as may concern the main object you have in view. Suppose, for example, that you go into a garden with the intention of spending an hour in admiring the flowers, but that immediately upon your entrance you see

a butterfly, and waste your whole time in trying to catch it, you will not have accomplished what you came for. Or, again, if you devote yourself entirely to one flower, you will miss all the rest.

This must be borne in mind during the wonderful study which now engages us, for the simple reason that each step will discover to us new beauties which will tempt us to stray from our purpose, and, if we go out of our way, we shall not make any solid advance. Your body alone would lead us into half a dozen different sciences, which would divert us from our main object—and that is, to know enough about the wonderful being which God has given you to make you prize the gift and take proper care of it.

2. In the first place, it will do you good to consider how marvellous is the construction of your body—so marvellous that the first thing to be done with it is to entrust the care of it to that dear good God who made it. Why is this necessary? Because He alone knows all about it.

From the very earliest times there have been men who have spent the greater part of their lives in studying the construction of the human body; nay, there have been those who have passed a long life in trying to find some one little thing about it. For instance, one man has taken the ear and another the eye for his life's study, while another has devoted himself to the intricacies of circulation of the blood. After all, to what do their united endeavours amount? What have they discovered? So very little, that it is still a subject of wonder

THE WONDERFUL CONSTRUCTION OF THE BODY. 15

where life comes from, and how it can possibly be kept together without something going wrong?

Take one example of this wonderful piece of mechanism. It has been discovered, after hundreds, I may as well say thousands, of years, during which man has dwelt upon the earth, that each throb of the heart sends his blood from the left side through various channels to every part of his body. The larger of these channels which go through the main parts, branch off into smaller ones, and these penetrate every extremity down to the very tips of the fingers. There are thousands of these little channels round the eye alone, which will give an idea of the smallness of many of them. These channels are called arteries. Through another set of corresponding channels just as small, called veins, the current starts back again, discharging itself into larger veins, and passing into what is called the right auricle, which is a kind of antechamber on the right side of the heart. From this the blood passes into a chamber below (the right ventricle), and is then driven by means of a special artery into the lungs, where it is purified. After this it is carried by a corresponding vein into another ante-chamber on the left side of the heart (the left auricle), from which it passes into another lower chamber (the left ventricle), where it is ready for another throb of the heart to send it forth to repeat its journey. By putting the hand on the heart this process can be felt, and it is because the beating of the heart is so distinctly felt on the left side that many persons suppose the heart itself to be there, whereas its position is almost a central one. If the wrist or ankle be taken hold of the stroke can be perceived there as it can also in other parts of the body, because the finger is placed upon an artery to which the pulsation is communicated. You may, perhaps, say to me that, after all, we do know a great deal about the human body, and may doubt my assertion that God alone can properly understand it! But have these men who have found out so much, discovered what sets this force-pump in motion, and what causes it to work with such untiring regularity? Not at all. After all their grand discoveries they have come to a stop, completely baffled by a mystery of the power of God.

This reminds me of the story of that learned man who, having devoted himself to the study of this very thing—the circulation of the blood—and examined with the greatest care the smallest artery and the minutest vein, became so terrified lest in moving he should break one of these fragile vessels, that he almost starved himself to death! Thus we see that the more carefully the construction of the human frame is studied, the more certain it becomes that only to the hands of Him who made it can we look for its preservation.

3. It is true that a very worthy class of men devote themselves to the study of these things, and they are right in so doing, because God has ordained that there should be physicians for the curing of the sick, although they often act without success, because, as the most learned of them will tell you,

science is very imperfect, and many are the mysteries which it has not fathomed. These doctors will tell you, too, that if you can do without them so much the better for you—that your Creator has, in fact, placed your best advisers within you. If a slight thing is the matter, these wise men will say: Let nature cure herself; let hunger be the doctor to tell you when to eat, and thirst the physician to prescribe drink, and so on.

4. Surely I have said enough to impress upon you that your body is a wonderful thing, and that your first duty in relation to it is to leave its preservation confidently in the hands of Him who made it. Indeed our dear good Lord Himself has insisted not only upon the duty of entrusting the care of it entirely to Him, but on the folly of being anxious about it. Listen to His words, for they are very beautiful:

"Therefore I say to you, be not solicitous for your life what you shall eat, nor for your body what you shall put on. Is not the life more than meat and the body more than the raiment?"

"Behold the birds of the air, for they neither sow, nor do they reap, nor gather into barns, and yet your heavenly Father feedeth them: Are not you of much more value than they?" (Matthew vi. 25, 26).

See how in these beautiful words He would point out to you that He who takes care of the sparrows, which He made without a rational soul, will take much more care of His dear children if they will but trust in Him. Again, in order to show the folly of supposing that we can preserve our bodies by our own care our Lord asks a curious question. He says: "Which of you, by taking thought, can add to your stature one cubit?" (Matt. vi. 27.) As if He would say: As you cannot add one inch to that body which I have given you, you should trust the care of it to me who made you as you are. You have seen that your body is very wonderfully framed, and that it contains many minute and delicate parts. That knowledge is not intended to create fear; you are not to be like the foolish man who was afraid to move lest he should burst an artery! No. But if from what you have seen of your own formation you learn to trust more implicitly in the loving God who made you, you have learned much, and yet there is more which it is quite as important that you should know.

The God who made you has placed within you, as I said before, various guides which tell you all that lies with yourselves with regard to the care of the body; and they are the very best guides because they were given to you by your Maker. Now if through self-will you disobey these advisers, you always do so at the risk of injuring yourselves. If gluttony lead you to indulge in over-eating, or the love of nice things induces you to take what is injurious, the fault will be avenged upon yourselves, and you should think not merely of this almost certain punishment, but should look upon your body as a sacred charge entrusted to you by Him who made it, and you should, with a holy fear of injuring His gift, beseech of your Father in heaven to keep it for you.

5. The fruit of what you have learned should be gratitude and confidence. Every day in your morning prayers you say: "Give us this day our daily bread." Let these words contain an act of thanksgiving and an act of confidence that He who has hitherto taken care of his gift will continue to do it. Let them contain also an act of obedience, by offering that gift to Him to obey Him for ever. To do this it needs but a thought, yet a thought which will render you very very dear to God, who loves gratitude, and who protects with an especial Providence those who do not forget this their bounden duty.

CHAPTER III.

Your Senses.

1. WE must now take a glance at a subject which is both curious and amusing: but in speaking of the senses I do not intend to say a word about their wonderful construction, any purpose which could be served by doing so has been carried out in my last lecture, and what I might say on the subject would trench upon sciences which are better studied by themselves. God has, however, supplied us with five senses—sight, hearing, touch, taste, and smell—and the mechanism of each of them is a philosophical wonder to be explained, and explained often very imperfectly by the science which undertakes its

elucidation. We will, however, leave that part of the subject alone for the present, and shall find plenty to amuse, instruct, and edify us in examining the senses, as gifts of God intended for our use and benefit, without entering at all into the mysteries of their formation.

2. Let us see, then, in the first place, how admirably we are served by our senses. Although we have not yet begun to treat of the soul, you know enough about it, my dear young friends, to understand all that I shall have to say about it upon this occasion. The five senses, then, are at the same time the servants of our bodies and of our souls, although properly speaking they belong to the body.

They do not, however, all serve the soul and body to the same degree; touch, taste, and smell serve the body a great deal, and the soul but little; while sight and hearing serve the soul very considerably, although they also serve the body. As a matter of course, then, sight and hearing are those senses which are of the greatest importance.

3. It is remarkable that persons who are, as is usually the case, in the enjoyment of all these five senses, should so little care to examine how beautifully they accomplish the purposes for which they were given, so as even to wonder why some things should be so agreeable while others only excite disgust. Suppose, for example, that you are taking a country walk, and drinking in with delight the morning air of spring, but that all at once you come upon an unsightly object in the shape of a

dead bird hanging from a tree where some farmer has placed it to frighten away its fellows! Time and a partial state of decay have rendered it offensive both to sight and smell, and you turn aside and hasten away, saying that it is a horrid thing. Does it not strike you that it is your wise Creator who has taught your sense of smell to love the morning air which is good for you, and has made both sight and smell shrink with disgust from an object which in fact taints the very air with poison from its state of decay. So you see that your senses like one thing and dislike another, in order that they may preserve your body, and because God has given them to you to be your servants.

In a little time, too, that cord will break, that unsightly object will fall to the ground, and industrious insects will drag that poor bird beneath the soil, where it will not only cease to be offensive, but will actually help to make the grass grow and the lovely wild flowers flourish.

Let us go a little more deeply into this subject. God has ordained that we should sustain our bodies by taking food, and it is wonderful to see that He has so ordained our senses as that what is good to eat is more or less agreeable to them all. For instance, a rosy-cheeked apple is nice and tempting to look at; the smell of it is also nice, and it is smooth to the touch. But take hold of one that is partially decayed, and its very touch is unpleasant, and it is extremely probable that you may drop it in disgust.

Now, although it does not always happen that what is good to eat is beautiful to the eye, yet such things are never repulsive. A bird that is flying about is certainly more beautiful than one which is roasted, nevertheless the latter is by no means unpleasant to look at, especially if set before us when we are hungry. So you see that relish or disgust are imparted to your senses to teach them what food is good and what is to be avoided.

We may notice here, too, how carefully Divine Providence has provided for your safety in the matter of choosing wholesome food. He has allowed one sense, namely, that of taste, to tell you when food is good and to guard you against what is bad and unwholesome; but He has also, in many instances, caused four out of the five to unite in causing aversion. And why? The reason is plain. As you have many kinds of good food to select from, it matters not much should you miss one or two of them, whereas it is of great importance that you should refuse everything that is unwholesome, because a very small quantity of such things may do you great harm, nay, may even go so far as to destroy life.

One word more upon this subject and I have done. There are certain drugs and medicines which, although very salutary, are so far from being pleasant that the very thought of them creates disgust. Why are these things, which must occasionally be taken, so bitter and disagreeable? This is only another instance of the wise ordering of Divine Providence. These things are only intended to be used in small quantities and seldom; therefore God has ordained that, when they are necessary, we should do violence to our feelings and swallow them by an effort. Who cannot see the wisdom of this?—for were the drugs in question pleasant there would be danger of their being consumed to excess, and, instead of being the restorers of health, they would thus be converted into poison.

4. We will now pass to the sense of touch, with which, as it were, the good God has armed every portion of our delicate sensitive bodies. Instructed by it, not only do we recoil from a pin prick, and start when we come in contact with a thorn; but we even feel an aversion for clothing which is rough and coarse, and pleasure in that which is soft and smooth. Let us examine the various ways in which the sense of touch is affected by the many external things which the circumstances of life, in this material and somewhat rough world, bring into contact with our bodies.

In the first place, the skin is averse to everything which of its own nature has a tendency to hurt it, such as a hair shirt, or even very coarse linen, because their use is productive of pain. But people endure this pain sometimes by way of penance for their sins. To what end in that case does this aversion serve? It is still useful, because, although the persons we speak of endure suffering for the sake of the soul, pain tells them when the substance rubs too hard; they flinch from it, become cautious in their movements, and this sensitiveness prevents the skin from being rubbed into a state of unhealthy inflammation by the coarse cloth or hair. Thus you see the pain caused by the friction of harsh materials against the skin gives warning against the more serious injuries which might occur, and the preference which the body has for anything smooth and soft makes us, as a rule, keep near it those things which suit it better.

Again, your sense of feeling gives you a strong objection to receive a blow from any flexible substance, especially if it be slender, a whip for instance, because you know that, however flexible, its slender nature and the way in which it is used render it dangerous. Neither do you like to be struck by anything hard, because you know the skin will be bruised or possibly more damage occasioned. Thus pain, a thing which none of us like, is converted into a positive blessing, because the dread of it guards us from injury.

5. I will mention another thing connected with the sense of touch, because it is both curious and useful. Although God has endowed you with this delicate sense, which preserves you in many ways from real danger, it is not to be expected that, living as you do in the midst of the hurry of this world of toil and bustle, you should always be able to avoid scratches, bruises and wounds. Now, nature has a wonderful way of preventing our body from retaining in it either a substance, by which it has been wounded, or any foreign matter that may happen to insinuate itself into our flesh. For instance, you get a thorn into your finger. It is very likely that you may

not *see* it, but it will not fail to make itself felt. It will occasion a smart, and so long as it is there you will have no rest. If you do not remove it, the place where it is buried will swell and fester, and in time will cause great pain, ending, in very extreme cases, even in death. Take out the thorn and the wound will heal. The same thing will occur if you allow dirt to get into a wound.

The thing seems very simple; you are aware of it; and you may possibly have experienced it many times without asking yourself why your Creator permitted you thus to suffer. Yet, when you reflect, you will easily see what a merciful provision it is against the admission into our flesh of what would poison the system and make havoc of that body, the wonderful construction of which I have endeavoured in some degree to explain to you.

You will easily admit, my dear young friends, that the desire for comfort is closely connected with the sense of feeling. I will therefore conclude this part of my subject, by speaking to you of something in which your natural tendency to seek comfort may be indulged with great benefit to your health—I mean the practice of cleanliness which is also demanded and enforced by another special provision which I shall point out to you.

It naturally happens during the course of our daily labour and recreation, that we continually come into contact with dust—the very smoke from our chimneys forming no small portion of the grimy matter which adheres to our hands, our faces and whatever portion of our bodies may be exposed to it. But God has ordained that the very exertion which brings you into contact with this dust, causes moisture to exude from the pores of the skin and to keep foreign matter outside of your skin. But what is the result? The perspiration, combined with the dust, makes you so uncomfortable that you are forced to wash in self defence, and thus to cleanse and cool and refresh your skin.

Are there not two or three very useful lessons in this chapter? Yes, my young friends, there are. In the first place, all I have said goes to prove the wisdom of that good God who made you, because it shows how He has provided that your senses should serve to guide your body to what is good, and to preserve it from harm even without your taking the trouble to think about it.

In the second place, there is a lesson in that natural dislike He has given you for what is unsound and corrupt, which tends to teach you that the farther you keep such things from you the better.

Lastly, by the way in which God has provided that you shall throw off all the exterior defilement engendered by contact with this dusty world, He teaches you to love cleanliness; and be assured that those who do not love it can hardly have the proper respect which the children of God ought to have for that material being which He has given them; whereas those who do love it for the sake of that dear good God whose beautiful present the body is, can hardly help loving that innocent purity of heart of which cleanliness is the image; and hence the truth of that old saying: "Cleanliness is next to godliness."

CHAPTER IV.

Your Senses continued—Sight and Hearing.

1. WE have only spoken hitherto of the senses so far as they serve to promote the welfare of the body, and, as a natural consequence, have said very little indeed about sight and hearing. There are so many things which might be said, and which it seems a pity to leave out if we enter upon the subject at all, that I am tempted to remain silent and to leave you to appreciate these senses only by their quiet enjoyment.

Perhaps, however, the better plan, in order to make you understand their full value, will be, avoiding carefully all that may lead me astray, to point out to you, 1st, How these senses convey knowledge to your soul; 2ndly, How they assist your will to act; and, 3rdly, How they assist your soul to take care of your body.

2. The eye is very small, my young friends, and yet how great is its range of vision. It takes in the sun, which is much larger than the earth and thousands of miles away; it measures mountains, seas, and valleys; with it we admire the beauty of living creatures, of trees and plants, contemplate multitudes of men and women, examine things great and small. It shows us the perfection of the most

insignificant of the works of God, and assists us to discover the comparative worthlessness of those of man. By its aid we learn to admire the ingenuity which enables our fellow-men to make wonderful things; in fact, the eye revels in the beautiful and the marvellous, and each object of vision brings knowledge to the soul. From the immensity of God's works we learn His greatness—from their beauty and perfection, His wisdom and power—from His care of the least of His creatures, His watchful providence. From the fact that He made them all for us, we become aware of His goodness and His love.

3. But everything cannot be seen. Must, then, knowledge be arrested on this account? Oh, no! Much of that even which you have seen you do not properly understand, but there are those who comprehend that in which you are deficient: they can explain—you can listen and learn, and thus the sense of hearing perfects the knowledge you have acquired by means of sight. Again, there are people who have seen that which you may never see; and they can transfer to you their information.

4. But has any one been to heaven and returned to tell us what is there? Must we remain in ignorance upon this all-important subject? No. The Son of the living God, the Master of Heaven, has been here and has told us all about that blessed place; and what He has told He has given to the Church to keep, and she has put it into the Catechism, where all may learn it and meditate upon it. Thus it is that sight and hearing bring knowledge

to the soul. And, before we proceed, let me ask you, my dear young friends, what is the first use to which we should put these senses? Is it not so to employ them that, seeing the beauty and greatness of God's works, and hearing of so many things concerning this world and the next, we may daily learn to know better that good God who has given us these senses for that very purpose, and has, at the same time, filled our lives with joy by means of these His gifts.

5. Nothing is more certain than that any person who should be deprived of the senses of sight and hearing would afterwards be able to do very little indeed, and he who is unable to do anything that he wishes to do can hardly be said to exercise free will. The man who is kept in prison has the will to be free; but his will to be at large, instead of being a blessing to him, becomes a torture, because it exists only to be thwarted. Now, a person blind and deaf would be in a sense even still worse off.

There are those who are born deaf and dumb, and this is indeed a great affliction, and will serve to illustrate what I mean. The deaf child cannot learn to speak or to understand language, because it cannot hear the voice of the teacher; and, until those so circumstanced are taught in a way that supplies the want of hearing, they can understand nothing. The soul remains shut up in the body without acquiring any knowledge except the little that may be gained from what is seen of the external world, and even that little is understood very imperfectly. Certainly, to give oneself to the admiration of the beauty of God's world and to see his works in it, is an act of the will. But how is the deaf child to learn that there is a Creator? How is such a child to be enabled to exercise the first act of the will? He is taught it through the sense of sight. By means of signs he learns to receive ideas and to return them, and in this way also he comes to understand writing, and is to some extent enabled to participate in that knowledge which flows in so readily upon others by means of hearing, and he is also enabled to use his understanding.

But how would it be if these poor deaf and dumb creatures were also blind? What would then be their state? We cannot tell. But in our own case we know that by the aid of these gifts we can work and learn and indulge in recreation. It is, therefore, perfectly true to say of them that they assist us to exercise the will.

6. The soul is so intimately connected with the body that, although it might be said that sight and hearing help the body to take care of itself, it is more true to say that the soul takes care of the body, because the soul does for us what the senses do for other living creatures.

Yet there is a power implanted in us by which the senses assist us without any conscious act of our own. We know of course that our eyes enable us to discern what is good to eat and drink and assist us in finding what we want, that they show us where to go, and that, should anyone attempt our life, they would help to warn us of danger, and point out to us how we can defend ourselves; and also that they teach us to keep away from other perils—such, for instance, as a falling brick or a dangerous precipice. In all these cases we are distinctly conscious of the guardianship, so to speak, of the watchful sense of sight. But the beautiful Providence of God goes farther than this. It teaches that delicate organ, the eye, to take care of itself. Not only does the fringe, which is called the eye-lash, which depends from the lid, prevent anything from getting into the eye when it is open, but, should a blow be aimed at the eye, or any dangerous thing be brought suddenly near to it, without any conscious act of volition, the lid itself will close.

How many such instances do we not find of the wisdom and Providence of Him who made us! Shall we not, then, love Him daily more and more?

7. But I must say yet another word about the senses. Besides being given by God to promote the general well-being of your body and soul, these five wonderful powers are also sources of great enjoyment, and whoever should deny this would only be throwing a cloak over the truth. As sources of pleasure you have to a certain extent a right to use them; but you must remember that they are *servants*, not masters, and that it would be a great mistake to become the slave of any one of them, and to live for its gratification.

To avoid such an error it is well to remember that the over-gratification of any sense has the effect of injuring, or even of destroying it. Take that of taste, for instance. We all like delicacies, and to have such a preference is not wrong. But to eat to excess is gluttony, which is a sin most unworthy of the child of God. And the glutton cannot with impunity gratify his shameful inclinations, for he injures his stomach so much that he loses all relish for food, and thus, beginning by gratifying his taste, he ends by finding nothing which can please him.

Again, with regard to the sense of smell, there are persons so fond of perfumes that they must have them always about them. This is not so great a sin as that of gluttony, but it also exacts a penalty from those who indulge in it, for the scents they carry with them hinder them from knowing whether or not the air they breathe is pure and healthy, and not only so, but they overpower and render inappreciable the delicate and far sweeter perfumes of beautiful flowers.

Those of you who live in the country and have learned to value those scents which tell of the healthiness of God's own nature—who love the exhalations from the hedge-rows, and the countless blossoms which spangle the meadows, know what a privation this must be; and even such of you as are dwellers in cities, to whom country walks are of rare occurrence, can understand the folly of so indulging in artificial luxuries as to lose the taste for natural ones.

There are other persons who are so fond of ease that they actually dread any kind of exertion. We see even children who are too lazy to play, and who prefer to lounge about. This is the sin of sloth—a sin which God's children will avoid for the love of Him. What is the effect of sloth? It deprives those who indulge in it of exercise, which is as necessary as fresh air, and it has such a weakening effect upon the constitution as to produce a feeling of perpetual weariness; so that, although strange, it is true, that no one feels so tired as he who does nothing. There is, moreover, this peculiarity in the weariness of the lazy—that he cannot, like a tired man, enjoy rest.

Some people there are who must always be listening; listening is a passion with them—they want to know everyone's business; they are called eavesdroppers. Such persons tell others what they have heard, and, as a consequence, breed quarrels. These people are disliked and dreaded by all, and as, according to the old saying, listeners hear little good of themselves, they end by being miserable.

Lastly, there are persons who covet all that they see. This is one of the most unhappy dispositions that can be imagined; covetous people are wretched.

The covetous person reminds me of a dog begging beside a dinner-table. No sooner has he got one piece of meat than he begins to look out for another; and it has often occurred to me to wonder whether he is more intent upon enjoying the first or in longing for the second; and as his master cannot give him his whole attention, the waiting part of the business is usually much the longest. The disappointment of the covetous person, in being unable to satisfy the cravings of this passion, must be very like that of the poor dog, whilst his master seems occupied by everything except himself.

Thus you see, my dear young friends, that although the senses are very enjoyable servants, they are very bad masters. Let us, then, use the senses—God's precious gifts—in the first place, as the means of knowing Him better, of increasing His love in our hearts, and of doing His blessed will; and in the second, for the purpose of taking care of our bodies, which are worth our care, because it is He Himself who has bestowed them upon us.

CHAPTER V.

God's Image and Likeness.

1. THE Catechism tells us we are made to God's image and likeness, and that which is in us, which is stamped with this likeness is, what I have now to speak of, that is to say, the soul. What has up to this time engaged our attention—the wonders of that mechanism with which our Creator has fitted our bodies to form part of the material world in which they are intended to move, and I may say to rule—has, I hope, my dear young friends, interested as well as instructed you. The soul, which we will now consider, of itself excludes all material attributes, and is, of course, a higher subject of contemplation.

As God lives in His own essence, without displacing one material being which He has made, or being displaced by any of them, and yet His power preserves everything, so your soul lives in your body without taking up any room, and yet it is that very soul whose presence gives life to your body and preserves it from becoming a corpse. However simple in its grandeur your soul might be, if it were in any way material, we might divide it into parts and speak of each. But this we cannot do, for this reason—that, being a spirit, it has no parts.

From the very nature of the things of which we shall have henceforth to speak, we shall require a more than human guidance, if we would attain to a certain knowledge of them, for the simple reason that they must be, to a great extent, beyond human reason. They therefore require a guidance which we have as yet had little necessity to use, namely, that of divine faith.

2. As, however, the object of these pages is to ground you well in the knowledge faith gives you of yourselves, and by that means to make you proof against the foolish mistakes into which those have fallen who have wilfully forsaken all divine guidance, mistakes you will every day come across in print in this unbelieving world, it will be useful to point out one or two extremes into which these wilfully misguided beings have plunged.

As you know, my dear young friends, that rebellion generally begins in pride to end in folly, you will hardly be surprised to hear that there are men who, refusing, as they say, to clip the wings of their glorious understanding, have persuaded themselves that their souls are an emanation of the Divinity, in fact, God! To come, however, to this conclusion, which pleases their pride, they have of course to deny the existence of the Creator whom you adore, and to persuade themselves that God, instead of being the maker of all things, is the very things themselves, and manifests Himself in various ways in the different parts of that universe which they mistake for Him its author!

Thus, of course, as the intelligence of man is the noblest thing they know anything about, the proud conclusion follows, not so much that their soul is God (a silly thought), but that it is the noblest part of God, whilst visible things are parts of God as well. Really, my dear young friends, this looks so strange on paper that I hardly liked to put it down. However, I suppose a good look at it is its best answer, and if those who hold such doctrine would not hide its enormity and folly under a cloak of fine phrases, it would require no other!

You can see plainly enough what this doctrine comes to! It is called Pantheism, which means "all God," but it is in reality what is called Atheism, or "no God;" being, in truth, a roundabout way of getting rid of the Creator, by denying that the world required a maker at all, and of arriving at the proud conclusion that man is the noblest being in existence.

It has been said that the pith of a lady's letter is always in the postscript. This wonderful theory is very much like a lady's letter, then, in this respect, that the whole of the fabrication is got up for no other purpose than to account for the little consequence slipped in at the end of it, namely, that man is the greatest being in existence.

Thus do these deluded men come to amuse themselves with a vain idea of their own excellence! But in doing so what must they not lose? They must give up all belief in the dear good Father who made them, all belief in the kind Providence that takes care of them, all belief in the eternal reward He has prepared for them; and when they come to die will their Pantheism serve them then? No. They get frightened then at that God they have tried in vain to deny, and fear to appear before the face of Him whose existence, apart from and independent of His creatures, they pretended to ignore.

Is not this a melancholy fate for which those who reject the guidance of faith exchange the certain knowledge of and filial confidence in a Heavenly Father.

3. It has been truly said that as our Blessed Saviour was crucified between two thieves, so falsehood always robs God of souls by dragging men into two extremes. Thus while some men, on account of the gift of understanding, try to exalt themselves to the skies, there are others who, forsaking also the guidance of faith, have come to the conclusion that they have no soul; but are only a more sagacious kind of animal, which by a wonderful process of perfectability have improved instinct into intelligence. Thus, dear young friends, those who forsake the light appointed by God to direct them to the know-

ledge of things of which their own powers can give them but very imperfect information, must end by running either into one extreme or another.

If, however, the delusion ended with life, it would not be of so much consequence. But it does not. "*The fool who has said in his heart, there is no God,*" and that other fool who says he has no soul, will appear one day before the God to whose revealed truths they have refused to submit, to account for the soul whose existence they have perhaps denied; and then of what use will be their theories?

Oh, pitiable indeed will be the lot of all who stand trembling in the presence of the Supreme Being, whose commands they have not only neglected to obey, but whose word they have refused even to believe.

4. I have mentioned these things because you will, no doubt, meet with men who hold such opinions, and with books which are poisoned by them. Let them have but one effect upon you—to make you bless your happier lot. Well grounded in the faith, that is to say, accepting with firm confidence from your holy mother the Church those truths which God has revealed, and which He has entrusted to her care, happy are you! Like a man walking on a safe bridge with sound handrails, you may look down with compassion on those who flounder and sink in the mire below. You may watch them as one by one they disappear and are lost, whilst you bless that bridge and Him who built it.

You may do more. You may try to persuade those who are not yet too far gone to retrace their steps, and tell them that this bridge is for them as well as for you; and if they heed not your word you can pity and pray for them. Standing in safety, you can contemplate as you travel on, the beauty of the surrounding scenery, which those who wander below do not notice, being too much engaged in their vain endeavour to find a pathway through the mire.

A bridge of safety to your steps, lit up by a divine light, such is to you revealed truth which you hold by faith. A dreary and impassable bog without a pathway, such is the vaunted liberty of those who call by this high-sounding name the rebellion of their understanding against God.

5. But enough of this contemplation of the misfortunes of others; let us consider more at length our own blessings. It is not sufficient that we possess, in the keeping of our holy mother the Church, endless treasures of divine wisdom. The bread of God's word must be broken to God's little ones. In other words, it was necessary that these truths should be put into a small space, so that they could be easily learned, and kept ready, as it were, "at your fingers' ends." Such is the Catechism. Divine truth and wisdom in a nutshell!

6. We shall take it for our guide in all that I am now writing for you, my dear young friends, and as we have to consider something which being invisible you cannot see, but which from internal consciousness you can to a great extent know, the worth of this guidance will soon appear. To teach you, indeed, what value to set upon your Catechism is

one object of this book; let me, therefore, tell you how your Catechism will guide you to knowledge.

The nature of the soul, although it could not be perfectly understood without the addition of higher knowledge than our own, might be partially inferred from our own internal consciousness. Finding themselves gifted with reasoning powers and free will, men have come to the conclusion, even by this means, that they have within them some sort of a spiritual being, of what kind they can hardly tell. The Catechism neither contradicts nor changes this knowledge, but brings us to it without difficulty, so that the facts which many have made out after much puzzling and after losing themselves amid doubts and conjectures, and which many have after much seeking and diligence altogether failed to discover, is made known to us in the Catechism with certainty and without further trouble.

In olden times, before the coming of the Saviour, there were men who, because they gave themselves up to the study of wisdom, were called philosophers. Some of these, after much study and conjecture, contrived to understand something about the soul. Let us suppose for a moment that you could meet one of these men, and that he began to use many arguments to prove the existence of a spirit within you, with what astonishment would you not look at him and say—" I could have told you all that when I was but seven years old—nay, more, if you will kindly listen I will tell you other things you do not seem to know, and correct you in some wherein you are in error "—and you could do it, of course, because your Catechism has led you straight into the truth, and made you clearly to understand that which your learned antagonist has only partly arrived at through his inner consciousness.

7. But there are things which no earthly wisdom can teach, even in the smallest degree, and of which the Catechism tells us plainly. What inner consciousness, for instance, could reveal to you that your soul is gifted with a power which could enable it to see God in the way which faith tells us will happen? Nay, it is more than doubtful whether any earthly intelligence could enable you to find out for certain the immortality of the soul! As, however, the disclosing of those things of which faith alone can give us the idea is the pleasant task which lies before me, I will say no more about them now, but will go on using the Catechism as a guide to the comprehension of our present subject, viz., The Soul.

8. "In what is your soul like to God?" says the catechism; and gives for answer—"In this, that my soul is a spirit, has understanding and free will, and is immortal." This short reply is all that we shall require in this and the two following chapters.

9. First, then, as to the soul being a spirit. We know that God is a spirit; that is, we know that He is a Being who exists without having a body. Our knowledge on this subject is not great—it is rather the knowledge of what He is not than what He is; but our ignorance on this subject springs from our weakness.

From the fact that we have a body, and that our souls use that body to get ideas of things, we are apt to confuse the notion of being with that of matter. Now, matter is a thing, which, although it may take many beautiful forms, only belongs after all to the lowest order of God's works. We know that God created a whole host of glorious beings called angels, who have no bodies at all, and that the soul, the noblest part of ourselves, is invisible. In fact, just as a man who looks through green spectacles fancies that everything he sees is green, so our souls, looking out of bodily eyes upon the world, would make material images of everything.

10. Nevertheless, faith tells you that God is a being immense and infinite, filling all the universe with His presence and His power; that He is the cause of the existence of every spiritual and of every material being that exists, and yet that He is Himself a spirit.

Now, what is the soul? Being a spirit it is like God. Filling, as it does, your body with its life, it is again a sort of image of the way in which God causes by His presence the existence of every material thing. Beyond this the likeness ceases; nay, it becomes a contrast. Poor little thing! The lowest of all spiritual beings, giving life to a wonderful little body remarkable for its helplessness! Peeping through marvellous little senses of clay; looking with wonder on things around; and trying to gain some idea of the vast creation in the midst of which it is placed! Wonderful little being indeed! And yet so insignificant, that if it were banished from the face of the world to-morrow it would hardly be missed, save by the good God who made it, and who for that reason takes an interest in it, and by a few fellow-beings to whom relationship or friendship have made it dear. In what are you, my dear young friends, like God? He is all-powerful, you so fragile that it requires the power of your Maker to preserve from moment to moment the being He has given you! He is infinitely good. Are you good? I hope you are, yet if you examine your goodness you will find in it so much selfishness and so little generosity, that you would be ashamed to claim for yourselves any such designation! God is all-wise. Are you wise? Yes; for God has put into the Catechism His own wisdom, and has given it to you! Without this, however, where would be your wisdom?

Nevertheless, your soul is a spirit; and in that at least you are like God.

CHAPTER VI.

God's Image and Likeness continued—Understanding and Will.

1. But if a spirit is a thing of which we can hardly get a proper idea, there is one way in which we are capable of comprehending it. We know a spirit by the power which it exercises.

Thus even, without the teaching of the Catechism, you know that you have a soul, because that soul reveals itself by its power of understanding. Your Catechism tells you, that soul is like God because it has understanding. God is infinitely wise—He knows all things.

Your understanding is truly a grand thing in its way, and makes your soul like to God, inasmuch as it has received from that Divine Being who knows all things the power of knowing something. This power of your soul is quite evident, and the conscious possession of it has made known to those who had no Catechism to guide them the fact that they had a soul. If you had not this gift it would be useless for me to take the trouble I am now taking for your benefit. It is the hope that you will bring your understanding to bear upon what I am saying that makes my doing so a labour of love. You use your understanding to learn from others what you do not know, to comprehend what goes on around you; in fine, under the useful form called common sense, you use it to guide you, not only in great things, but in all the daily actions of life.

" 2. Your understanding, although it is very limited in comparison with other intelligences, those of the angels for instance, raises you immensely above everything that does not possess this gift. Ask the magnificent sun that rises every morning and sets every evening whether it has any pleasure in its existence? It is much larger than you and much grander, yet its existence is nothing to it, because it is perfectly unconscious. Ask the same question of the elephant, the lion and other powerful beasts!

They enjoy their existence in a certain sense, they are endowed with pleasurable instincts, but nothing more, they have neither knowledge nor understanding. These creatures cannot comprehend what it is to have been fashioned by the hand of an all-wise Creator, nor can they know anything about His greatness, or admire His works. Thus, you see, understanding adds to your wonderful being a tenfold joy!

3. This soul of ours, however, is not known by the capability of understanding alone. It has another power by which it evinces itself still more plainly, namely, free will.

Whether man's free will has generally the effect of making him more like God is another question, upon which we will not at present enter. One thing is certain: that we have free will, and desperately free it is.

The first thing we must notice about this free will is, that its power to disobey God would almost lead us to suppose, at first sight, that it made us more unlike Him than any other creature He has made.

The sun and moon obey God, whilst sometimes even little children do not. Every living creature except man obeys the instincts God has placed within him for his preservation and well-being. Man alone, in his wilfulness, often does wrong, although he has an understanding to teach him what is right. Are not, then, those creatures that never do wrong more like God than man is? Not so; for this reason. The animals do what God has ordained they shall do, because they cannot help it. In these creatures there is no imitation of God's goodness. It is God's goodness you see in them, not theirs, for they have no free will. Everything God does He does because He is good, through the goodness of His divine will. He is infinite goodness. Now, when the sun shines upon you, or the birds sing, or the lambs in the meadows amuse you with their gambols, it would hardly enter into your head to thank them for the benefits or the amusement they afford you, because you never suppose that it is through any real goodness of theirs they do these things. On the contrary, you turn your thoughts heavenward and say, "What a good God that must be who implants in His creatures so much of goodness and beauty!" You see that it is the goodness of God Himself that wills the things that you admire, not the goodness of the creatures themselves, which have no goodness, simply because they have no free will.

4. But God has given to us a free will, that we may have the merit of a small portion of goodness, which He deigns to find worthy of a reward much greater than we could ever imagine. That God has given us a will for no other end than this is clear enough; it is not, however, at all so clear that He will find much goodness in our will—He will find much wilfulness no doubt.

But let us now see what is that goodness which He wants to find, for I am quite certain, my dear young friends, that you would like to give it to Him.

In the first place, then, He wants our hearts.

"My son, give me thy heart" (Prov. xxiv. 26). He says to each one of you, and if you ask me in what way you are to prove that you do this, He Himself tells you: "If ye love me, keep my commandments" (John xiv. 15).

The way in which God wishes you to exercise your free will is as easily seen as the reason for which He gave it. He gave it to you that you might have the merit of loving and obeying His law, and in doing these two things can you alone use it as He wishes. The more you know of Him the more you will love Him; therefore, He wills you to apply with great zeal and good-will to learn all you can about Him.

We must now say a word about what frightens some people, although, if looked at properly, it is only another proof of God's desire that we should love Him. To give us, as I have said, a little bit of goodness of our own, God has had to give us also a terrible power, namely, that of disobeying His law, in other words, of committing sin.

By this power we can actually refuse to obey God, we can even wilfully do what He has forbidden. In two ways this power is terrible; first, it renders us capable of doing what no other being on earth can do, namely, of insulting our Creator by defiance, and this is indeed terrible; and, secondly, this crime must of necessity bring upon the daring creature who commits it Divine vengeance, either temporal or eternal; and you know something, at least, my dear young friends, of what a fearful thing Divine vengeance is.

God, however, has put this terrible power into our hands, although He knew, far better than you or I, what it involved. But why did He do so? Simply because He would have from His children a free, meritorious love. What a desire, then, must be that of our God for the love of His creatures! Think what a terrible thing it must be for insignificant atoms like ourselves to be able to disobey God! Think again of that terrible place in which those burn who have died in revolt against Him! And then say to yourselves: "God has permitted all this rather than deprive me of the power of loving and serving Him freely."

But you will naturally say also, If God has made my soul like to Him, by giving me the power of being good, surely the power of being bad makes me very unlike Him. This is true, and is a very strong reason for striving after goodness.

5. Yet, even here, there is one thing in which the image of God is still in a certain sense preserved. When you do wrong you do it, not because it is wrong, but because, through some mistake, you think a thing to be good which in reality is not so, or at all events not good for you.

Our first mother, Eve, saw the apple which God had forbidden her to eat. It looked very nice, and when the devil told her it would give her the knowledge of good and evil, she took it and ate it. Why did she do so? She was very wicked, and foolish too; but she did not eat the apple because she thought it was bad. No, indeed! It would have been well for her had she thought so, for then she

LESSONS TO BE LEARNT FROM THE WILL'S NATURE.

would have left it on the tree! What led her to eat it was this: In the first place, she saw that the apples looked good; in the next, she knew that knowledge is to be desired; and, turning her thoughts from God and His command, she believed the wicked serpent and acted upon his suggestions.

This is the way in which sin is always committed. No one desires a thing because he thinks it bad; but because, turning from the thought of God, he only looks at what appears to him good. So you see that, in spite of sin, the will of man always maintains that one property, that what it takes to be good it must love, what it takes to be bad it must hate. From this you can learn some good lessons.

Since God has made your hearts such that you must of necessity love what you take to be good, learn all you can about Almighty God, that, seeing His goodness more and more clearly, you may love Him more and more.

6. Secondly: Although all the creatures which God has made are good, they are not always good for you, and are never so when His commandments forbid you to make use of them; you must therefore learn not to set your hearts on them too much, lest they prove a temptation and the occasion of sin to you, as the apple was to Eve.

Thirdly: When you get fond of anything, never do as mother Eve did—never turn away from the thought of God and the voice of conscience, which tells you that what seems good is not good for you! It was by this that she committed so terrible a mistake.

Lastly: Always follow the guidance of your conscience and the commandments; and remember, that to disobey God is to pay too high a price for anything, however good it may seem to be. Above all, take care to learn to know God, to hate sin, and to turn to God and our Blessed Lady in every temptation. If indeed you love God, His love will teach you that nothing in the world is good enough to be purchased at the price of one venial sin.

7. God has then given you, my dear young friends, the power of being good; it is, therefore, your duty to exercise it by knowing Him, loving Him, and keeping His commandments. Who are they, as a rule, who commit sin? Those who take no trouble to know God, those who turn away from and forget Him. If, then, you would not use the gift of God against Himself, there is but one course open to you, and that course is your only safe refuge from crime and from misfortune! Fly to it, I beseech you! It is a sweet as well as a safe refuge, and it consists in the life-long study to know, the life-long endeavour to please, your dear good God.

CHAPTER VII.

God's Image and Likeness continued.
Immortality

1. WE now come to the third attribute in which, as the Catechism tells us, our souls are "like unto God;" they are immortal. We have now arrived

at a point in which the resemblance can indeed be seen.

The immortality of the soul is one of the first truths which we are taught. This very fact may furnish a reason for its being little dwelt upon by us, for it often happens that what we have always possessed is looked upon as our right. But let us consider how utterly we depend upon God for this gift.

There cannot be a greater mistake than to suppose, as some people do, that after God had created them and given them life, He left them to themselves, only bestowing upon them now and then a little help and guidance by His Divine Providence. Far from this being the state of the case, it requires in fact the same power on the part of God to keep all creatures from annihilation, as was at first needed for their creation.

This is true with regard to our soul as well as our body. Let me ask you now what it is to have an immortal soul? Simply this: that God, having once created you, will, by His omnipotent power, keep your soul in existence as long as He shall be God! That is, for ever!

2. Do you now perceive the amazing nature of this gift? It is such that it affects your whole being, and makes you entirely different from what you would be without it. It gives a special character to your existence here, and bestows on you hereafter an eternal destiny.

We will say no more at present about the gift itself, but consider our being, here and hereafter, in the light which this gift sheds upon it. I was just going to say that this gift upsets all that goes to make up our lives in this world, but had I said so I should have made a great mistake. It re-arranges everything, and puts everything beautifully in its place.

3. Some things, which to a creature not immortal would be of serious importance, it reduces to utter insignificance; and, again, circumstances which a mere mortal would look upon as misfortunes are changed, by the fact of our immortality, into positive blessings. Immortality may be compared to a pair of scales in which you must weigh yourselves; and, tested in this manner, you will find yourselves to be very different creatures from what you would otherwise imagine. If I neglected to speak to you upon this point, my dear young friends, I might as well have never begun to teach you self knowledge, for all I could have said would only have placed before you an imaginary being, which, for want of this our gift of immortality, would have been no true likeness of you.

When Saint Augustine and his companions came to England, to convert our Saxon forefathers, it happened that the king of one of the provinces into which the country was at that time divided was holding a Wittenagemot, or council. In that assembly there was an old Thane, or brave noble warrior, who had listened very attentively to the missioner; and when he was asked what he thought of these strange men, who had come from such a distance to teach the doctrine of salvation, he got

IMMORTALITY MAKES TIME PRECIOUS.

up and spoke somewhat as follows: "Often, O king, when we were assembled here in the winter and the fire was blazing, we have seen a little bird fly in at one door, flutter about for a while, and at last find its way out again; but whence it comes or whither it goes we none of us know. Up to this time we have been like this bird. Man walks the earth for a few years, but what precedes his birth, or what is to follow after his death we cannot tell. Undoubtedly, if the new religion can reveal these important secrets it must be worthy of our attention."

This beautiful and simple parable of the little bird flying into the hall, and after fluttering there for a little time, passing out again, made use of by the rough old warrior, is a very good figure of those who, not possessing the gift of faith, are unconscious of their immortality, and therefore ignorant of their own greatness.

4. Now, as faith has taught you this truth, it would be a great mistake to deny to immortality that consideration and place which it imperatively claims in whatever would legitimately pretend to give you a true knowledge of what and how noble you really are. Let us begin then. Being immortal, man is not a being created to live for a time and then die and disappear for ever; he is a being created to live for a time with his soul united to his body, after which time his body will die, and his soul will continue to live separated from it, until, after the last judgment, they will be re-united for all eternity.

Immortality, then, makes this life the beginning of what will never end, and shows us that it is given for a special purpose, which, but for our immortality, it could not have; it is a period allotted to us by God, in which to merit a glorious happy eternity.

Eternity makes every moment of our lives precious indeed.

We may understand this by an illustration. If you were taken to a grand palace and shown heaps of gold and jewels, from which you were told you might take as much as you could carry away in an hour, surely you would consider that hour too precious to be spent in sleep. In the same way we are in the world for a certain time, and our fortune for eternity depends upon the way in which we use that time. God has prepared for each of you a throne and a crown, which, if you forfeit not, will be yours for ever; but that throne has to be beautified, and that crown made more brilliant by jewels which you can make your own every moment of your lives.

Do you know what the jewels are?

Every act of love and obedience which you perform during your mortal life. And these acts can be made every moment—yes, in the most insignificant action, if offered to God and done in conformity to His will.

5. Again, these jewels are of different degrees of splendour. In what does the difference consist? In the greater or lesser amount of love with which your actions are done. Does not immortality, then, render life very short and very precious? Waste it

not, my dear young friends—let every act you do be very full of the love of God. Remember always that you are immortal beings, here but for a short time, working for eternity.

6. But if immortality makes time precious, what does it do with the joys and sorrows of life?

To a being created to enjoy merely for a time the life given to it by its Creator, every joy of its existence would indeed be precious, and even the slightest sorrow or suffering might be accounted great. But to immortal beings, whose life here is but a moment compared with eternity, what is either joy or sorrow? Surely next to nothing, except inasmuch as they may be turned to profit for eternity. In this sense both may be made precious to those who use them aright, while to those who do not, each may be hurtful; yet, even when they are turned to profit, sorrow is, as a rule, more valuable than joy. Is it not wonderful how immortality changes all things in their relation to ourselves? If sorrow be used as an occasion for the practice of patience and resignation, suffering will become a treasure for eternity; and even joy, if you use it as a source of gratitude and an encouragement to go on serving God, will itself be made worthy of an eternal reward.

7. But what I want especially to point out is, that it enhances the other gifts by which our Creator has made our soul like unto Him—namely, understanding and free will. In speaking of the former I purposely abstained from dwelling on the chief boon which it confers upon us—the power of knowing God; and I did so because the mere gift of

understanding is in itself magnificent; and when God gave it He added immensely to our happiness as creatures: for who can deny that consciousness increases every other joy? For this gift alone we owe to God more than we can ever repay. But when He made us immortal, destined to serve Him here for a time, and after that to live for ever, He gave us something outside ourselves. He gave us the power of knowing and admiring our Creator from His works—He gave us the power of knowing a great deal more about Him by the light of faith—and He has also given us the power of one day seeing Him face to face with our understanding strengthened by a divine light, and of finding eternal bliss in the contemplation.

What, then, is it to be made to the image and likeness of God? What did God really bestow when He made us immortal beings capable of knowing something? He bestowed upon us nothing less than His own infinite Self, to be the object of our knowledge and admiration now and for ever. Yes, my young friends, He has given us Himself, that we may see Him in His works, and may know Him as faith reveals Him, until He shall make us eternally blessed, in the sight and possession of our God for ever. What return, then, can you make for such a gift? For it is your very own, and nothing in this world, except sin, can take it from you! The very thought should be enough to make you fall down in silent adoration, blessing God for having given you a soul made to His image and likeness!

But we have not yet done. We have already, guided by the Catechism, seen how God, in order to enable you to have a little goodness of your own, has given you a will capable of loving Him, so as to make you worthy in His dear sight of a reward; and we have even trembled to think what this gift involves. But you must reflect upon what life would be without love before you can feel what a wondrous gift is that of free will. Already have you, I trust, used this gift over and over again in making warm acts of love for Him who gave it—and yet, perhaps, it has scarcely struck you what it was that God really gave when He bestowed it, making you also immortal.

8. Immortality teaches you to look at your existence as a continuous whole, of which the present life which God has given you to work in for eternity is but the precious beginning. The occupation He gives you for this life and the next is one and the same, namely, to love Him; and, lest occasions should fail you to prove your love for Him, he bids you love your neighbour for His sake, accepting what you do for your neighbour as if it were done for Himself. He has, in fact, designed your life to be a life of love whichever way you turn: teaching you to find in your fellow-creatures objects in which to love Him. He has given you Ten Commandments, by keeping which you may prove your love for him. He has revealed to you by faith His beauty and His goodness, in order that such knowledge may force you to love Him; and when life is over He will take you to Himself, where you will be

rewarded, by loving Him for ever, for every little thing you did for His love here.

9. What should you do, in return, for that God who has made you to His own image and likeness? Make Him any worthy or adequate return you cannot, because your whole being, offered to Him in adoration and love,—your whole mind employed in trying to know Him more and more perfectly,— your whole heart and soul employed in loving, and all your powers in serving Him, could not repay Him for having given you your understanding and your will! And as for making Him a return for giving you Himself as the object of your knowledge and your love, the debt is such as to render all hope of paying it out of the question! Nevertheless, if you give Him all you can, He will be satisfied; and not only will He be satisfied, but He will reserve in store for you an eternal reward for doing all you can, although it be infinitely less than what you owe.

Give Him, then, your whole being, and never forget, as long as you live, that to devote your whole understanding to the knowledge of God, and your whole will to His love, is only a small part of the debt you owe to Him who, out of His infinite bounty, has given you a soul made to His own image and likeness.

CHAPTER VIII.

Yourselves.

1. I CANNOT better commence this last chapter of the first part of my book than by calling attention to a passage in the history of creation, as it is given in the first book of the Bible. The words are these: "And the Lord formed man of the slime of the earth; and breathed into his face the breath of life, and man became a living soul" (Gen. xi. 7).

Why did God call man a living soul, in relating what he became when he was created? Would it not have been more correct to say that he became a living man? No, my dear young friends, the words used by Almighty God express the truth better than any other words could do. They express more than they say. You know that the soul is the noblest part of man; but these words mean more than that. They mean, in the first place, that the soul which God gave to man, possesses of itself a life quite independent of the body, and that it will still live, even when separated from it.

In the second place, these words show that it is nothing else but the soul which gives life to the body, so that without it, it would have remained a corpse, just as it will become a corpse whenever the soul leaves it. Principally, however, they point out that the life which the body leads, is really the soul's life in the body, so completely does the body lead the life which the soul chooses to allow it to lead. Is it not wonderful what an amount of truth these words express?

2. Perhaps, the title of this chapter may lead to some speculation as to what I can have to say upon the subject. I have already told you where you come from; I have spoken of the wondrous construction of your body; I have said something about your senses; and, finally, I have treated of your soul. But I have spoken of all these things separately: they do not however so exist in you; they are united, and the result of that union is a curious combination—in fact, yourselves.

How shall I describe you? I will take the words of Genesis and apply them. You are beings for whom God has made a body formed of the slime of the earth, and into whose faces God has breathed the breath of life, so that you have become living souls. Living souls indeed! In fact, almost all soul, so that your body is scarcely more than a connecting link uniting the spirit within you with the visible world.

I will show you what I mean. As I told you before, you are very different from the brute creation, which enjoys life to be sure, but in a purely animal fashion. In your case, on the contrary, all life springs from the soul, which makes the body a sharer in its emotion. Is the soul sad?—the body participates in its sadness; is it glad?—the body also may be said to rejoice.

3. Although, however, the body owes its life to the soul, so that without such an inhabitant even its own senses would be of no use to it—of what service are

eyes and ears to a dead man? Nevertheless the soul receives in return a great deal from the body. And the difference between the human soul and other spirits which God has created is, that the former was made to act in and through the body, so that, although it will be for a time separated from its companion, it will afterwards be united to it again.

Now, as your soul was made to be the soul of a living being who should have a body, God made it such that it gets its ideas of things and gains knowledge of them through the senses. So true is this, that if you try to imagine something you have neither seen nor heard of, you cannot do it. If you make the attempt, you will find that you have only been putting together, in a distorted kind of way, things of which you had before some kind of knowledge.

4. Your soul, then, being so formed as to obtain its ideas through the body, it would be hard to tell in what other way it could get them. Whatever it may be able to do after its separation from the body, it is certain that it has not hitherto had the opportunity of obtaining them in any other manner, because it was shut up in the body as soon as it was made. Thus you see that the body forms the connecting link between the soul and the visible world; for whilst it partakes of the joy which the soul imparts to it together with life, it also gives back to it the knowledge of all those things which its eyes see, its ears hear and its other senses perceive.

5. The body and soul also re-act upon each other in pain and pleasure, in joy and in sorrow. Whence

comes the sadness which overpowers us at times, when we are sick and in pain, but from the sympathy of the soul with bodily suffering? And when the soul grieves, does not the body lose its activity and grieve with it, sometimes even to the extent of becoming a prey to sickness? This latter extreme, however, is seldom reached, save through our own fault; but the fact of its possibility sufficiently demonstrates that the body does sympathize with the soul. There is no need to insist upon the effect of joy of soul upon our bodily frames. Every one knows the delightful elasticity which springs from such a cause, and how even suffering becomes light when the spirit is rejoicing.

6. Now let us see in what manner the will affects the body and the soul. You will often hear or read of the wickedness and folly of being governed by the passions and desires of the body, instead of making the body obey the soul. Even your Catechism, to show you the importance you should attach to your soul rather than your body, asks the question: "Which must you take most care of, your body or your soul?" and answers: "Of my soul." Now, at first sight it would seem by this as if the will sometimes obeyed the body. Yet this is not strictly true. The will is a power of the soul, and exercises a complete control over the body, which it obliges to do its bidding.

But, although the will does not obey the body, this is what happens.

On account of its intimate union with the soul, the body is able to impress upon it the desirability of comfort, of ease, of pleasure—and there is no harm in this provided that these desires do not imperil a greater good; and the soul, finding these inclinations enticing the will, comes to desire them, and sets both body and mind to work to obtain what it needs. Thus you see that even in things which immediately concern the body, it is, after all, the soul which sets it in motion. In many cases it is absolutely necessary that the soul should use the body for its own preservation, and that the will should act in accordance with its requirements, as, for instance, in taking food and drink, rest and recreation. The Catechism and other spiritual books do not mean that the body should be neglected, but that the care of the soul should be our chief concern. There is no reason to insist upon the care of the body, however, because the soul loves it too well to be in danger of overlooking its necessities—the fear is rather lest it should be careless of its own affairs.

7. I will conclude this first part of the "Mirror of Faith" with one further reference to the principal subject of this chapter, namely, the will; for I wish to impress upon you that your body, soul, and understanding, being all subject to this controlling power, the right use of it is of supreme importance.

If you have any duty to perform towards God, it is your will which must accomplish it; and whatever may help you in discharging the obligation must be inspired to do so by the will.

Our first duty is to love God, and in order to love Him we must know Him; yet, when knowledge shall have taught the will to love, that will can command the understanding to seek more, and yet more, of that heavenly knowledge, in order that love may increase a thousandfold. After all, love is the only thing our good God cares for, and the proof of love is obedience. Let, then, your will, which is free, be conformed to the will of God in everything, for the attainment of this is perfection. Yes, my young friends, the sum and substance of your duty is to love God always, to do everything you can to please Him, or, in other words, to devote your whole being, soul and body, to the doing His will and the keeping of His commandments.

8. You know that our Blessed Lady was the one most pleasing to God of all pure creatures; but have you considered what it was which had the greatest share in her holiness? It was that, from the first moment of her creation, she offered her whole being to God, and to the end of her life used all her powers of soul and body to do His will. Now, in this you can, every one of you, imitate to a great extent the dear Mother of God, whom God has given to us to be our mother, and thus only can you be her true children. If, then, you desire to attain conformity to the will of God, ask the Blessed Virgin, whose conformity was so perfect, to help you. Say to her constantly, with ardent devotion, "Mary, my mother, teach me to love Jesus and to do His will."

PART SECOND.

WHAT SIN DID TO YOU.

CHAPTER I.

Your Prospects.

1. LIFE is a holiday. In saying this, my dear young friends, I am making use of a paradox, or an expression contrary to apparent fact, but one which is perfectly true when-explained. I repeat the assertion, however startling: Life is a holiday.

The body with its wonderful senses—the soul with its more wonderful powers—are each of them teeming sources of joy; and, springing from the very fountain of life, this joy receives new additions at every step, joys from within—joys from without, joys varied as the world we live in, joys united into one mighty gladness by that power of consciousness which is in itself the greatest joy of all.

Yes; life is a holiday. To know, and to seek further knowledge—to love, and to act through love—are pure pleasures; and our fellow-creatures are the partakers of our joy and sources of further happiness, since they are beings on whom we can spend the overflowings of our love to God and from whom we can receive similar kindnesses, rendered from the same motive.

2. God's beautiful world is one vast pleasure-ground filled to overflowing with beautiful things, placed there by our Heavenly Father, that their loveliness and variety may raise our thoughts to Him from whom they receive their every charm, to Him whose power, wisdom, and goodness fashioned them all. Feelings such as these may be, perhaps, without their knowing it, the cause of the gladness of little children; but at any rate such feelings should be ours. But do the realities of life bear out my picture? Ah! that is the question! For to raise buoyant hopes which might turn out illusory would be but cruelty, and cruelty which would at the same time be useless. No, this is no illusion. Is not this world a pleasure-ground to him who sees reflected in every flower the beauty of that dear good God who made it? Is not the body with its senses a joy to him who thanks God for them, and who feels that while he is innocently enjoying them he is pleasing in the sight of his Maker? Is not knowledge delight to him who in every creature sees a book to speak to him of the goodness of that Father to whom he belongs, and who makes use of the beautiful truths which faith has made his own to go beyond the limits of human knowledge, and to look into heaven and feed on what he finds there?

And what is life without love? A dreary waste. Yet is it not certain that no one can either love or be loved unless the love of God makes him amiable, whilst the love of divine goodness enables those who love God to love for His sake every shadow of that goodness which is found in the creature; and he who for love of God loves his fellow-man cannot but be the object of love in return.

 Then, surely, to obey the impulse which springs up within us to devote our whole being to God is in very truth to secure happiness, and to turn life into a holiday.

 3. But why do I take so much pains to impress this truth upon you? Because I want to put you on your guard. I wish to show you every obstacle that you will meet with in giving yourselves cheerfully to God, so that you may not be astonished at difficulties—I want to point out to you hidden enemies, so that you may not be knocked down in the dark—and I want to do this without damping your ardour—in fact, I want to make use of the very brightness of your life to nerve you for the task of living for God.

 Take an example. Is sport the less a pastime because it may be somewhat laborious? And is not opposition itself often the life of a game and even got up for the very purpose of adding spirit to it? Therefore, difficulties are not sufficient to prevent life from being a holiday; but, on the contrary, as opposition makes the player give all his attention to the game, instead of allowing himself to be distracted with other things, and makes him put out all his strength in the hope of gaining a victory, so in your case the difficulties you will meet with in life must make you give all your attention to the service of God, looking your enemy straight in the face, and putting out all your strength in the cause of Him who is watching over you both to give you the victory and to reward you for gaining it.

4. To carry on the simile: what I want to do is to make the game fair. There are many persons who with the best intentions in the world do exactly the reverse, because they object to let you know with what enemies you will have to contend. They are afraid, possibly, of damping the pleasures of youth; but such a course defeats its own object, and is about as reasonable as would be the conduct of a friend who, seeing a joyous young party just starting off on some delightful expedition, should omit to tell you of a missing lynch-pin, or some other thing he had perceived to be wanting to your equipage, and allow you to meet with an accident, almost at the outset, rather than damp your pleasures by putting you on your guard and causing you to provide against danger! I believe that this line of conduct is often pursued with children, and that it is very fatal in its consequences. For imagine a little child taught to believe that it is very easy indeed to love the God who made it, and to do His will, yet who finds, to its astonishment, that its mind wanders away during prayer-time as if all kinds of thoughts had been waiting for that moment to come just when they ought not; or perhaps the child feels on a certain morning that it has a more than ordinary inclination to be out of humour! It finds there is something wrong, and it does not know what, and the natural conclusion for it to come to (and one which I believe

many children do come to) on being disappointed in its first efforts to serve God, is that it is perfectly useless to try to do so. Such an idea once imbibed may be retained for a whole life; and when once a person gives up trying to serve God, it becomes every day more difficult to begin again, for not to serve God is in fact to go away from Him.

5. Suppose you were knocked down two or three times in the dark, what would you do? It is extremely probable that you would say: "If I do not want to be knocked down again, I had better remain where I am; for if I do not get up, I cannot be knocked down!" God preserve you, my dear young friends, from such a miserable conclusion!

6. But the real question is, Why should you be exposed to such danger? And since there is no reason why you should be so, I am determined to guard you from it.

In serving God you will meet with enemies; enemies whom you cannot see. This is certainly a troublesome prospect, but that is not a reason why its truth should be hidden from you. The man who has to fight likes to be warned, likes to be armed, and likes to know the nature and number of his assailants. To know nothing whatever is to fight on very unequal terms. If you are forewarned, you will see that, with the arms God has given you, you are more than a match for all your antagonists, and that you have at your side One who is always fighting with you and for you, and who is stronger than all of them together. It is darkness that makes your enemies seem unconquerable, and it is only the not being warned that can prevent your being properly prepared for an encounter. To this darkness you shall no longer be a prey, nor shall you meet your foe unawares, if I can help it. That which has thrown difficulties in your way, is a storm which came and is gone.

Like other storms, it has been dispelled by Him who rules the elements. Like many other storms, too, it has left rough traces behind it. These traces we shall have to study, and the subject will not be void of interest and even amusement, for it is quite possible to find interest in the contemplation of a ruin, and amusement in recounting a disaster. Far from depressing you, this study will nerve you to greater effort; and, before we enter upon it, I will tell you why.

The traces of the storm which our good God has suffered to remain within us, He has left within us out of love, making them, as it were, the excuse for so many more palpable proofs of paternal care, so many more manifestations of paternal love, that I shall have to write two more parts such as this in order to tell you about them. Yes; these traces of the storm have caused so many good things to be provided for you, that they have actually made it hard to say whether you are not better off now than you would have been had that storm never come near you! This is so true, that the great Doctor of the Church, St. Augustine, looking at the love of God in the Redemption, cried out concerning the fault of our first parents which left those traces behind: "Oh, happy fault, that needed such a Redeemer!" that is, that made us the centre of so much love.

If then the traces of sin within us are so insignificant as to leave it doubtful whether they render our condition better or worse, who would be so foolish as to endeavour to conceal them? Let us therefore examine them in our succeeding chapters.

CHAPTER II.

The Storm.

1. WE have had quite enough general talk about obstacles and hidden enemies, and were I to dwell more upon them they would begin to grow up into giants. Let us, then, come to something definite, and in the first place consider the storm which came upon humanity and was dispelled by the power of our Merciful Father.

Of course I allude to the sin of our first parents.

But before I speak of this sin—which was, like all sins, at the same time a blunder—I must say something of that arch-blunderer whose crime was all the greater in that he was clever enough to have known better.

Long before God created man, He made a vast host of spiritual intellectual beings, whose intelligence is so vast, that in one moment they can know more than we can learn in a life-time. These creatures, being made out of nothing by the pure benevolence of God, that He might make them sharers in His happiness and glory, owed, as we do, a great debt of gratitude to Him, as well as the total consecration of their whole being to His service.

How long a time God gave them to earn, by the free exercise of their will, their eternal reward we know not. One thing is certain that, from the magnificence and clearness of their understanding, it ought not to have needed much to show them the claim of God upon their allegiance, or to bring them to His footstool in adoration and love. Nevertheless we know as a fact, that one-third of that mighty host, with Lucifer at their head, refused to acknowledge that God who had made them out of nothing, with a folly rendered, as I said before, all the greater by the clearness of their understanding—took pride in the beauty of the being God had given them—and, in punishment of this their sin, were changed into hideous devils, and sent into that hell prepared by the outraged majesty of God on purpose to receive them.

2. There is something very terrible in this; yet, when we consider all the circumstances, we must perceive the justice of the sentence. What a picture have we here of the fate of those who dare to rebel against God, and to fly in the face of Him who made them out of pure love, and for no other purpose than that they might earn by free love a share in His own felicity. And there is a special point to be observed about the arch-blunder of the devil, which is, that having made it and gone to hell for it, he cannot correct his mistake. In spite of his understanding, which serves him well enough in

doing mischief and in misleading those who are so foolish as to become his followers, he is in one respect no match for the veriest child. He still looks upon that pride, which made him rob God of the honour of his creation, as a noble act of independence, instead of owning it to be what it really is—a piece of mean robbery. Yes, indeed, a cowardly, mean act was this one of the first of all robbers—an act in which he has been followed by too many of those who, having received understanding from God, declare for its independence, declare in fact that they will not submit it even to the guidance of God's revealed truth, and who revile the keeper of truth, the Church, to whom God has enjoined obedience as the sole act of submission He requires from them.

What do these persons get even in this world by their rebellion? They fly, with unshackled wings, as they express it, into the regions of doubt (and most unhappy regions are they), where they remain, speculating, and perhaps discovering many things, not one of which can lead to happiness, if indeed they fall short of sinking to a yet lower depth where independent spirits, who rage against every restraint of law, order and obedience, rebelling against the Commandments of God and man, become slaves to masters who degrade them below the level of the very brute creation.

As you, my dear young friends, are certain to meet in your path through life with various phases of this devilry, calculated to confuse, more or less, your ideas of things, and to induce you to mistake the so-called liberty, the seeking for which is a repetition of the sin of the fallen angels with the liberty of the children of God, I would advise you to mark well, both the nature of the transgression itself, and the consequences to which it always leads.

Every form of proud rebellion, by which any part of the being God gave you, refuses to pay its first homage to its Maker, is a repetition of the devil's sin, in so far as it comes from pride which seeks to rob God of what belongs to Him, and it generally ends in leading its foolish victim into misery and confusion here, as it also carries with it a special right to a share in the devil's lot hereafter.

3. How different, how noble, how truly grand, was the conduct of the other angels, with the glorious St. Michael at their head. Astonished, indignant, and horrified, at the treachery and folly of Lucifer and of the third of their number who joined him, the great archangel, as his very name of Michael signifies, cried out, "Who is like unto God?" and two-thirds of the heavenly host joined in the cry!

No sooner is that cry uttered and responded to, than the act of humble homage it contained sealed for ever the eternal bliss of all who uttered it. Then were the angelic hosts divided under two banners; then it was that the tug of war commenced; Satan was driven with his rebel host into hell, St. Michael locked the door upon them, and having done so was received with all his faithful companions into eternal bliss.

"Who is like unto God?" Mark well the expression. It is the watchword of the saved. You have heard of holy humility. What is humility? Is it the wholesale acknowledgment of guilt? No. Humility is noble honesty—it is the act by which the creature says: " Who is like unto God ? " and in that act acknowledges that all that it has, however great, is but the gift of God.

" Who is like unto God?" said St. Michael; and, saying so, he looked upon his magnificent nature, and paid homage to the God who gave it to him!

" Who is like unto God?" exclaimed, in her heart, the humble maid of Nazareth, when she saw herself, lowly as she was in her own esteem, raised to a dignity compared with which the dignity which staggered Lucifer was as nothing!

" Who is like unto God?" say the saints; and, in proportion to the sincerity with which they say it, does God, fearless of robbery, heap upon them his choicest graces!

" Who is like unto God?" says the humble penitent; and whilst the devil gnashes his teeth in impotent fury, the chains of sin fall off, and Satan's slave is free!

" Who is like unto God?" cries the faithful child of holy Church as he bows his head to receive every article of faith which God for his enlightenment has left in her keeping; and straightway he finds in the Catechism food for contemplation, if he be learned—or knowledge of the truths of Divine wisdom, if simple.

" Who is like unto God?" cries the obedient child of God, as he sets himself in earnest to keep God's commandments, and thus begins to walk on the road to heaven!

4. Yes; mark the expression: "Who is like unto God?" It is your watchword—your battle-cry! Forsake it but for one moment, and every step you take will be a step astray! Keep it, be guided by it, and it will lead you where it led St. Michael, safe to the gates of heaven, which will fly open at the sound of those familiar words.

And now, having consigned the prince of blunderers to his home, and left him there to carry on his evil deeds, we have gained, in doing so, some useful information, and may be said to have learned a lesson at the expense of the devil. So that you see even the arch enemy may do us a service by teaching us to avoid his own folly!

5. But there is more to come, Lucifer, by sinning, caused a third of the heavenly thrones to be vacated, and Almighty God did not intend to have them empty, and thereupon determined to fill them with other creatures.

What does He do? As He Himself beautifully puts it, He takes counsel with Himself. In other words, the blessed and undivided Trinity take counsel, and come to the conclusion to create man. God says: "Let us create man to our image and likeness." (Gen. i. 26.)

Now, as there is nothing wrong in guessing, if it be done in humility, at the reasons which our Father may have for what He does, let us ask ourselves in this spirit why God chose to make creatures such as we are, partly spirit and partly matter, to fill the empty thrones in heaven? If we consider for a moment what it was that turned the angels dizzy, we shall perceive that it was pride in in their grand spiritual nature! Perhaps, therefore, Almighty God determined upon making a creature that would have no such temptation to ruin itself, and so he created us with a spiritual soul, indeed, but with a body as well—a body which, although very wonderful, is after all only made of clay!

6. Besides, as God created also a material world, He determined to place upon it a being which should contain within itself something of everything, and therefore made man with a material body like the clay, with growth like the trees, life like the animals, and a spiritual soul like the angels; and this, of course, aroused the wrath of Satan, who, resolved upon doing all the mischief in his power, immediately began to endeavour to get man to commit a sin of pride, in nature like to his own.

7. When God created our first parents it was, of course, necessary that their fidelity should be tried in order that they might have the merit of obedience. Therefore, as you are well aware, God placed them in the beautiful Garden of Paradise, and only forbade them to eat of the fruit of one tree. Instantly the devil begins to compass their destruction, and resolves to persuade them, if possible, that this tree has about it some special quality which makes its fruit peculiarly desirable. Coming into the garden, under the form of a serpent, which at that time was a beautiful creature, Satan then approaches Eve, and craftily points out to her the

beauty of the forbidden fruit, asking her at the same time why she was not allowed to partake of it. Now, Eve should have simply answered that God had a right to issue what commands He pleased, and that it was not her part to question them; but, instead of doing so, she first evaded the question, and then cast a doubt upon the truth of what God had said—"Lest *perhaps* we die" is her expression; and, oh, how that "perhaps" must have delighted the fiendish malice of Satan.

Sure, from this time, of his game, and liar as he always is, he now proceeds to press his point by directly impugning the word of God and blasphemously insulting Him, by suggesting that the Creator had motives of His own for His command. "No," he says, " you shall not die the death"—mark the boldness of the words—"for God doth know, that in what day soever you shall eat thereof, your eyes shall be opened, and you shall be as gods, knowing good and evil" (Gen. ii. 45). See, my dear young friends, the devil's stamp here. He has not forgotten the temptation that ruined him, so he, first by insinuation, and then by a bold lie, connects a temptation to pride with the forbidden apple, and tries to persuade the mother of the human race to disobey God. You know the result. Eve takes it in her hands, looks at it, tastes it, and gives it to Adam, who also tastes it, and then the fatal act is done. Thus God is offended, and thus every human being, with the exception of our blessed Lady, is involved in the sin.

8. But, before we consider the effects of this deed,

let us see if we cannot learn something from our first mother's blunder, by examining the steps which led to it.

The first mistake she made was in parleying with the serpent at all. No sooner did she listen to him than, as we have seen, she herself began to question God's word. So true is it that "evil communications corrupt good manners!"

Now, you, my young friends, will often come across people who question what Almighty God does, as if they knew better what should be done than He does. You must carefully avoid joining in what they say; for if you do not God, will allow you to suffer the penalty of those who tempt Him; and you will imbibe false opinions and habits of scoffing if you listen to them with pleasure.

Eve ended by believing the devil when he came out with his bold lie: this was mistake number two.

What right had she to believe the devil? Had he any claim upon her that she should believe him when he spoke against the God who made her? Yet she did believe him without any reason, when she had gone so far as to doubt the word of God.

You will meet with many who have brought themselves into the same dilemma, and it will be well for you to put this down amongst the maxims for your daily guidance: that all who, after doubting, reject the revealed word of God, are sure to pay the penalty of their infidelity by taking up, as if they were true as the Gospel, the most absurd speculations, which they believe without either rhyme or reason to support them.

CHAPTER III.

The Effects.

1. Now, however, it is time for us to see how grievously disappointed our first parents were when they had eaten the forbidden fruit. They expected to have their eyes opened, and to know good and evil. Their eyes were indeed open to the knowledge of evil, but not to that of good.

Had Eve been loyal to Almighty God when she heard the blasphemy uttered by the serpent, she might have known that, except in him and his companions, there was no such thing as evil; while, as for good, in knowing God she knew the only good. Now, however, she learned to know evil.

2. I will try, by means of a simile, to show you the confusion into which the whole being of man was thrown by sin.

Suppose you were invited to a concert, to hear a famous musician play the piano, and that in the midst of a magnificent performance which filled you with delight, a number of disorderly persons were to rush into the room, hurl the musician from his seat, and each hammering at a note, produce a fearful din; although the instrument would be the very same from which but a short time before such sweet sounds proceeded, would not the subsequent discord be overwhelming? This is very like what occurred at the fall of our first parents.

Suppose, again, that after this confusion had gone

on for some time, one of these disturbers, stronger than the rest, having borne for a certain period with the universal uproar, should seize the musician, blindfold him, place him at the piano, and oblige him to play just as one rough after another holding his hand may happen to please, until at last the strongest, driving away the others, should make him obey him as a slave! This would be a picture not only of what happened to Adam and Eve, but also of what we all occasionally feel, and is in an especial manner the picture of those who, forsaking grace, deprive themselves of its beneficial influence. I will explain.

3. God made man like a beautiful musical instrument composed of many notes. The musician to play upon this instrument is the will, enlightened by reason and the knowledge of God. The notes of the instrument are, I will not say our passions, because sin has caused passions to be a term of evil import, but our inclinations.

Now, my dear young friends, if you will only examine yourselves, you will find that your inclinations are not bad of their own nature, but are only so when they play out of tune. They are, in fact, every one of them good, when reason, guided by God, employs them in a proper way! Take, for instance, greediness or gluttony; what is it? An inclination which God has given us to seek food, for the health and life of the body. But when, this inclination is abused, it injures the body, instead of doing it good! I have shown you before that each of your senses has its inclinations, which, if made a wrong use of, tends to injure you instead of doing you good.

These inclinations of the body, then, we will compare to the treble notes of the instrument, because they attract more notice, perhaps, than those of the soul, being, like their prototypes, shrill, although not deep.

These inclinations are useful when kept in their place, but, like high notes played out of harmony, are very confusing when suffered to assert control over us. It was the tyranny of these inclinations which made our first parents ashamed of themselves; and God allows us to feel these same inclinations very strongly at times, although at the same time He enables us, by a particular grace, to gain perfect mastery over them.

That shame, which was in the first instance simply an effect of sin, God Himself has sanctified and blessed—modesty, the guardian and protector of one of the most beautiful of Christian virtues, namely, holy purity, by which we adore and honour the sanctity of God in our bodies, by keeping them in continual subjection as a sacred charge committed to us by Him.

We have seen enough mischief done by one of the deep notes (the inclinations of the soul), namely, pride; and we need not wonder at this, since Eve allowed the devil to put his finger upon it! And yet—is pride an unmitigated evil? I question it. Certainly, the mean, thief-like pride of Satan was evil in its essence and evil in all its fruits.

But what was it that made St. Michael say,

"Who is like unto God?" Was it not a noble comprehension of the paramount claims of justice, and a spontaneous acknowledgment that the payment of a just debt is true nobility!

And call it by what name you will, I hope that you will ever cultivate the truly noble inclination which urges you to give to God all that you owe to Him. Mean, cringing spirits are not the stuff that saints are made of! Be humble, for humility is truth; be honest with God and man, because honesty is true nobility.

I need not go much further into this subject, except to repeat that every passion of the soul is a deep note in your nature, jarring indeed, when played out of tune, but only tending to the harmony of the whole, when played properly. Yes, even two words tell us as much as this: envy is a passion, but is not emulation a source of good? What, however, is envy? It is emulation carried so far that, not content with excelling, it would injure others! Again, anger is a passion as zeal is virtue; but is not zeal sometimes a just anger against that which outrages God? And now I think you understand the application of my figure.

4. No sooner had Adam and Eve sinned than the light which God had shed upon their souls disappeared: so that, instead of knowing good, a cloud of ignorance at once overshadowed them, and every passion of the soul and body began to cry out, each for its own particular gratification. This was an opening of their eyes to the knowledge of evil which they had little expected. No wonder they were

astonished, bewildered, and ashamed at the wild confusion which sin brought into their whole being. Up to that time the perfect harmony which had existed within them had left them ignorant of many different impulses, just because they acted so sweetly as to escape their notice. Then with what intensity must they not have hated their deed, and the vile serpent who had deceived them into it!

5. But what, you will say, means the rest of the picture? Just this. You have heard of the predominant passion; and you know that whatever you do, you do through your will; and that whatever your will does, it does it because your understanding tells it, whether rightly or wrongly, that it is good so to do. Therefore, when I said that the strongest of the disturbers brought back the musician, I meant that a passion stronger than the others, deceives the will, and makes it look upon as good what this passion desires. Now, this is what the strongest passion always does; and although the others all make the will obey them in turn, it often happens that one passion is so strong that it predominates over all the rest, and, taking full possession of the man, makes him do whatever it likes. Thus we see men devoting every energy of body and soul to rise to a higher position, driven on by ambition; others, carried away by avarice, devote themselves to the acquisition of riches; and others, again, ruin body and soul by dissipation, until they are worn out by their own excesses.

I have now shown you what a terrible storm sin has brought into the world. It is a storm which

Adam and Eve felt—a storm which involves in wholesale ruin many who, through their own fault, expose themselves to it, by forsaking God.

It is, however, thank God, a storm, the clouds of which your heavenly Father has dispersed from your soul, leaving behind only traces of it—for reasons which, as we shall see, are more than sufficient to make you rather glad than otherwise that it once took place.

CHAPTER IV.

The Sun of Justice.

1. I AM not going, my dear young friends, to enter at present into the discussion of that mystery of divine compassion and mercy, through which atonement was made for sin by the Son of God, who, for the love of us, became man and paid our debt. No, this mystery is in itself sufficient for endless meditation, but it would lead us far from the subject we are now considering. I have compared the havoc made in the soul of man by sin to a storm, and verily a storm it was.

Picture to yourself a beautiful tract of country dotted all over with farmhouses and cottages, each with its neat little garden and orchard, with pleasant lanes, sweet-smelling hedgerows and verdant meadows, with green-pastures, where herds of cattle and flocks of sheep are peacefully grazing, and with rich fields of growing corn. Add to the landscape majestic forest trees which afford shelter from the heat, and let a glorious sunshine shed its fulgence over all. Imagine this, and it will represent to you the soul of man clothed in its original justice.

2. Evening comes on. The inhabitants of this lovely country retire to rest, and soon with trembling anxiety listen to the wind which begins to rise, and is soon followed by vivid lightning and loud claps of thunder. The rain and hail come down in torrents, and everything is threatened with destruction. Yet on the morrow, possibly all is calm again. But the hurricane has left its traces. The glistening raindrops, which beautify and freshen wherever they fall, are not the only marks of what has occurred. Deep furrows have been left by the new-made rivulets as they rushed across the country—here a noble oak tree has been rent by the electric fluid, there lies another torn up by the roots—perhaps a cottage or a farmhouse has been struck, and its terrified inmates are running wildly hither and thither seeking for shelter, and bewailing the loss of their property and their homestead; certain it is, that on all sides you would surely see evidences of a great catastrophe, although the sunshine had reasserted its influence, and a gentle shower had washed from every leaf and bud the mire and dirt strewn over them by this convulsion of nature.

3. Thus has it been with ourselves. Before we were born, the sin of our first parents had come like a hurricane, and had stamped upon our being the marks of the evil which had been done; so that, when we came into this world, all the powers of our souls and bodies bore the traces of that fatal storm. Sin

disfigured each one of us with its foul stain, and so universal was the taint, that only one of all simple human beings escaped original sin, namely, the ever Immaculate Mother of God, and she escaped it by the special interference of her Divine Son, who shielded her from its approach.

No sooner, however, had sin been committed, than the compassion of our Heavenly Father began to show itself. Yes, "God so loved the world as to give His only begotten Son, that whosoever believeth in Him may not perish, but may have life everlasting" (John iii. 16). In other words: God, seeing that the outrage committed by man was infinite, and could only be atoned for by a being at once divine and human, instead of being moved by vengeance to punish mankind, by a beautiful invention of His divine compassion, heaped new favours upon him. Oh, wonderful compassion of our dear good God! Father! could Thy children but see what it embraces, would there be one tongue that would cease its thanksgiving, one cold heart that could refuse Thee its love!

Yes, man's salvation was determined upon as soon as sin was committed. At that instant was the Redeemer promised! So that, without one moment's delay, salvation was provided for man by faith in a Redeemer to come—salvation even before the coming of the Redeemer—salvation by faith, "that whosoever believeth in Him, may not perish, but may have life everlasting" (John iii. 16).

4. My dear young friends, long before you were thought of, the Sun of Justice had appeared; had

put an end to the ragings of the storms; had shed again a bright radiance over the world of human beings; giving them light, hope and guidance to help them on their way, and strength to walk in it. although that storm had encumbered it with obstacles, and even enfeebled the powers of man! The Son of God incarnate, for love of you, has come, and He says of Himself: "I am the way, the truth and the life" (John xiv. 6). "The way, that you may know how to live pleasing in my sight; the truth, that you may be saved from error; the life, that you may have help to make you capable of keeping my commandments."

CHAPTER V.

He is well cared whom God takes care of.

1. LET us quietly look our life in the face and ask ourselves, now that the storm is over, what we have lost by it, and what we have received in its place.

We have lost original justice. That is to say, we have lost the harmony produced by our numerous inclinations acting in union under the control of reason, reason being subject to God.

But when our first parents possessed this original justice, was it sufficient to keep them from going astray? The light of reason did not prevent their being deceived by the old serpent. Their upright will did not restrain pride from breaking out and separating them from God! No, as the result proves, all their advantages were insufficient to preserve them in justice, whilst, on the other hand, they had not so great a claim upon God's compassion as we have.

2. If they had not fallen, should we, their children, have been safe under the same circumstances ? God alone knows. At any rate, God is our keeper now, and He has left us blind and lame for no other reason than that our helplessness may keep us humble, and our very misery may make us objects of compassion to our Heavenly Father, moving Him to direct us that we may go right, and to bear with us when we go wrong.

The traces of sin remain within us, many of the penalties of sin remain upon us, weighing us down. We are blind and lame, subject to the assaults of passion on the one hand, while, on the other, God has become the light of our eyes, the director of our steps, our strength in weakness, and because of our helplessness, has also thrown His boundless compassion around us; and this compassion has very often more to do with our salvation than all the other blessings He has given us.

3. The chief traces of the storm within us and their counterbalancing blessings are the following:—

1st. A blinded understanding, of which God has Himself become the light.

2nd. A wavering, unsteady will, of which He has become the stay.

3rd. Tumultuous and unruly passions, which God Himself, by His personal intervention, assists us to keep in subjection.

4th. A life subject to suffering, with the merits

of Jesus Christ for our solace, and His leadership for our example.

5th. The last but not the least privilege of our fallen state, our claim upon boundless Divine compassion.

4. But, before I speak of these things, let me say one word upon a subject of which later I must say a great deal, namely, the refreshing shower, even Baptism, which has washed from your souls the stains cast upon them by original sin.

You came into the world not merely with the traces of sin, but with the very sin itself upon you. Clothed in this foul mantle, you were separated from God; and if not the objects of His wrath, you were at least objects of abhorrence to Him by reason of it—you were deprived of His friendship—you were incapable of entering heaven! But the Son of God, who had long ago purchased forgiveness for sin, would not leave you under a guilt in which you had no personal share, and so His divine blood, like a gentle shower, washed your soul, restored you to His friendship, and left you a being whose lot had indeed been altered, yet, thanks to our dear Lord, hardly rendered the worse by sin.

CHAPTER VI.

The blinded understanding, and Faith.

1. I SUPPOSE there are few things more self-evident than the terrible blindness with which sin has stricken the human understanding.

What, for example, can be more absurd than that

reasonable beings should imagine heaven to be peopled by a whole host of rival deities, whose history, far from exhibiting signs of divinity, reveals actions unworthy even of men, instead of acknowledging that every creature must owe its existence to One Supreme Creator, infinite in every perfection, and who, consequently, must claim the entire worship and homage of all! Yet, in spite of the strong aspirations of a section of humanity towards something more perfect, this has been the belief of the larger portion of it for more than 4000 years!

Common sense, you will say, should have been sufficient to teach men that there could be but One Being, who, uncreated Himself, had created all else; and it is true that common sense always did teach men this! The mischief was, that then, as now, common sense was blindfolded, or, it may be better to say, smothered, by human passions.

These so-called deities were far from being God-like in their deportment; they were said to have made strange revolutions in heaven, to have played curious tricks upon each other, to have fought, intrigued, and treated each other very badly. Common sense had, in reality, nothing to do with the worship of these gods; when it asserted its rights, it made game of them; they were worshipped in open defiance of it: but why?

Because men saw, in the fables of their own invention, images of themselves! Not of themselves as God made them, but of themselves as the slaves of sin and ignorance which they had become, and they needed gods to suit their fancy.

2. This was, indeed, a strange upsetting of the order of things, and shows that man had always within him, like the devil, a desire to make Himself like God! Fallen into ignorance, and become the helpless slave of passion, far from showing any trace of being like God, he finds himself unable to act as a reasonable human being. What then does he do? At all events he shows wit and invention, if not wisdom—he makes gods like himself, seeing that he cannot make himself like God!

He sees that pride, ambition, avarice, and sensuality characterize himself, and, according to this pattern, he invents heroes, attaches to each a history of wonderful exploits, and fills an imaginary heaven with beings who differ from himself only in this—that they are even more wicked than he. To these beings he offers his adoration, making to himself gods, who are nothing else than gigantic specimens of his own most degraded passions and vices.

Such, my dear young friends, is the explanation of paganism, and it certainly shows that the understanding of fallen man has become terribly blind.

The folly of men did not, however, end here. Not only did they adore, under the name of God, their own vices, but they made, with their own hands, images of these gods, and, with a stupidity perfectly unaccountable, worshipped the very things they had themselves manufactured. No doubt the devil, who even in hell takes a miserable satisfaction in stealing honour which belongs to God, sometimes helped them in their folly by dwelling in their stone and wooden gods, and deceiving his foolish votaries by a sort of conjuring which, in their ignorance, they often took for manifestations of a divine power. These tricks were, however, oftener played by cunning rogues, who lived by serving the idols, more than by means of evil spirits.

4. With this history before us, which is, to a great extent, that of 4000 years, we need not, I think, be astonished at anything we may hear of the blindness of the human understanding; nor will it be difficult to comprehend that man is in need of some very plain guide, without which even redemption itself would be but of little practical use to him. Yet, there are men who, with the historical facts of paganism before them, have the folly to cry out against every attempt to interfere with what they call their glorious gift of liberty. When we see this, are we not tempted to come to the conclusion —and it is, indeed, the true one—that such men are as blind as the pagans themselves, only their blindness has taken another form.

So much for the paganism of the past. It is an historical fact; no one can deny it. But as God only knows what will not be denied by some people, we find proof of the possibility of such a state of things in the fact that there are pagans existent even now. Take, for instance, India, China, Japan, and Persia. In Persia there are men at this present day who worship fire; as for the Hindoos, you are well aware what hideous monsters they adore as gods.

5. We need not, however, go so far afield to look for proofs of the blindness of the understanding of

those who do not obey a better guide than their own reason. Even before the coming of our Lord this blindness could be avoided. The chosen people of God had at least the knowledge of the true God, and this fact was pretty well known to other nations; and, besides, when the people of other countries—as, for instance, Job, the man of Huz— were simple-minded, and obeyed the law written in their own hearts, God revealed Himself to them, so that, unless wilfully blind, every one could be saved by belief in a Saviour to come, and that this Saviour was sufficiently known by tradition is proved by the Book of Job. Yet in those days men were obliged, in a sense, to go out of their way to see the truth. Blindness and falsehood (produced by passion and in contradiction to common sense) were round about them, and were the first things that met their view. Little wonder, then, that when once their own blind passion had made falsehood acceptable, men should lose sight of truth for ever, and should fall under the yoke of the prevailing error, however absurd.

6. Now, however, my dear young friends, things are altered. The Sun of Justice has arisen; His gospel has been preached; the civilized world even glories in the name of Christendom! What then? For one cause or another, in one way or another, men have refused to be guided by the light of faith. A divine power on earth is in their very midst, and, instead of acknowledging it, they ignore it, and turn away their eyes from it, lest, haply, common sense should tell them that it was divine. In spite,

however, of every opposition, it daily gains new strength, and proves, by its undying life—by its unity—by the sanctity of its doctrine—by its power of converting nations, and making its obedient children something more than human, that it is divine: and yet men will not see this, but either rage with anger against it, or else, like the men of old, who attributed the pentecostal gift of tongues to the effects of new wine, get rid of the evidences of divinity, and of their own credit for common sense, at one and the same time.

By the sophistry of some foolish arguments, or even without any reason at all, they reject the evidence of their senses; and why?

Because this divine thing, God's living voice on earth—His Church—by His own authority, bids them listen to its voice, and receive from it those revealed truths which He has committed to its keeping! Have we not proof here of the wilful blindness which clouds man's understanding, in the obstinacy with which it refuses and rejects this divine guidance?

7. This, however, is but the beginning of absurdities; for, after rejecting the truth contrary to the dictates of that sense which makes him a human being, man throws open his bewildered mind to falsehood, extravagance, and wild speculations of every shape and form, as varied as they are outrageous; and the sight of these vagaries might be a source of amusement were not the subject one of too serious a nature for sport.

We have, as I said before, men so carried away by

the conceit of their own reasoning powers, as to reject altogether the idea of a Creator, and, confounding Him with His creature, imagine all things to be emanations of the Deity; so that, as they consider their own souls to be the most noble emanation, they put themselves at the head of all things, and make themselves, in fact, a sort of God.

8. And others there are who, taking up a theory of development and progress, come to a conclusion they are almost ashamed to own, namely, that they are nothing more than the lineal descendants of monkeys.

To vary the scene we have religious maniacs, who, taking the Bible as their watchword, but removing it from the only foundation on which it can rest, namely, a divine and visible keeper and interpreter, dissever text from context, pulling it as it were to pieces limb from limb, and making these maimed and mutilated members contradict every doctrine they were written to teach, and prove every absurdity which can be devised, until many honest men, with no particular principles of their own, come to the almost pardonable conclusion that religion and the breaking of unorthodox heads are synonymous terms.

9. Then we arrive at a phenomenon, which, try as we may to retain our gravity, will make us laugh in spite of ourselves: I mean that droll creation, the State Church. Certainly this invention formed no part of the design of Christianity's Divine Founder, although we may conclude that He has permitted it in order to render a human substitute

for religion: in itself a most absurd thing—ineffably more absurd.

You have seen one of those collections of cats, mice, rabbits, rats, pigeons, &c., denominated a happy family! The State Church is something like it. It is a religious happy family, shut up in a box and kept in order by State formalities and State pay. In the real affair, good feeding prevents the cat from eating up the rabbits, rats, and pigeons; and by some similar arrangement the members of the State Church are kept from devouring one another—although I cannot but say that if the two happy families are compared, that of the irrational animals will appear to be by far the most peaceable. In the State Church, indeed, there has been at times something like peace, so long as a comfortable indifference to all forms of Christianity has lulled the whole family, as it were, into a nap. But at other times it has been otherwise; and just now, unfortunately for the tranquillity of the cage, a peculiar species of animal has made its appearance within it, and has aroused every one of the inmates. This creature goes by the name of the Romanizing tendency, and is the only thing to which the religious happy family has any decided objection.

It would, however, be as great a mistake to suppose that this Romanizing tendency is in any sense related to God's Church, as it is to imagine that a monkey could be related to a man! The Romanizing tendency is absolutely ignorant of divine faith. It can, indeed, with the ape's power of imitation, copy some Catholic practices rather deftly; and, by the right of private judgment, it protests that it holds as opinions some of those things which the Church knows by faith. Then comes the disturbance. This interloper has enough of the appearance of Popery to set the whole menagerie by the ears, while in reality the position it takes up makes it most essentially Protestant. The Romanizing party is only another instance of the blindness of man's understanding. It is doubly Protestant, for it protests at one and the same time against Protestant Sectarians and the Catholic Church. It even abuses its own Bishops, and accuses that Church which it calls its mother of rejecting the truth and of falsifying the promises of God.

10. I think I have now said enough to show what proposed, namely, that the understanding of fallen man is capable of any absurdity, however much opposed to common sense, and it is now time to see what remedy our good God has provided to save us from the ravages into which we might be led by a fatal blindness.

Multiplied as have been at all times the proofs of this blindness, it is nevertheless true, that from the very moment when the Redeemer was promised to our first mother, man was not left without a light to guide him. His want of discernment of it was a wilful closing of the eyes. That light was faith: first, faith in a Redeemer to come; then, faith in the Redeemer when come; and now, faith in the truths which He has committed to the keeping of His Church for our sakes.

This light was not a guide to the Jew alone; tradition put it at the disposal of the Gentile also; and no nation was so remote, no individual so hidden, as to be beyond the reach of this light—for if every other means failed, God Himself would reveal it to the soul who in simplicity sought to know Him. Yes, the knowledge of God was written on the heart of man, and could only be blotted out by passion and by wilful blindness.

The truth of this is apparent in the history of holy Job, who, in the midst of his sufferings, uttered a truth which, for doctrinal correctness, might have come from the mouth of a well-instructed Catholic, although he belonged to a Gentile nation: "For I know that my Redeemer liveth. And in the last day I shall rise out of the earth, and I shall be clothed again in my skin, and in my flesh I shall see my God. Whom I myself shall see, and my eyes shall behold, and not another: this my hope is laid up in my bosom" (Job ix. 25, 26, 27).

Lest, however, blindness should overrun the earth, and the Gentile should have no means of verifying the traditions of the future Redeemer, a nation is chosen by God, in which the worship and knowledge of the true God shall be preserved.

But how was this to be done? and how was a nation, itself prone to imitate the idolatry of its neighbours, to be kept in the worship of the true God? Ah! here we can see God's remedy for human blindness; here we can perceive how, by means of faith, God speaks to man.

Yes, continually was the light of faith kept burning amongst the people of the Jews, and by the very same means by which it is kept burning now. In that nation God raised up first one human voice and then another to speak to His people, and to claim from them to be heard and believed with divine faith. What was Moses, who, armed with a divine authority by the visible power of God, who said to him, "Go, and I will be with thee," but a voice of God, speaking to God's people? What were the signs and wonders that accompanied his mission? Were they not evidences of the authority by which he spoke? What were the judges? What the prophets? Were they not all living voices of God? Did not each speak with the same certainty? Was not each stamped with the same evidence?

11. And when our Lord Himself came, although He was the Son of God, He asked not to be believed, except on the strength of the evidences of His divinity.

12. It was the same with the infant Church. It was the living voice of God; it showed the evidences of a divine presence within it.

The same voice speaks now—it shows equally now the evidences of a divine presence. Why, then, you will perhaps say, do so many now refuse to believe that voice?

I will answer that question by asking two or three more.

Why did rational men who were present at the sermon of St. Peter at Jerusalem refer his gift to the effect of new wine?

Why did the Pharisees who heard our Lord Himself, call Him Beelzebub and attribute His miracles to the devil?

Why did some of the Jews rebel against Moses?

Why was Pharaoh incredulous when miracles were worked before him? Because men who allow themselves to be governed by passion and unruly desires are blind—wilfully blind. That is the reason, and no other.

13. In two or three places in the Gospel our Blessed Lord spoke of the necessity of people becoming like little children if they wished to be saved: " Unless you be converted, and become as little children, you shall not enter into the kingdom of heaven" (Matt. xviii. 3). Perhaps you will ask in what must people become like little children in order to be fit to enter heaven; and I will tell you. Were I to say that children knew more than their elders, you would laugh, knowing that this is not the fact. And yet a tolerably sharp child is often more clever than many grown up people whose inclinations are engaged, in judging whether what is narrated ought to be received as truth, or rejected as foolish and absurd. The reason of this is, that the child's judgment is less darkened by passion than that of the grown-up person. I do not say, that you cannot make a child believe what is false, if what you tell it carries an air of probability—but I say, that to make a child reject against sound judgment what is true, and receive in preference what is false, is quite impossible.

Here we have the reason why people who wish to be saved must become as little children.

14. It was this spirit of childhood which taught Abel to sacrifice to the one God. This it was that taught Job and the other Gentiles to find traces of the knowledge of God in their own hearts. This it was that made Abraham, Isaac, and Jacob God's faithful servants. It was this that taught the faithful Israelites to see at all times the evidences that accompanied God's voice, wherever it was. It was the spirit of childhood which drew our Lord's disciples round Him. The same spirit drew "daily" into the early Church "such as should be saved." It is this same spirit which teaches faithful souls to bow their heads down now to God's living voice on earth, the Church. This spirit it is which makes all give heed to divine guidance—a divine voice speaking through the little Catechism.

15. Yes, to such an extent is this true, that from this same book children learn their lessons, the poor and simple become wise, learned philosophers draw food for the mind, and saints gather matter for contemplation.

Faith saves man from every vagary and bestows on him every light.

Would you know the mysteries of the Godhead? You have them in your Catechism.

Would you know something about yourselves? I am teaching you from the Catechism.

Would you be safe from all serious error in matters of science? Never believe anything contrary to the Catechism. Would you know the way to heaven? It is taught you in the Catechism.

Would you learn how to find help on the way? You will find this also in the Catechism.

16. Do you not now see, my dear young friends, the remedy which God has provided against a blinded understanding? He has told us certain truths about Himself, and has given us the assurance, by a special heavenly voice, that these truths come from Him. In fact, He has made us so certain of what He has spoken, that He has even made us a present of His own certainty; so that, although we are incapable of knowing what God knows, still we can in one sense say, I am as certain (for instance) that there are Three Persons in one God, as God Himself can make me, by giving me His own certainty. Such is the real meaning of divine faith.

17 One word more. Although this is the privilege of every child of Holy Church, all do not make proper use of it. Some have faith, and yet take little trouble to know much about God, and so do not love Him, and even fall into a horrible forgetfulness of Him. This is ingratitude; and to such persons faith itself will only bring a more severe judgment.

There are others to whom faith teaches the way to heaven, and holds out the help by which they may easily get there—who will not walk in the right way, but will rather choose any other, and who also utterly refuse to make use of the help offered to them.

18. Faith is indeed a great blessing; but it must be a practical faith—a faith which will make us love and serve the God it teaches us to know—a faith which

will make us walk in the way that it points out, and use the arms it puts into our hands.

Let such, my dear young friends, be your faith, and then you need never fear to have a blinded understanding, because God has made you a present of His own bright truth to guide you safely on your way.

CHAPTER VII.
The weak Will and the Gospel.

1. It is difficult sometimes to separate, for the sake of explanation, things which of themselves are intimately connected with each other. It is not easy to say how much of the weakness of the will towards good proceeds from inherent feebleness of the will itself, and how much proceeds from the way in which different passions, as I have before described, drag the will now in this direction, now in that, imparting to it a wavering disposition. A glance at the way in which the understanding influences the will may possibly help us out of our difficulty, and show us that its weakness has its origin in a combination of both causes. Although, in the last chapter, I laid more stress upon wilful blindness of the understanding than on simple ignorance, still I think that what I have said shows very plainly that sin has cast a great curse of ignorance upon the human mind—an ignorance only to be eradicated by religious education, or. better still, by the practice of a Christian life. Now. as I have said before, the will depends for guidance

on the understanding; and it follows simply enough, as a consequence, that the will cannot get firmness of purpose so long as ignorance leaves the understanding a blank. It can have no purpose of good at all, because good is not pointed out to it. So much, then, for the will's inherent weakness.

2. On the other hand, however, the noisy passions are always showing to the understanding each its own little hobby. One shows it how nice it is to gratify vanity; another, what a grand thing it is to be rich; a third, how pleasant it is to have nice things to eat; a fourth, what a gratification it is to have revenge for some fancied injury! Thus is the understanding dazzled and the will pulled about, until not only has the latter no firmness in keeping to what is good, but is like a child in the midst of a swarm of butterflies, who runs first after one and then another, until in the end he catches none at all.

3. Now, you see that, although in the next chapter I shall have to speak about the disturbance caused by the passions, it is impossible not to allude to the subject in this place. If, however, these two curses which sin has brought upon the will are so closely connected, the remedies for them are not so, or rather our good God has been so generous in His methods of cure, that I can afford to apply a distinct one to each case. I will speak now of the eternal remedy which God has given us in the guidance, warnings, invitations, and promises contained in the Sacred Scriptures, and I shall include everything which a child of the Church has at his disposal

under the general name of the Gospel, and will afterwards say something upon grace and other helps.

4. When I described to you the various absurdities into which man has been led by blindness of the understanding, I did so at some length, because I know that many of you, my dear young friends, will certainly be thrown a good deal amongst the spiritually blind, and I think that knowledge on the subject is calculated to save you from astonishment at finding the world, so to speak, turned upside down, and also, that to dispel ignorance is to destroy the best chance of propagation which such follies can have.

5. The case is different here; for, although we have indeed to deal with evils which are quite as widely spread, they are of such a nature that there is no advantage to be found in knowing anything about them; nay, it is your duty to avoid them, even in thought. They are evils which you cannot even approach without being dragged into whirlpools of misery, which it is much easier to get into than to emerge from again. Nevertheless, I have one duty concerning these evils, viz., to say something toward off the mistake into which you might possibly fall, of believing that, after all, the service of God must present some great difficulty, since so many people are found to neglect it. To avoid so fatal an error, I will not shrink from saying enough to prove to you that the very opposite of this is the case, viz., that the service of God is the only thing that can save you from falling under a very hard yoke indeed.

6. The first thing which strikes us, in the spectacle

of forgetfulness of duty and neglect of God which is presented to us by the world, is that these things do not spring from any deliberate refusal to serve God. The will of a child is not so much like a mule which stands still through obstinacy, as it is like a steam engine which stands still because the fire which raises the steam to propel it has not been kindled. The clouds of ignorance are still upon the mind. The will is not moved forward by the love of God, because, through a mistaken idea that the child is still too young for such teachings, or else through negligence, which is even worse than a mistake, the little one has not been taught to know God, the knowledge of whom can alone set the heart on fire.

7. These errors are, alas! too common; and those who fall into them are little aware of their fatal consequences. By neglect of early teaching, that precious time is wasted in which, perhaps, better than at any other, the seeds of virtue can be sown—for then the child, with its genuine impulses all fresh, would, if treated properly, spring forward to God, and become a very giant of divine love—a warrior fully armed, before even the first real assault of passion had time either to dazzle the mind or ensnare the heart.

In confirmation of this, look at the lives of saints, and in particular of our own holy founder. No doubt from earliest infancy he showed signs of being possessed of supernatural graces; but what was the course pursued by his pious mother? She stilled his childish petulance with the crucifix: "Look, my child," she would say to him, "what Jesus suffered for the love of us!" From his earliest years St. Paul of the Cross was trained in the love of God; and from his earliest years that love, strongly burning within him, enkindled love to man, so that he taught his brother and his young companions to love also! How many young saints there have been who, but for the love of God, would have been young sinners? And, piteous thought! how many possible young saints have had their holiness lost, endangered or delayed, through the want of this early training?

What, however, generally happens? The child grows up innocent indeed, but also how empty! Poor silly thing! how can it have learned to love the God whom it has not learned to know? What is to prevent it from offending, by numberless venial sins, a God it has not been taught to love?

But if parents waste precious time and delay, one thing will not delay. As surely as that child carries within it the seeds of Adam's sin, so surely will passion dazzle the mind; and, without love, without strength, without grace, why should not its allurements steal away the heart?

8. But sometimes another mistake, not less fatal than the first, is made. Instead of the child's being taught to offer its heart to God by fervent ejaculations and short acts of love, it is made to join in long family prayers, the meaning of which it cannot understand. The duty of family prayer is a lesson which Christian parents will not neglect to teach it. So far, well. Nevertheless, if children were taught to love God, it were better to let the love of God

teach them to pray. Let us examine what is in reality conveyed to children by the prayer-lesson, and I think you will agree with me that the system is not a good one, and often teaches that which should never be learned, and what will perhaps never be forgotten during the whole course of a very long life. In the first place, the limbs of children are at once soft, and tender, and full of life, requiring almost continual motion. Lesson number one, then, consists in connecting the thought of prayer with aching knees and a constrained position—and I believe many children never entirely get over this impression.

Lesson number two is worse than this. One of the first things a child is taught is, that wilful distractions at prayer offend God. Now children must think about something; and, if they do not understand what they say, what can people expect them to think about? So almost of necessity the child learns to say a number of prayers, and to think of everything that comes into his head whilst he is saying them. Here is indeed a fruitful lesson! It will fetter the child with at least one habit of venial sin to accuse himself of, with sorrow, at his first confession, and, God knows, perhaps at his last as well!

9. So much for these mistakes, the consequences of which I would advise you, my young friends, to avert, by taking the matter into your own hands, and learning, as soon as possible, not only to love God, but also to occupy yourself with the thought of God's love, making ejaculations whenever you

find it difficult to attend to particular prayers at which you may be expected to assist.

10. Let us, however, go on and see how men fall into a confirmed neglect of God. From what we have seen, it is plain that it is impossible for the will to move forward in the service of God until ignorance is from some source or other changed into knowledge. It is far otherwise, however, as to the power of going away from God. Nothing is so easily deceived as an unformed mind: it is ripe for deception and follows the first false light shown to it. Thus, is innocent ignorance only a beautiful thing to be wept over—a victim surely destined (as, alas! too many are) to destruction, or to be carried away captive in the devil's chains. Thus it is that children are led away from God's service. There is a very familiar truth which, however, people seldom realize. It is that *mortal sin kills the soul*. To ask, then, why those whose innocence has been thus destroyed are hurried from one sin to another, and why they do not immediately return to God, at least when they find themselves galled by the devil's yoke, is very much the same thing as to ask why a corpse does not return to life, or why it is not disgusted with the worm which is feeding upon its heart. Perhaps it is the compassion of our dear good God, who so often raises dead souls to life, which makes it difficult to realize this truth. Nevertheless it is true; and there is another thing not less so, which, however frightful, I will not hesitate to tell you, because it will serve to make you cling tightly to your baptismal robe of innocence, and

resolve never to part with it. It is this: that *when once mortal sin is committed, unless God by a miracle restores life again to that soul by the grace of repentance, it can never get it back, and is practically lost for ever.* God alone knows how many young persons, after once forsaking Him, have become miserable slaves of vice, and are dragged through its mire during a whole life, until, guilt laden, they fall into the eternal abyss.

11. I think I have shown you now that the sight of innumerable sinners around us does not necessarily prove that the service of God is hard. Far from it. Hear what our Lord Himself says of it: " My yoke is sweet, and my burden light" (Matt. xi. 30); and so it is, to those who make use of the means provided by God to turn our hearts to Him.

12. Before, however, we begin to speak of this, let us take a look round and see if the devil's yoke is a pleasant one. Let us ask ourselves one question, and answer it honestly, and that will be sufficient. What does sin do ? Sin fills prisons, lunatic asylums, and hospitals. Sin causes wars and adds to their horrors. Sin breeds quarrels in families. One vice often takes away the means of getting a livelihood, by depriving a man of his situation. Sin very often turns good pay into a producer of increased poverty and greater wretchedness than small wages. In short, as sin first brought evil into the world, so it has ever since brought into it every misery ; and, although the innocent sometimes suffer with the guilty, yet evil always falls on the unfortunate slave of vice, even when others escape its bitter fruits.

Always remember this, my dear young friends, as it is a very valuable lesson, and a lesson, moreover, which it is better to learn from one who tells it to you, because he loves you, than to find it out by sad, and perhaps fruitless experience.

13. It is now, however, time to turn to those sweet and strong influences which our dear good God has provided for us in the Gospel—in order, first, to draw the weak will to serve Him; next, to shield it round about, lest it should forsake Him on the road, and then, to fire it with new courage at every step.

14. Before we begin, let me remark what a different feeling comes over me in dealing with a subject like this, from that which I experience when speaking of human miseries and follies. In touching upon such things one feels, as it were, a sort of freedom, as with subjects in themselves requiring little explanation, because they are self-evident, and may be summarily dealt with, just as an artist, with two or three strokes of his pen, can bring before us the peculiar expression of some familiar public character.

But when I have to discourse of what belongs rather to heaven than to earth—of those beautiful creations of God's love for His children—I feel as if I were going to spoil something which is too glorious for my clumsy handling, yet which must be spoken of, for fear that silence should cause it to be passed over, and which must even be crowded into a small space, because God has strewn around us so many other things which equally claim our notice.

Such being the case, I must beg you to take for granted, once for all, that anything I may say on these subjects is not only ineffably poor, compared with what I have to describe, but also, that I do not say nearly so much about it as might be said.

I am now going to point out to you, in a few words, under the general name of the Gospel, the various influences (of which the Gospel certainly forms the centre) with which God has ordained that the weak will of man should be supported in good.

15. From what I said in the beginning of this chapter, it will appear that the first influence required is one that will set our hearts, as it were, on fire with the love of God. Is this influence wanting? That God made him is, I suppose, the first thing a Christian parent teaches his child. What an influence is here! It actually requires no reflection. A look at himself—no, not so much as that—his very consciousness of being, and then straight to the throne of God goes the child's first act of love, and the child's will is given to God.

16. Then he must be taught his prayers. He learns the "Our Father," and, in the first word of it, is the idea of having the dear good God for his Father made familiar, while it is taught, with child-like confidence, to ask for those things which He wishes to be asked for, in the very words put into it by God Himself.

17. After this children are taught the "Hail Mary" and the "Apostles' Creed." I will not separate them. Here, after the doctrine of the Unity and

Trinity of God, comes the true love-story: the history of the Son of God made man, and living, suffering, and dying for the love of us. I am not going to enter into this mystery just now: it would lead me too far. What, however, does it all come to? A look at the eternal Son of God; a look at His beautiful, pure Mother; a look at God's annihilation, through love; a look at the beautiful, yet, oh! so small-created nature He took and made His own—that nature He would never part with—in which He lived, suffered, and died, and in which He will live and reign for ever! What influences are here to draw a child's heart to love God! And are not these the very first things that Christian children hear of? Then, again, they are told of the beautiful heaven which is to be theirs, if they love and serve this dear good God; and, when they get a little older, they read in the Gospel and in their prayer-book of those things of which they learnt to lisp in childhood.

18. Does it not seem that a great deal more might be made of these lessons than is usually made? Do not these beautiful truths lose weight from the thoughtless way in which they are learnt? Sometimes they have sunk very deep into children's hearts, when learnt from the lips of very holy mothers. Oh, would that all mothers were holy, were it but to teach these truths to their children! Still, the matter principally concerns ourselves: with us it lies to make these first influences effective which God brings to bear upon the will.

19. Much more might be said upon this subject.

From this point of view, the whole Gospel, and the whole history of religion, are, like magnets, drawing our hearts towards God by the greatness, as well as the variety, of their manifestations of God's astounding love. Here, again, I could not go far without getting beyond exterior influences, so much is one thing connected with another. Each of the Sacraments provided for us by our Saviour is not only a means of grace, but an attraction, drawing you sweetly to love the God who gave it. It is, indeed, true what St. Paul says: "The charity of Christ presseth us" (2 Cor. v. 14). But it is not sufficient for God that He should thus, as it were, steal your hearts: He must warn you to persevere in His service. No one can read the Gospel without being struck by the way in which our Blessed Lord takes for granted man's lack of perseverance. Not only does He show there, how well He knows His creature will tire of living in the daily fulfilment of his duties, but He seems, in warning him, not so much to insist on his doing this, as to bid him take care not to be surprised by death whilst neglecting it. "Watch ye, therefore, because you know not the day, nor the hour" (Matt. xxv. 13). Again: "This know ye, that if the householder did know at what hour the thief would come, he would surely watch, and not suffer his house to be broken open. Be you, then, also ready, for at what hour you think not, the Son of Man will come" (Luke xii. 39, 40). Thus it is that Almighty God would, as it were, wile us into leading a good life, by the fear of being surprised by death; although, did we live a hundred years, they could never be spent so well or so happily as in His service.

20. Then, what shall we say about the promises of God? It seems as if Almighty God would almost force Himself to save us, He has promised heaven to so many different things. Can any one, after reading the Eight Beatitudes, talk of the difficulty of being saved? Do you want heaven to be yours? Be poor in spirit, or suffer persecution for justice sake—it is your own.

Do you want an eternal inheritance? Be meek, and possess the land.

Do you want comfort? Mourn over your own sins and those of others, and you shall be comforted.

Would you like to see God? Be pure of heart, and you shall see Him.

These are only a few of the promises our God has given us.

Judge not, and you shall not be judged. Be merciful, and you shall find mercy. Forgive, and you shall be forgiven; and so on of the rest.

21. Then the weak will want help. Well, in the Gospel we are told two things: in the first place, not to confide in ourselves: "Without me, you can do nothing" (John xv. 4); in the second, where to go for help, with a promise of succour: "Whatsoever you shall ask the Father in my name, He will give it to you" (John xv. 6).

22. Then, as for guidance, there is so much in the Gospel, that every book which has been written on the subject, and every sermon preached on it, find

their text in the sacred pages—so that, if I wish to bring this chapter to an end, the less I say upon the subject the better. I have, however, said enough already to serve my purpose, which was to show you that, while the fall of our first parents has made our wills weak and wavering in good, God has not left us without the means of remedying the defect.

23. Take, then, my dear young friends, your destinies into your own hands. The Gospel is your own property. Jesus Christ has placed it safely in the keeping of your holy mother the Church, in order that you may have it pure and entire. You will find it not only in the Bible—you will find it in the first prayers your lips learn to utter. You will find it in your Catechism. I may almost say, you will find it in the Catholic atmosphere you breathe. Would your will learn to love? Cherish and meditate on the lovely truth the Gospel reveals. Would you persevere in God's service? Listen to the Gospel warnings. Would you be encouraged in good? Dwell with delight on its promises. Would you, in short, be guided safely through life? Everything which can influence your will and strengthen it in good, you may, if you like, make your own, if you only confirm your will in good with that which God has given you for the purpose, namely, the Gospel.

CHAPTER VIII.

The Power that rules the Storm.

1. Although it may, perhaps, seem to some of those into whose hands this book may fall, that I take a cruel pleasure in holding them up as objects of merriment, I cannot, for two or three reasons, give up doing it. In the first place, because these persons take up absurdities as if they were facts; in the second, because the kindest personal feeling for their sensitiveness on the point cannot absolve me from the duty of saving God's children from a mistake which they might easily fall into if I treated with gravity what is, after all, the wildest of follies, namely, the supposing, that what is simply a farce can have any right to the cloak of sanctimonious, long-faced seriousness which it has thrown about itself. And I have yet another motive—one of kindness towards those who are deceived by appearances.

Yes, there may be many souls gifted with that child-like spirit that gives clearness to the mental vision, who, when they find these human vagaries laughed at, may end by not only joining in the laugh, but by being led to separate their lot from that which makes them objects of laughter—although it is rather the position in which they were born and educated which makes them ridiculous, than any folly inherent in themselves.

2. Before I begin, then, to speak of the human soul

in its two phases—either as a scene of contention of rival passions, each trying to obtain the mastery, or as a battle field on which the will, aided by grace from above, fights with these unruly disturbers, and with more or less of success keeps them under control—I have a few words to say as to the origin of a peculiar form of so-called Christianity. And, as each human vagary had its rise in some passion-blinded human understanding, it will hardly surprise you to hear that many of them sprung from passion itself rather than from reason.

This is true of Paganism, true of Pantheism, true of Atheism, and, if we examine closely, will be found true of nearly every other strange fallacy to which a blinded understanding has given rise. The particular phenomenon, however, to which I wish at present to call your attention is Calvinism, which has also a development known as cant. This peculiar form of spurious Christianity had its origin in nothing else than the passions of a man, and is a proof of that which it is my duty to show you in this chapter, namely, that man, without the aid of grace, is entirely at the scant mercy of the raging passions within him.

3. Calvin was a man who lived upwards of three hundred years ago, and who, being morose and proud, overstepped the wholesome limits of God's commandments, and went far from that source of grace, whose aid can alone make a human being master of himself. Of course, as might be expected, he suffered the consequences, by becoming the slave of passions which, in spite of himself, caused him

annoyance by the uncomfortable conviction they brought with them of his own depravity. Remorse, which is nothing else than self-conviction of evil deeds, is anything but a pleasant companion.

Now the devil soon perceived that, if he wanted not only to sap the morality of the world, but even to bring Christianity into disgrace, by effecting this demoralization in its name, he could not have a better assistant than John Calvin. With an impudence, therefore, altogether diabolical, he suggests to his tool that, since he is already the helpless slave of passion, he may just as well cast the blame upon Almighty God, by quietly assuming that it is of no use trying to be anything else! In other words, that his very nature makes him sinful, and that everything which man does is full of sin. As, however, respectable Calvinists are ashamed to own to their full extent the blasphemies uttered by this impious man, I will not dwell upon them.

So much for impiety. But how to give a religious turn to impiety was the next question, and one which it needed some cleverness to solve—for impiety itself could not be called religion. . Let us see how he managed this. In the first place, he must have a counterfeit of virtue. Nothing easier! Humility is a virtue easily counterfeited, and it was found appropriate to the business. Utter sinfulness and spurious humility, these were Calvin's stock-in-trade. He must teach men that humility consists in acknowledging his utter sinfulness and his utter inability to do anything but sin; and so he puts this dogma into a catechism to be drilled into children before they are able to walk, and to be their staple food on Sundays and week-days throughout their lives.

Whether or not they learn, under such an influence, to realize the truth of their own doctrine, we will not say; at any rate it would be no wonder if they did. Three years' experience in a Calvinistic country, many of the people of which I learned to respect, and even to love, tells me that a great many do not. The fact is, that the principles of right and wrong are too deeply implanted in human nature to permit of their doing so. This, however, only serves to make this false Christianity more ridiculous. Instead of their religion being an assistance to their morality, they are upright and comparatively good, by reason of their better nature appealing against the very principles they profess.

This is not all, however. When a child of God's Church commits sin, he knows very well that he must repent before he can find peace. Not so the Calvinist. He can be a sinner and a devout Christian pretty nearly at the same time. How can he be anything else? For how can he give up that which he is taught to believe to be part of his nature? We will not say, that he has leave to sin as much as he pleases; no, a devout Calvinist would scout such an idea, therefore we will say nothing about it.

This, however, we must say: that if he believe in the Lord (whatever that may mean), and leave his sins for his Saviour to atone for, he will be all right. I will leave it to you to decide whether such tenets have a good or a bad influence on poor fallen human nature. First, there is the doctrine of utter sinfulness; then the habitual drilling into children of this one idea under the name of humility; and, lastly, the calming of the conscience by outward religion.

4. Is this anything at all like the promise of the angel, "He shall redeem His people from their sins?" He shall redeem His people *in* their sins, would be the proper Calvinistic rendering!

When we see well-meaning people deceived by the cloud of false religion with which, as a cloak, this strange system has covered itself, we can but wish that the man who invented this salve for his gashed conscience and vice-wounded soul had but kept it for himself, instead of offering it to others, disguised beneath a mountain of cant, and thereby deceiving good people, who would otherwise seek for grace to make them truly noble, and who have no sympathy whatever with the vice which gave rise to this doctrine.

5. I should not, perhaps, have said so much about this form of so-called Christianity, were it not that it is represented by a whole section of literature of its own, which might, if you were not duly warned, easily deceive you by its canting religious tone, but which you may easily recognize by its talk about sinfulness, and its nice way of taking a hop, skip and jump over the work of a real and true repentance for sin.

As appropriate to this, I really must introduce here an anecdote which I met with lately, as it shows so plainly the utter absurdity of such teaching. An amiable young lady, whose zeal, like that of many others of her class, was worthy of a better cause, was instructing in a Sunday school, and of course intending to impart those doctrines which she had herself imbibed from the Calvinistic catechism, without, I am quite sure, being in the least aware of its impure origin. Innocently adopting its tone, she proceeded to teach little children what she took for Christianity, and coming to a little boy of four years old (mark the age), asked what he had got besides his sinful body. Fancy a baptized child of four years old having a sinful body! The reply she received was delightful: "I have a nice new pair of trousers at home!"

6. What would you think, dear young friends, if I were to talk to you about your utter sinfulness! My ambition, however, is to teach you something very different; and I hope that before I have done, you will have learned from the Catechism, upon which I ground all that I say, to entertain such a reverence for your bodies, that you would not willingly harbour a disrespectful thought concerning them. This will be more like Christianity than talking about sinfulness to children, who should be innocent. In fact, the one is truth—the other a diabolical lie, with a cloak thrown over it.

7. But, you must not think, because circumstances forced me to explain that which you will often doubtless meet with, that there are not also persons in the true Church who are the slaves of passion, without even error to encourage and, in a certain sense, excuse them.

Yes, my dear young friends, man is a free creature, and it is in his power either to use or reject the remedies which God in His compassion has given him. Thus we see that, in spite of all the remedies which God has provided for blindness, he can still be blind; and, in spite of the Gospel, he can turn from God, reject His graces, and become the slave of sin.

From this very cause it comes that the fallen children of the Church often stand out prominently in malice amongst those who are not of the Church, when, forsaking the path of justice, they unite with them. Thus, in a country demoralized by false religion, Catholics sometimes show less regard for morality than Calvinists themselves. Do you know why? They insensibly copy their manners, and in doing so sin against the light; and the reproaches of conscience, in defiance of which they act, cause an amount of violence which gives a dash of impudence to their acts, which does not appear in those who sin without ever having had faith to enlighten them. My duty, however, lies now with the power of grace which God has placed within your reach, and which makes you masters of yourselves, rather than with the fate of those who reject it and refuse its aid. But, whenever we do look at the case of such persons, we must think of it as the effect of a wilful rejection of grace.

8. Let us now consider what grace is. Being more desirous of giving you a practical idea than of adhering to theological definitions, I shall say grace is an assisting power given by Almighty God to

every human being, without which it is impossible to do anything pleasing in God's sight, according to God's own word: "Without me you can do nothing" (John xv. 4). Thus, you see, grace is given to all men; so that, although man can do nothing of himself, still each man will be able to save his soul, if he uses properly the grace which God gives him.

The next thing we know about grace is, that man can either accept it and correspond with it, or refuse it and throw it away.

Again, there are various kinds of grace which may be classed as follows:

Helping grace, which is given to man even whilst he is separated from God by sin.

Habitual, or sanctifying grace, which means the friendship of God; and, lastly,

Actual graces, which God bestows plentifully upon his friends.

Helping graces God gives to all, and it is by corresponding with them that man obtains sanctifying and actual grace. Thus helping grace draws infidels and heretics to seek to know God and the truth. Faith and hope are both, in this sense, helping graces, because they remain in the soul in spite of sin. The grace of repentance is a helping grace, because, unless God gave it to man at the very time he is His enemy, he could never regain His friendship.

From what I have said, you will see plainly that we shall not have much to say about helping grace in this chapter. The Power that rules the storm is, in fact, that habitual and actual grace which accompanies God's friends : with this our duty lies.

9. "Without me you can do nothing" (John xv. 4). With dormant passions within us—with a will of itself possessing all the power which the above words guarantee, and not an atom more, such are the prospects with which we start in life. The consequence of such a state of things is plain : slavery to the first passion that assails us, or grace from above by the aid of which we become masters of ourselves.

There is no other alternative.

But then you may say, We have habitual grace from Baptism. True; but if, by any chance, this grace should be lost, where are we then?

See you not, that the assault of passion puts this very grace in danger, and that we have arrived at a very important crisis of our lives! Well, mark that. It is truth number one, and you can very easily comprehend its weight.

10. Perhaps, however, a child may have passed a few years enjoying the light of reason before this crisis takes place; and what happens during these few years requires remark.

Actual grace, which always more or less accompanies God's friends, depends a great deal upon correspondence. Every time you correspond to a grace, or do something pleasing to God, you earn a new one. Thus it was that our Blessed Lady, who alone corresponded to every grace, multiplied, as it were, her sanctity every moment she lived. Then, on the other hand, every grace you reject is, to say the least of it, a grace lost; every neglect in the service of God, an opportunity for strengthening your love for Him gone; and every deliberate or careless venial sin, a stain on your baptismal robe of innocence, a weakening of the love which exists between your soul and God.

What then? Everything depends upon how this period is spent. Whether the important crisis of life shall find the child a young giant of divine love, with grace strengthened, and the love of God grown, and I may say multiplied within him; or whether this same crisis shall find him weak, empty, with his baptismal robe all stained, and God's love within him so cold, that the least temptation would be sufficient to destroy his innocence. Behold truth number two.

11. These truths are soon told, my dear young friends, but they have been in my mind for years. For years I have contemplated this work on account of them. For years the thought has followed me—"Why should children, the best loved of God amongst all human beings, grow up and be led away, and have their hearts drawn from God at the first dawn of reason, because the explanation of truth is kept from them?" I have found no answer to the question, so I have resolved to speak, that parents and teachers, and all who are responsible for these little ones, should know how to teach them to keep their white garments stainless, and that young people who are able to understand me may be masters of their own lot.

12. I have, then, shown you the first step towards

making your own, the power that rules the storm. Look on this side and on that, and see the choice you have: God's blessing or His curse in this life, and your eternal happiness or misery hereafter; it is in your power to decide now for one or the other, with more advantage now than at any other time. I do not say that you can now choose God's curse, temporal and eternal. No, God is too good for that. If you lose grace you may yet regain it. But, even if you get God's blessing afterwards, it will cost you a hundred times more pain than it will to choose it now; whereas, God knows! you might possibly sink into wickedness out of which you would never return. On the other hand, you may make a choice now for eternity, which will strew your life with God's choicest blessings, and lead you safely to a very high place indeed in heaven.

Of course you will have to persevere; but then the first choice, having been a good one, will have made the keeping of God's commandments, as it were, a second nature. Yes, for the Holy Spirit says: "It is a proverb: a young man according to his way, even when he is old he will not depart from it" (Prov. xxii. 6). At any rate, your own good sense will show you that you must not part with the grace of God afterwards by mortal sin; and that, if such a misfortune should befall you, it would be the most foolish thing in the world to remain in that state, because one who should do so would again become the victim of his passions and be at their mercy.

But this is, you may say, exactly what people do. True enough, but it is something to be accounted for—not to be imitated. Let us, then, account for it.

In the first place, these people never grow as strong in the love of God as I hope you may do. Then they have done something which you must not do—they have fallen into carelessness and venial sin, until the love of God has grown cold within them. They have most likely brought themselves into this state by neglecting the Sacraments, the sacramental grace of which we shall have to talk about later on. As to their subsequent apathy, it is easily accounted for, by one of those truths of which I spoke to you before, which I said should make you cling with a kind of fear to your baptismal grace. Their stupor is, in fact, the stupor of death. Their soul is dead, and cannot live again, until God, in His compassion, rouses it, by that wonderful helping grace which He gives so often that people forget it is a miracle.

14. Then, again, there are graces which our good God has promised to prayer. As you know; He has been so merciful to us on this point, as to say that He will give us whatever we ask in the name of Jesus Christ. What a wonderful power of assistance we have here, and yet one which places us under an obligation? We are bound to pray whenever temptation comes, or passion strives to wile us into sin.

Again, our good God likes to honour His Mother and His saints; He likes, also, the beautiful virtue of humility: He is especially pleased if, besides praying ourselves, we ask our Blessed Lady and the saints to pray for us, and always listens when we ask them to join our prayer.

15. I think I have said enough now, my dear young friends. You have seen how unfortunately desperate is the position of those who, forsaking faith, have practically delivered themselves and others into the hands of their passions.

You have seen how, by beginning to love God in earnest, you can start with the power that rules the storm strong within you. You have seen how important it is for you always to keep in the friendship of God. You have seen, in fine, how necessary it is, if you would be masters of yourselves, to seek by every means, what you will find easy, if you go the right way about it, namely, to remain during your whole life closely united to Him by love, to be near whom, is power and strength. For not only is He your dear good God, but for love of you He has deigned Himself to become, within the souls of His children, the Power that rules the storm.

CHAPTER IX.

Your Leader in sufferings and death.

1. FROM all that you have seen, my dear young friends, I think you cannot but agree with me that there is a very good path through this vale of tears, and that God's children, who keep in the way of duty, have very decidedly the happiest lot, even in this world. Yes, this is a great truth, worthy of

grey hairs and old age, and one which experience and old age have always taught; but those who, in childhood, are persuaded of it, are far better off than those who learn it by experience.

The reason is plain, for experience can only teach those who have strayed from the right path; whereas those who have never left it enjoy all the happiness to be derived from such a course, and escape the toil and hardship necessary to regain it, after being sunk in bogs or quagmires, even if they should be happy enough to avoid the possible contingency of being dashed to pieces by a fall over the unseen precipice.

2. What you have seen has also been sufficient to make you understand what is meant by the freedom of the children of God. It must, I am sure, have struck you, that there is no true freedom but subjection to Almighty God, which makes us complete masters of ourselves, and delivers us from that worst of all tyrannies, the tyranny of passion, which, like a cruel monster, would tear us in pieces. This is another useful truth—for there is no greater misery in the world than being under the control of a number of foolish desires, each seeking its own gratification. Even if such desires are not all very bad, they are, at least, tormenting, because it is not possible to satisfy them; and, if not kept in subjection to reason, they must be the cause of endless disappointment. Whereas, the man who is master of himself can contentedly enjoy all the beautiful things with which God surrounds him.

3. You can understand also how, while the way to

heaven is, as our Lord describes it, straight and narrow, His yoke is at the same time sweet, and His burden light. Yes, the path is, indeed, narrow; and many a time you will have to fight hard to prevent being pushed from it. It is a narrow bridge, but it spans a torrent which roars between deep precipices, and it will save you from destruction.

4. You have seen all these things, and in doing so have looked at so many rugged places in life—places made rugged by sin—that it must have occurred to you that the world is a rough playground, and is more fitted to be the arena of warfare for strong, brave men.

5. In a certain sense this is the case; but there is something in a child's nature which specially fits it to overcome; and if we can only join the simplicity, honesty and ardour of children's fresh young hearts to the firmness and courage of riper age, we shall, indeed, be soldiers fit to hold our own in this rough world—aye, and to uphold in it the cause of God as well.

6. We have considered some of the things which make our present life one of suffering and of toil; but there are other trials, too, which make this world deserve the name of a vale of tears. Sin brought death into the world, and with death, sickness, poverty, and various ills; and God has left these traces of sin, as well as those we have considered. I have promised to give you a fair view of what you have to undergo, and I will do it. "Through many tribulations we must enter into

the kingdom of God" (Acts xiv. 21). Such are the words of Truth Himself, and I would not even wish that you should find it otherwise.

7. I will not insult you, my young friends, by supposing that any of you could, even in your hearts, complain of the sufferings brought upon us by the sin of our first parents. Ere I have even mentioned the subject, a form must rise up before your mind's eye—the familiar form of Jesus, God and Man, extended on the cross—and the question must force itself upon you: "Do I not owe all to suffering?" "Why is not," you will say, "this world to me a dreary waste, in which I am bound to dwell without knowledge of God to draw me to His love—without a Gospel to tell me what way to go—without grace to save me from the effects of sin? Finally, why is not this world only for me the prelude of eternal woe?" And does not the answer rise up before you: Because all these miseries have been changed for me into blessings, by the Son of God made man living in poverty and submission, to make me rich in grace—preaching in the midst of contradictions the way to heaven, that I might walk in it, and dying in the midst of agonies, to buy grace for me during life, and entrance into heaven after death?

Saved by sufferings, surely you could not expect the life of redeemed man to be free from pain. You would not hope to escape the penalty of sin—death—when your Divine Redeemer became man on purpose to die for you, and when His sinless Mother also died. No! You would not, if you could, be members, free from pain, of a head crowned with thorns!

8. Talking, however, of sufferings, how much will you have to endure? In the first place, you will have, as we have seen, less of real suffering in God's service than you would have in the service of the devil, for the dreariness and want of consolation in trial, consequent upon the forsaking of God, are miseries impossible to God's children.

9. I will tell you how much you will have to suffer. Just enough, in all probability, to prevent your life from being one unbroken chain of bliss. Just too much, I hope, to prevent you from forgetting God. Just enough to make your dear Saviour see in you a faint resemblance to Himself. Not an atom too much to make you ashamed of the small share you have in your Saviour's Cross.

10. And more! Jesus has given you all His merits, so that you have only to unite your puny crosses to His sufferings, and every one of them becomes worthy of earning for you a new grace here and an eternal crown of glory hereafter.

Then, again, these sufferings themselves make you like Jesus Christ; and which of His loving children does not like to be like our Blessed Lord? Are you poor, and obliged to work for your living? Jesus was poor and worked also, subject to His Mother and His foster father, for nearly thirty years. Do you suffer contradiction? So did He. Do you suffer pain? Oh, how light are your pains compared with His!

11. You will have to die. He also died. And what will death be to you if, as I hope will be the case, you have loved Him during life? Will it not,

indeed, be sweet to fall asleep like an infant on the bosom of its mother, armed with a holy confidence in Him whom you have loved, and for whose sake you have willingly suffered ; and then to open your eyes in heaven, where they reign for ever, who have been like Jesus in suffering here?

12. What say you then? If sin has made this world a world of suffering, has not Jesus Christ rendered suffering itself glorious? Nay, has it not almost become a joy? Yes, it is a joy; but without at the same time ceasing to be suffering. You will feel it keenly at times, but not so keenly as did Jesus. Did it not draw from Him those words which proceeded, as it were, from His afflicted humanity: " Father, if it be possible, let this chalice pass from me "? (Matt. xxvi. 39). Yes; but this was followed by those other beautiful words: " Nevertheless, not as I will, but as Thou wilt" (Matt. xxvi. 39).

13. Thus, in suffering, Jesus became, also, your example—an example which, if you follow through life, you will do well indeed. You will also do well to follow that other example He gave—the example of forgiveness of injuries—when He said : " Father, forgive them, for they know not what they do " (Luke xxiii. 34).

To conclude, then, our Blessed Lord, lest you might be discouraged, has made Himself your leader. Hear His words: " If any man will come after me, let him deny himself, and take up his cross daily and follow me " (Luke ix., 23).

14. Behold His invitation! Surely you are willing to follow such a leader ! But what does this Cross,

this denial of self, mean? Nothing else, after all, but His yoke, and that yoke we know is sweet. Self-denial is nothing more than that restraint which all must exercise over their unruly passions, unless, indeed, they would pay the penalty incurred by not ruling them. Such, then, is the Cross, which your Saviour, by a sort of loving exaggeration, deigns to call by that name, and with which He bids you follow Him. Need I ask you whether you will obey?

You can hardly call it a Cross to be obliged in answer to His call to spend your lives in loving and serving your God, and in bearing in union with our Lord, with joy of heart, those little trials which make you fit members of a head crowned with thorns—like to your Saviour in sufferings, and true followers of that divine leader, who, after bearing the Cross, died upon it, to open heaven's gates to you.

CHAPTER X.

Divine Compassion.

1. To analyse the air we breathe, and at the same time to forget that it is supplying us with a necessity of life, would be very much like treating coldly of divine compassion, with no deep sense of how much we owe to it. A moment's thought must tell you that you owe it to divine compassion that I can address you as God's dear children; whilst, as for me, I write this with the feeling that every letter

should be a tribute of eternal gratitude to Him to whose compassion I owe, not only the privilege of being allowed to address you with the authority of one of His ministers, but that I am in life to address you at all.

To come to the point, however, I can do nothing here, after all, but call your attention to a few of the manifestations of divine compassion, for the subject is so vast that, were I to write till doomsday, I could not exhaust it.

The compassion of our dear good God is, in a particular sense, the inheritance of fallen man; and that Almighty God allowed the children of God to feel in themselves the effects of their first parent's sin for no other reason than that He might extend to them immeasurable compassion, may easily be believed, if we judge by the length to which this compassion goes in man's regard.

2. No sooner, indeed, had man fallen, than the hand of God's compassion was, as it were, stretched out to him; for surely the promise of a Redeemer, belief in whom brought salvation to the believer, was nothing else? Again, when sin had overspread the earth to such an extent that God determined to destroy it by the deluge, compassion made Him save eight souls, whose descendants would learn to spread sin again! How does Almighty God avert the consequences? Is it by threatening mankind with a more sudden destruction? No; it is by binding Himself, out of compassion, not to destroy him: "And the Lord said: I will no more curse the earth, for the sake of man; for the imagination

and thoughts of man's heart are prone to evil from his youth: therefore, I will no more destroy every living soul, as I have done " (Gen. viii. 21). Surely this reason, which God gives for not destroying sinners, is one that would scarcely satisfy anything but His compassion!

3. There is another instance of God's compassion related in the Old Testament, which is so beautiful that I cannot refrain from speaking of it. It is that of Jonas and the city of Nineveh. This city was so very wicked, that God sent the prophet Jonas to prophecy to it that in forty days Nineveh should be destroyed. When, however, the King of Nineveh heard the prophecy, he himself and all his people did penance in sackcloth and ashes.

As is very often the case with men, Jonas, caring more for his reputation as a prophet than for the welfare of his neighbours, was vexed that his prophecy was not fulfilled. To punish him for his faults, and to give him a lesson, God, first of all, allowed a piece of ivy to grow over his head, to shade him from the sun; and then, when Jonas had gone to sleep under it, God allowed a worm to come and destroy it, so that, before the poor prophet awoke, he got well scorched by the sun and by the burning wind. Jonas was actually so troubled by this that he prayed to die. Hear what Almighty God says to him: " Dost thou think thou hast reason to be angry for the ivy? And he said, I am angry with reason, even unto death. And the Lord said: Thou art grieved for the ivy, for which thou has not laboured, nor made it to grow, which, in one night came up, and in one night perished. And shall I not spare Nineveh, that great city, in which there are more than a hundred and twenty thousand persons that know not how to distinguish their right hand and their left, and many beasts?" (Jonas iv. 9, 10, 11).

The first thing you see here worthy of remark is, how strangely the petulance of the prophet contrasts with the patience of Almighty God, with his bad humour. Then, we see how God finds a reason for His compassion, in the thought of the innocent children who were not old enough to commit sin. How much must He not love innocent baptized children, when, in the innocence of those who were not baptized, he found an excuse for His compassion.

4. Now let us look at two or three remarkable things concerning the wonderful inheritance of compassion which belongs to us.

I have shown that even Baptism, while it takes away sin, leaves behind it traces of blindness, weakness, and passion.

What food is here for divine compassion!

Yes; compassion pities our blindness, and straightway sends us the magnificent gift of faith.

Divine compassion pities our weakness, and gives us the Gospel.

God sees our passions, and pities us, and out of that pity come such abundant graces, that our life is completely hedged in by them—by helping grace—by habitual grace—by actual grace—by sacramental grace!

5. Then, how is it that there comes to be such a thing as deliberate venial sin? I am sure that you see nothing wonderful in the fact that a cool deliberate sin against God drives Him away from you, makes you His enemy, and is even punished by eternal damnation. But what is extraordinary is, that, out of compassion, God has ordained that certain offences—by which His commandments are broken with just as much coolness—shall not have power to separate us from Him, or to constitute us His enemies!

Now, if any one were to give you a blow in the face, although he did not kill you, he could hardly be considered your friend. But our good God is far more compassionate with us than we are with our fellow-creatures; He wishes to leave us as few opportunities as possible of becoming His enemies, knowing how very easily we are drawn away from Him.

6. Nevertheless, every sin is a grievous insult to Him; so great, indeed, that no temporal calamity is any evil in His sight, compared with one venial sin. He, indeed, warns us that venial sins lead to mortal ones. Still, until the mortal sin is committed, He will not leave the soul. No; the hateful sight of numberless venial sins will not compel Him to go. On the other hand, how does He not, by His love, try to shame us from committing them, and, as it were, compel us to get them pardoned by an act of contrition Is not this compassion indeed? Yet, which of us could dare to say He could do without it?

7. Then, again, there is the conversion of the sinner! Have I not told you that the commission of a mortal sin is the voluntary renouncing of salvation? How, then, is it that men fall and rise, until they forget that it needs a miracle to make them rise? Our Lord has provided a sacrament of divine compassion for the daily working of this miracle—the sacrament of Penance.

8. How is it that Jesus has not only made Himself your food in the Blessed Sacrament, but has made freedom from mortal sin the only condition for receiving it? Compassion again—always compassion.

9. Then, look at God's patience with the sinner—the Holy Sacrifice of the Mass to stay His hand from striking—His making His Blessed Mother the refuge of sinners—and allowing the saints to intercede for them. Again, He teaches His friends on earth to pray for them, gives weight to the words of preachers to convert them, threatens them with hell to frighten them into His friendship, and finally provides special means to deliver them, at death's door, from the devil's grasp.

10. Such is divine compassion! Shall the study of it make us lax and careless? Indeed, it should not. This inheritance of our fallen state is precious; God knows we could not do without it. It does sometimes help to make people careless; it is, however, because they do not consider it. If you meditate on it, my dear young friends, it will shame you, as it were, into the love of Him, who, after having given you, as I have shown, such ample compensa-

tion for the traces of the fall, has also bestowed on you, in addition, an inheritance of Divine Compassion, which seems to go beyond them all.

PART THIRD.

REDEEMING LOVE.

CHAPTER I.

At the Right Hand of God.

1. As this work, my dear young friends, consists simply of a description of yourselves, and is not to be looked upon as a treatise on the mysteries of faith, it must not be expected to contain a full explanation of the wonders of redeeming love; although, without a section devoted to the illustration of the new and beautiful relations between you and your Creator, which arise out of the fact, and still more out of the manner of your redemption, any description of you would be strangely incomplete.

Thus your Maker's love, which drew you out of nothing, and made you the wonderful creatures you are, required that one part of this book should be devoted to it. The change wrought in your circumstances, by the fall of man, is so marked, as to require another; while Baptism, bringing with it so many special subjects for consideration, cannot be compressed into a less space, and will furnish a fourth division, leaving for this, my third part, the glorious honours and duties involved in the wonderful mystery of redeeming love.

When we consider the sublime beauty of this subject, we feel that it can be done justice to only by an inspired writer; I, therefore, can scarcely hope not to mar the picture by my clumsy handling. Yet, with God's help, I will try to bring its beautiful truths before you in such a way as to give you some idea of the dignity to which you have been raised, and with the hope that they may influence you with new love, and with a nóble ambition to lead lives, at least in some degree, worthy of God's adopted children—the images of Jesus Christ in the flesh, your eldest Brother, and the children of Mary, His Immaculate Mother.

2. By a happy coincidence, I sit down to this, my task, upon a day which, of all others, is, perhaps, the most capable of inspiring worthy thoughts on such a theme—upon the festival of our Lord's Ascension.

What are the reflections which, on this day, go home to every Christian heart? Does it not suggest the words of the Royal Prophet David: " My heart and my flesh have rejoiced in the living God "? (Ps. xxxiii. 3). Let us, then, delay for a moment, to consider what happened on that day. It was on the day of the Ascension that, for the first time, the gates of heaven were thrown open for the entrance of a human being. He who entered did not enter as you hope to do—your soul separate from the body, to remain so separate until the day of judgment; no, He entered body and soul. It was a human foot that crossed that threshold—a foot which, on earth, had been weary, and had felt pain—a foot which retained, and which still retains, the mark, now glorious, of the terrible nail which had pierced it through and through. It was a human hand, moreover—wounded also for love of us—which, by its own right and power, flung heaven's gates wide open, never to be closed again against any one marked with His precious redeeming Blood. It was a human nature, which, united for ever to the divine nature and person of the Son of God, on this day took its seat at the right hand of God.

3. Surely the remembrance of these things is enough to make us congratulate ourselves in proud, exulting joy, when we see our nature so exalted, united to the God-head, seated at the right hand of God; and still, in the person of the Son of God, does our nature maintain its throne. Near that throne is another, and on it sits a pure human creature, the Immaculate Mother of God, whose body—that undefiled human fountain-head, from which Jesus Christ's blood first came—was not allowed to moulder in the tomb, but was transported to heaven, and united to her blessed soul, where she reigns triumphant, heaven's bright Queen, seated near her Son.

I need say nothing here of our dear Lord as advocate with His eternal Father, showing Him His wounds. I need say nothing of the intercessory power of her who sits near Him. My object in recalling these beautiful visions to your mind is a different one.

4. I bid you look at Jesus, God and Man, and at Mary, His Immaculate Mother, and see in them the representatives of the human race. I ask each youth amongst you to see, in Jesus, Him of whom you yourself are a living image. I bid you see, in His Immaculate Mother, her who should make you look with deep respect on one who bears to you a like relationship to that which Mary bore to Jesus. I bid you, also, learn from that sight to cherish, with tenfold affection and respect, the sister who is to you as the image of Mary, sanctifying your home.

As for you, dear daughters of Mary, I bid you look up, and learn to love and respect the mother who gave you birth, and to be proud of the protecting guardianship of your brother, who should be to you the image of your eldest brother, Jesus Christ, and also of your own likeness to the purest of creatures, whose veins were found most worthy to supply blood for the incarnate Son of God Himself. It is thus, with a holy pride, I bid you, dear children of God, look up at these two thrones in heaven.

5. Such thoughts, however, naturally suggest the question—Why bring these things especially before us? I will tell you.

Although our redeemed human nature is far from that degradation which wicked men would impute to it, in order to soothe their pride, by blasphemously attributing their sins to the being God has given to them; nevertheless, the state of warfare in which the fall of our first parents has left us, obliges us to keep down, with a strong hand, the unreasoning inclinations of our lower nature—hence the necessity of that self-denial which our Lord bids us practice, and which St. Paul calls "chastising our body."

Just as thoughtless children, who begin to chatter and laugh in school, sometimes require the master to cry silence in rather a stern tone, and even to enforce his command by threatening the cane, so man's natural inclinations call for something of the same kind from the commanding voice of reason, the sense of duty, and, above all, the love of God. So great is human weakness, that sometimes under one form, and sometimes under another, man has always had a tendency to forget the sanctity to which God destined him, and to take consolation in, and excuse its wilful shortcomings, on the plea of the impossibility of sanctity in human flesh and blood. This is the reason why I have brought before you, in so prominent a manner, not only the sublime dignity to which our human nature has been raised, but have also laid special stress, as I shall do throughout this part, on the dignity of your flesh and blood, that you may become holy both in body and spirit.

6. This way of drawing God's children to a holy life is no new idea of mine; yet I think that the things I am going to say are usually kept too much in the background, and when I lay stress upon them I am but following the method of St. Paul. For what does he mean by these words which I have placed as a second motto upon my title-page? "I, therefore, a prisoner in the Lord, beseech you that you walk worthy of the vocation in which you are called" (Ephes. iv. 1). And again: "You are bought with a great price, glorify and bear God in

your body" (1 Cor. vi. 20). Indeed, were I to quote all that St. Paul says about Christians being members of the head, Jesus Christ, temples of the Holy Spirit, &c., &c., I might recapitulate his epistles almost from beginning to end. It is not, however, so much St. Paul whom I follow—I am rather, with him, following what our Blessed Lord Himself not only taught, but forced upon us, by the very way in which He set about the redemption of man.

7. There is no doubt that, before our Lord came, the world had wilfully fallen into entire ignorance of God; and had, as might be expected, become very wicked, so much so as even to adore the worst vices. In what way, then, did the Son of God proceed to sanctify man? For we must not lose sight of the fact that Christ made Himself our model, as well as our Redeemer, when He came to save us.

He took that very human body and soul which man had disgraced by sin, and showed thereby that the body which God had fashioned was worthy of Him who made it, being worthy even of union with the Divinity. He did more: He took it from a pure human source, as if by one stroke to make His children respect their human nature, and also the mother that gave them birth.

8. Then look at Jesus Christ; did He not pass through every stage of life, sanctifying each as He went, and showing man how to live from the cradle to the grave? As the late Cardinal Wiseman said: "Jesus touched the manger cradle, and by His touch made infancy sacred." Is not this equally

true of the other stages of life? Yes, it is true of boyhood; the history of our Lord's life is one of obedience, and is contained in these words: "He was subject to them" (Luke ii. 51). So also of the youth He spent in assisting St. Joseph in his trade; and true again of His public life, devoted to God's work, and of His sacrifice of Himself—"obedient unto death, even unto the death of the Cross," to save man and to do His father's will.

Yes, Jesus, the Son of the living God, like a dear elder brother, went through each stage of life, to show us how to live, how to be holy, and how to sanctify each stage of our lives by imitating Him.

9. You must not for a moment suppose that when our Lord raised within us that holy pride by which we glory in being like Him, He gave us no gift which would save our aspirations from being mere vain attempts to reach something unattainable. No, in consideration of the honour He had done our human nature, He bestowed on us a blessed privilege, which is the inalienable right of each of God's children, to be preserved by the use of graces easily within the reach of all—the privilege of being able to live, clothed in human flesh and blood, a life of most blessed independence of and control over it; a privilege so great, indeed, that it makes human beings the admiration of angels.

By a special call of God, many have been and daily are being drawn to lead the lives of angels upon earth, and thus, free from the ties of nature, they serve near the person of the King of Kings, their Spouse, stand at God's altar to offer sacrifice, or go, like ministering angels, to serve God in the suffering members of Christ, or to instruct the little ones of His flock. This is indeed a wonderful and high vocation; but the privileges bestowed by an Incarnate God upon His children do not end here. They penetrate the Christian family in a way perhaps almost more wonderful, and sanctify it with the presence of beings whose beautiful influence renders holy, not only sacred home itself, but all persons and all things which come into contact with them.

10. But this cannot be, unless the feelings of God's children on these points are raised to that height which will make them have all the strength of a holy pride—to give us which, Jesus Christ became our eldest brother; and to confirm us in which, He chose to pass through every stage of life, throwing a halo around each of them.

But, perhaps it will be said—Can pride be good? Fear not, my young friends: one of the effects of this pride, or, to call it more properly, self-respect, is, that it is the foundation of deep humility. We have seen before that an opposite spirit is only a salve for rebellious pride. What can make you so truly humble as a deep sense of the holiness God expects from you, of the wonderful aids which God heaps upon you to enable you to obtain it! We will speak afterwards of the continual shortcomings, by which you fall short of the mark on which your eyes are fixed.

How can I better finish this chapter than by recurring to what I said at its commencement, and again bidding you look up to heaven, and gaze on those two thrones, until the sight shall have rendered you proud, and more than proud, of the very blood that runs through your veins.

CHAPTER II.

The Eternal Father's Gift.

1. One of the brightest qualities of childhood, and the one which makes its spirit peculiarly adapted for gaining heaven, is simplicity. Whilst philosophers are puzzling themselves about the why and the wherefore of everything around them in this wonderful world, the child is drinking in the joys which these things impart, and blessing God for his happiness, without making any effort at all. The infant in its mother's arms does not consider whether that mother is beautiful, or powerful, or what may be the reason why she cherishes and protects him; it simply takes for granted that it is in the safest and best place that can be found for it, where it has all that it wishes for, and so it smiles in its mother's face, and claps its little hands, and if a stranger should come near, only clings the more closely to her for protection.

2. In this sense, that which is often called philosophy is the very opposite of the spirit of childhood. He who cannot contemplate the mysteries of God's love for man without asking himself why God did this and why He did that, may think himself a philosopher, but will hardly learn much. He is only

wasting time which might be much better employed in prayer, or in drinking in new fountains of love and gratitude, in the contemplation of those manifold proofs of paternal love which God has given him. Besides, the very presumption of such curious conduct is enough to bring blindness upon those who indulge in it, just as our natural eyes are blinded if we attempt to gaze upon the sun.

Indeed, it is as ineffably absurd, on the one hand, for man to suppose that he can fathom the reasons for the acts of God, as, on the other, it is eminently rational to take it for granted that he cannot. In order to be convinced of this, it is only necessary for man to examine himself and discover what sort of creature he is. He is a being possessing intelligence indeed, but of what kind? An understanding which derives most of its ideas through the senses, as through so many windows of its house of clay. A being with eyes to see that the grass grows, while its understanding cannot comprehend how! This is a being, indeed, to pretend to question the why and the wherefore of the actions of God!

3. Such thoughts especially impress themselves upon me at this time, and I set them down as they arise. If we would, then, drink in the rich streams of divine love which we are going to treat of, we must be as children in simplicity—nay, doubly childlike.

What is it to you and me whether the Eternal Father gave us His Divine Son to be our Redeemer and to become man, on account of man's sin, or for some other reason? What is it to you or me to know whether our Lord would have become man if Eve had not eaten the forbidden fruit? Shall we ask ourselves whether it was more for the sake of vindicating Divine Justice and atoning for its violation by sin, or more out of compassion to us, His poor fallen children, that Jesus was given to us? What we know is, that it is well for us that Divine Justice has received an atonement more than sufficient to blot out the sins of the whole world. Blessed be our Heavenly Father who has given us His only-begotten Son made man for our sakes! We have enough employment for our thoughts in feasting them upon the magnificence of the gift, without troubling ourselves with useless questions.

4. So it is. "God so loved the world, as to give His only-begotten Son, that whosoever believeth in Him may not perish, but may have life everlasting" (John iii. 16). In these beautiful words are expressed the magnificent gift our Heavenly Father has bestowed on His children.

The first thing that strikes us concerning it, is not the question whether or not it was given on account of man's sin—it is rather wonder at the love which, instead of taking vengeance on man's treason, took pity on the work of His own hands, and at the very time of man's guilt, promised him this gift.

5. But if we cannot ask the why and the wherefore of God's acts, we may yet admire them. Let us, then, see in how many ways our Heavenly Father's gift shows His divine wisdom and goodness.

Let us suppose, as we well may do, that Almighty God wished to make every human being such an object of His divine complacency, that not one sin, nor any amount of sin, could make Him forget that man was the work of His own hands. Surely we could imagine no way more effectual for this purpose than that chosen by the wisdom and goodness of the Eternal Father. He, as it were, forces Himself to see in every human being the image of His own Divine Son, by giving Him to us with our own nature united inseparably to Him.

Now, there is something in the heart even of a human parent which makes a child, even when wicked and ungrateful, nevertheless an object of love. Were a son about to die upon the scaffold for the murder of his own brother, there would be room in the mother's heart for pity! Now, if this be so, even with us poor mortals, with what love must not the Eternal Father cherish, not only His only-begotten Son, but that deified human nature so inseparably united to His divine nature! Through Jesus Christ we also have been made the sons of God; but sin has too often made the paternal compassion, and his likeness to Jesus Christ, man's only claim on the Eternal Father

6. Does not the providence of God still watch over us, even when we are in sin, as our Lord Himself says: "That you may be the children of your Father who is in heaven, who maketh His sun to rise upon the good and bad, and raineth upon the just and the unjust" (Matt. v. 45). Yes, the providence of God watches over all. And more, the

untiring patience of God keeps back the shafts of His justice, whilst a whole legion of graces sent by God's compassion besiege the sinner's heart, and almost force him to the feet of his injured God to ask His pardon.

Whence comes all this? Perhaps you will say it is from God's love for the being He has made. I dare say it does; but perhaps we should be nearer the truth, if we attributed the gift of His only begotten Son to some such cause as this. Offended justice, however, has its claims, and such a reason would not satisfy them. All this providence, patience, and compassionate restoration comes from the fact that the Eternal Father looks at His Divine Son and sees His image in the most sin-stained human being. The consequence of this is, and it is the first blessed consequence that comes of our Father's gift, that until final impenitence and death have sealed the traitor's doom, no human being is so covered with crime, as to make his God forget him, or cease to bestow graces, to bring him back to his God and salvation. Yes, because of Jesus, so long as there is life, so long is there salvation for the penitent sinner.

7. As I said, however, just now, justice has its claims; and so true is this, that in God, who is Infinite Justice, its claims must be satisfied. Here is a second subject of admiration at the wisdom and goodness of God. In this gift of the Eternal Father have the divine wisdom and goodness done nothing less than reconcile justice and mercy, so that, as David said, "Justice and Peace have kissed each

other" (Psalms lxxxiv. 11). Yes, the union of our human nature with the divine, and the atonement of the God-man in His human nature, has, as you know, given to God an infinite satisfaction for sin, that deed of infinite malice. It is, however, more with the consequences we have to do than with the fact, which you know from your Catechism.

These consequences are, that no amount of sin can require punishment from God's justice unless some cause prevents the blood of Jesus Christ from washing it away. Thus the greatest sinner in the world has only to repent, that is, sincerely to detest his sins for the love of God, and to make use of the means appointed by God for their remission; and immediately the blood of Jesus Christ washes them all away, and more than atones for their malice.

8. I cannot, perhaps, make this plainer to you, than by pointing out to you the opposite fact, namely, that the only place where the Divine Justice does not get an adequate atonement is really in hell, where those who do not repent are punished. The reason is clear, because, while all the torments of hell cannot satisfy the outraged majesty of God, the sinner, by his impenitence, prevents the blood of Jesus from more than doing so. Thus you see how sweetly divine wisdom has made Justice and Peace kiss each other. For in giving His only begotten Son to redeem us, Almighty God has so arranged, that the only way in which Divine Justice can be appeased, is through the application of the merits of Jesus Christ, which is effected by repentance,

and makes man the object of God's tenderest mercies at the same time.

9. You may learn from this how acceptable to your Heavenly Father must be the prayers of His dear children for the conversion of sinners, seeing that not only did our Lord die for their salvation, but that in that conversion alone can Divine Justice and mercy be properly satisfied.

Who can talk or reflect coolly on these things? The infinite justice of God locked in the arms of His mercy! Why, we are making calculations about that which is our life, our joy, our treasure, our hope here, and the contemplation of which will be our occupation for eternity! But let us learn some practical lessons from the subject.

10. When, in Baptism, the stain of original sin was washed from our souls, Divine Justice embraced mercy within us, so that we immediately became not merely an object of the divine mercy, but worthy in strict justice of God's love, and as St. Paul says of himself, our good works would henceforth be actions justly demanding reward. Thus St. Paul says: "As to the rest, there is laid up for me a crown of justice, which the Lord, the just Judge, will render to me in that day" (2 Tim. iv. 8). Now, how can St. Paul lay claim to a crown of justice? Was it not he who assisted at the murder of St. Stephen? It was that, in his glorious conversion, "Justice and Peace kissed each other." Now, if (which God forbid) it should happen that any of you should commit a mortal sin, Justice and Peace would be again separated, so that immediately

your sin would begin to cry aloud for vengeance. Yes; and as long as impenitence should keep the atoning blood of Jesus Christ from your soul, this cry would continue, however much God's compassion might plead on the other side; and this cry would not cease until repentance had brought the blood of Jesus to you, and Justice had again embraced His mercy in your soul. From this you may see another reason why mortal sin is above all things to be dreaded, and why you should never be guilty of the double folly of allowing wilful delay to keep you in a state of separation from your God.

11. If we are to judge of the love of a giver by the greatness of his gift, and what that gift cost him, how much reason do we find to consider here how great must be the love of the Eternal Father for His poor fallen creatures, when we remember that it was His only-begotten Son, the Eternal Son of God, equal to His Father, that He gave us to be our Redeemer; and that, in giving us this His Son, the Eternal Father has given us also all the treasures that such a Redeemer brings to us, according to those words of St. Paul: "How hath He not, with Him, given us all things?" (Rom. viii. 32).

But this is not all. The Well-beloved of His Father, His own cherished Son, for the love of us must be annihilated; for love of us He must assume our poor human nature, and in that nature must suffer not only poverty, cold, weariness, and pain, but must become the very sport of divine vengeance, that you and I might be saved!

Think you, then, my dear young friends, that this

gift cost the Eternal Father nothing? Was He deaf to the terrible cry, "My God, my God, why hast Thou forsaken me?" (Matt. xxvii. 46.) Yet, nevertheless, He willingly made this Divine Son the object of His wrath, that we might be saved from becoming such; that, in short, our atonement for sin might be almost reduced to the making an act of contrition. It is by meditating thus on the gift, and what it involved, that you can gain some idea of the love of Him who gave up His own Son to all these humiliations to save you.

12. We have seen two effects of this gift, namely, the claim it gives man on God's pity, even when he is His enemy, and the way in which the Eternal Father has by it reconciled His outraged justice with His infinite mercy. The first was necessary, because man could never become God's friend unless God's love sought him even when in a state of separation from Him; the second makes, as it were, a clear road from the lowest depth of human misery to a perfect reconciliation between the sinner and his God.

This is, indeed, much: but the work does not end here. This reconciliation has a further object, and is, if I may use the expression, a beautiful resting-place where the happy soul of God's child gains strength for a further journey. "But as many as received Him, He gave power to be made the sons of God" (John i. 12). We receive God, in this sense, as soon as we come to the use of reason; we ratify, of our own free will, the obligation contracted in Baptism, of giving our heart to God. We receive

God also when, by repentance, we give Him back our will, which has been miserably separated from Him by sin. In all these things there is power given to become the sons of God; that is, to live the lives of sons, to enjoy the privileges of sons, and to partake in the inheritance of sons.

13. It is the mistake of too many thoughtless people entirely to pass over, what is really the sublimest part of the divine scheme of redemption, namely, man's call to be holy. They think, and unfortunately they act, as if they considered that nothing entered less into the mind, either of Jesus Christ, or of the Eternal Father who sent Him, than their sanctification through redeeming love. The effect of this mistake upon their lives, if it were not truly deserving of tears, would be almost amusing on account of the way it turns their whole life, as it were, upside down. God has given us a law, which is, I must say, nearly the easiest imaginable which could make man in any way like his elder brother, Jesus Christ. These people, however, act as though they would try how much of this law they may break without actually becoming God's enemies. They go further. If they find this law inconvenient, they break it outright, and still consider themselves good Christians if they make friends with God once, or, at most, three or four times a year. Of course they suffer various inconveniences, and load themselves with innumerable burdens and annoyances, as the natural consequence of such a mode of action. They seem to wish to try how little can be done to become holy without being lost; or how many risks

they can run of losing heaven, without being shut out. It seems as if they would be quite content to know that they should eventually get within the heavenly gates, after throwing away every opportunity of gaining the bright crown of sanctity which their Saviour died to place within their reach. But will heaven be attained at all after such a fashion?

Jesus Christ has provided for these people a bath of His precious blood to wash away every stain which may disfigure the likeness of God in the soul; He has given them, as we shall see later on, His flesh to eat, in order to change their very flesh and blood into Himself; and what do they do? They use that precious bath of blood as a convenient means of getting rid of a load of sin, instead of using it to increase the purity of the soul; and as for the sacred flesh and blood of Jesus, they seem to try how far they can do without it, without drawing upon themselves the penalty: "Except you eat the flesh of the Son of Man and drink His blood, you shall not have life in you" (John vi. 54).

Now, this terrible mistake, which involves so many evil consequences—such as the throwing away the means of sanctification, the wasting of life, and the terrible risk of salvation—comes from the fact that such persons pass over and forget that Jesus Christ became man and died, not only to save us, but also that we might become holy and perfect.

14. The helps which Jesus Christ has bought for us to enable us to attain perfection we shall speak of hereafter. I will content myself in this chapter with showing you one thing, namely, that the

sanctity to which you are called is nothing more or less than the perfecting the likeness of your elder brother, Jesus Christ, the Son of the living God, within you.

There is a great difference between an image and a likeness. A statue may be an image of a man, although it has no life. One man is always an image of another, and yet may not be like him. I have shown you that you are images of Jesus Christ, and so is every human being; yet how many are anything but like Him! To become holy is to become like Jesus Christ; the commandments are beautifully adapted to make you like Him, and we shall see elsewhere what powerful means He has given you of perfecting this likeness. What I wish to impress upon you is, that unless you are, to some extent, like Him when you die, you cannot be saved; and even if you are sufficiently like Him to be saved, anything that stains His likeness will have to be worn out by the fire of purgatory. Now, I cannot better show you how this likeness is brought out in your soul, than by making use of a simile of the Prophet Malachias. Mark his words. Speaking of Jesus Christ, who, infinitely holy as He is, must see His own likeness in you before you can enter heaven, he says: "Who shall stand to see Him? For He is like a refining fire, and like the fuller's herb, and He shall sit refining and cleansing the silver" (Malach. iii. 3, 4). Now, when silver is purified, it is put into a very hot furnace, and all impurities gradually disappear out of it. During this process the refiner sits closely watching it, until it is so clear that he sees his own likeness reflected in it, as in a mirror. Now, there are two fires represented by that of the refiner. The first is the fire of divine love, which will purify your soul, if you live such a life as to allow it to do its work, until Jesus sees His likeness in you, and you will be fit to enter His kingdom. If, however, death finds you with some stain on that likeness, although the image of Jesus be there, the severe fire of purgatory must finish the work. Must not such a thought persuade you, my dear young friends, to try and increase the fire of divine love in your hearts, even while you thank God for His compassion in creating that cleansing fire, which renders so many like Him who, otherwise, could not ever attain to that resemblance.

15. We have now, my dear young friends, seen what a gift is that which the Eternal Father has given us ; we have traced the effects of that gift as it gently draws man from the lowest depths of his misery, and clears a road for him, first from sin to pardon, and then from pardon to sanctity, and onward to the gates of heaven. Let, then, the thought of these beautiful things influence your hearts with love for Him who, out of His great love, has given you His only begotten Son, and let that love continually produce in you a more perfect likeness to Him who, as I said before, came upon earth to be your example as well as your Saviour.

CHAPTER III.

Bought by Jesus' Blood.

1. WE can scarcely do better in treating of the many beautiful subjects which here cross our path, than allow ourselves to be guided by what I may call the language of faith. There are certain simple expressions, "familiar as household words" to every Catholic, which yet contain in them the very sublimest doctrines of our holy religion. The contemplation of the truths contained in such expressions has made saints, inspired apostles, and missioners—familiarity with such truths has been the very atmosphere of devout Catholics, and has entered into the talk of little children; the denial of them has stamped men as heretics; and the utterance of them, without thought or care for their meaning, is both the mark of an indifferent Christian and the very cause of his indifference! Such expressions, for instance, as "the souls for whom Christ died;" or "souls redeemed by Jesus Christ," so often on the lips of every child of Holy Church.

2. It was the Catholic truth, that Jesus Christ, the Son of the living God, shed His blood for all men, without exception, that supported St. Francis Xavier whilst his arms ached with the labour of baptizing a thousand Indians in one day. It was the truth, that Jesus Christ shed His blood for their salvation that caused saints not only to make their own salvation their first consideration, but devote their energy to try to give Jesus a small return for

so much love. I have seen the same familiar truth make a little child of eight years clap her hands, because her father, who had been a Protestant, was, after having been received into the Church, about to make his first Communion the next day. If by what I shall say in this chapter I can prevent the possibility of this word becoming to any of you an expression without meaning (which may Jesus grant, for the sake of His precious blood), I shall have done a glorious work.

3. You know that by every right the creature is the property of Him who made it, so that on this score you could never belong to any one but God. Yet it is sometimes said that sin renders us slaves of the devil. It would, however, be more true to say that having become the victim of God's offended justice, and having been stolen from our Creator's love, deprived of that love we fell under the yoke of sin. At any rate, while in sin we did not belong to God in the way He wished, and at any cost He would have us back again, children of His love and mercy. Nay, He would make us His own by a double claim. He would buy us again, so that we should be His by purchase after being already His by creation.

But at what cost would He do this? At an infinite one! Are we, then, worth such a price as this? That is the question. The Eternal Father's mercy valued us at such a price. Jesus valued us at it also.

4. This is no matter for speculation. It is matter for meditation. You must drink in the truth and

JESUS ACCEPTS THE OFFICE OF REDEEMER. 165

let it light the fire of divine love within you. You must learn it as a lesson, and calculate, not how it can be—that it is so you must be satisfied to know—but what must be the value you should set upon the soul for which God has paid the infinite price of Jesus' blood. And this will lead you to think what amount of love you owe to the dear good Lord, who undertook so willingly to pay that infinite price.

5. You have seen how the Eternal Father, out of love for His creatures, sent His only-begotten Son on His mission of redemption. See how Jesus accepts it. Holy David, who, in prophetic vision, beheld all this, thus describes the Son of God accepting the Father's commission to redeem man: "Burnt-offering and sin-offering Thou didst not require: then said I, behold I come. In the head of the book it is written of me, that I should do Thy will. O my God, I have desired it, and Thy law in the midst of my heart (Psalm xxxix. 7, 8, 9).

Do not these words beautifully show, first, the uselessness of any but an infinite satisfaction for sin, then the expressed will of the Eternal Father, and lastly, the willing acceptance of Jesus Christ? Yes, and it was for love of you that He so willingly accepted the office of Redeemer with all its sufferings.

6. Still more. Love makes Him eager for those very sufferings, as the royal prophet again points out in the words: "He hath rejoiced as a giant to run the way, His going out is from the end of heaven (Ps. xviii. 6, 7), and, does He not Himself tell us of His yearning after sufferings to save you.

Hear His own words: "With desire I have desired to eat this pasch with you before I suffer" (Luke xxii. 15); and again: "I have a Baptism wherewith I am to be baptized, and how am I straightened until it be accomplished?" (Luke xxi. 50).

One would think that in this eagerness which Jesus had shown to pay the price of your redemption there is amply sufficient to feed the soul of His children with love, without going any further. This, however, is precisely what Jesus Christ did not think, as I have yet to show.

7. Although your purchase required a price of infinite value, it did not require what Jesus really gave. Here we have something more wonderful still to reflect upon. One drop of the blood of Jesus Christ, even one tear shed by Him, would have been amply sufficient to save not only you, but the whole world. There is one thing, however, which Jesus wanted, and which one tear, or one drop of blood, would not obtain for Him—something which He coveted, but which, even in spite of all He has done for them, His children withhold from Him even now, by forgetting His sufferings after He has endured them.

What is that, my dear young friends?

It is the love of our wayward hearts.

It seems strange, but it is true, that Jesus would endure the bitter agony in the garden, not so much because it was necessary for man's salvation, as that we should have that particular suffering to meditate upon, and out of that meditation might learn the enormity of sin, and at the same time be moved to make a few extra acts of love. Yet so it is with each of the mysteries of the Passion. What a thing to think of! Follow the Stations of the Cross. Think of the prodigality of suffering those stations reveal; then say to yourselves, Jesus suffered these things, and considered He had not done too much, because an increase of love in the hearts of His friends, gained in meditation on those cruel sufferings, and the devotion of the Stations of the Cross, has been the fruit.

8. Truly as St. Paul says: "You are bought with a great price" (1 Cor. vi. 20). Yes, at the price of every drop of the blood of the Son of God. Never, then, my dear young friends, let these words of the language of faith, "bought by the blood of Jesus," become meaningless to you. Let them be rather words filling you with an earnest care for your salvation. Let them make you yearn after the salvation of others. You have seen the eagerness of Jesus. Never let it seek in vain for the love of your whole heart. You have seen that Jesus not only shed His blood for your salvation, but that He shed it prodigally for your love. Give Him, then, that love; find it by meditation on the mysteries of the Passion. Surely He who has done so much has a right to claim that His love should not be in vain. No, it shall not be so. Far from allowing such a thing, your earnestness and your love will not only prevent Him from regretting what He has done in your regard, but will make Him rejoice for each drop of His precious blood that He has shed for you.

CHAPTER IV.

Your Eldest Brother.

1. To call Jesus Christ, the Son of the living God, by this name, looks at first sight like an exaggeration. Well, I suppose if you were to tell a person who had never heard it before, that God had assumed and united to Himself a human soul and a human body, it would appear to him a great deal more like an exaggerated statement than a truth. But our happy familiarity with the truth, that God became man, has taken away from it much of our feeling of wonder, although in reality His having done so shows much more loving condescension than His afterwards making Himself our eldest brother.

Nevertheless, I would not, on my own responsibility, address our dear Lord by this title; but St. Paul has not only given it to Him, but has also shown us that He made Himself our brother in order, in that character, to make us like Himself. These are his words: "For whom He foreknew, He also predestined to be made conformable to the image of His Son, that He might be the first-born amongst many brethren." After all, my dear young friends, what is a brother, but one who is the child of those who are our father and mother, and, after that, what renders the relationship more striking than a family likeness?

2. Now there are two ways of being made brother and sister, the one by birth, the other by adoption. You have become brethren and sisters of Jesus

Christ by this latter mode. By adoption you became the children of His father and mother.

I have already shown you that in giving you His only-begotten Son, the Eternal Father, to use the words of St. John's Gospel, "Gave to as many as received Him the power to be made the sons of God" (John i. 12). We shall speak by and bye of this adoption in Baptism; these words are, however, sufficient for my present purpose, for they show you that it is your happy privilege to have become the adopted children of the Eternal Father. But who is Jesus Christ? Is he not the only Son, begotten from all eternity of this same Eternal Father?

Yes, and therefore He is truly your eldest brother. But you are also the children of His Immaculate Mother. You are well aware when and how He gave her to you for a mother. It was, indeed, a time she is not likely to forget, neither can she forget what it cost her to have you for her child. She became your mother at the foot of the Cross, where she stood in anguish, watching her Divine Son accomplish the sacrifice of Himself for your salvation. Hear the words in which St. John, the Apostle, who himself represented you on that occasion, relates the event: "When Jesus, therefore, had seen His Mother and the disciple standing, whom He loved, He saith to His Mother: Woman, behold thy Son. After that He saith to the disciple: Behold thy Mother. And from that hour the disciple took her to his own" (St. John xix. 26, 27). And you, too, dear young friends, may also well take her to your own, well assured of the love she must bear you, seeing that she received you in the place of Jesus, and at the expense of sacrificing Him for your salvation. Every circumstance of this solemn scene is calculated, indeed, to give her all the feelings of a mother towards you, as was doubtless the very intention of Jesus in choosing that time. But we must pass on, satisfied with having shown how, by being the adopted children of Mary, as well as of the Eternal Father, Jesus Christ has become your eldest brother.

3. Now what have we to say about the family likeness?

Can you be in any way like Jesus Christ?

In the first place St. Paul says almost more. Speaking of Jesus' likeness to you, he says: "For what the law could not do in that it was weak through the flesh, God sending his own Son, in the likeness of sinful flesh, and of sin, hath condemned sin in the flesh" (1 Cor. viii. 3). Here St. Paul goes further than I dare; for, adopting, as it were, the language of those who have learnt almost to consider sinfulness the very property of fallen man has said, in as many words, that our Blessed Lord took the very image of their sin-stained nature, in order to shame sin out of them.

But why was it that, as I told you before, Jesus passed through the different stages of life? Why was He a helpless infant? Why a boy, then a youth? Why did He spend so much time in a simple routine of poverty, labour, and obedience? Why did He only spend three years in His public ministry? Truly it was that His life might be like yours. It was that you might have simple virtues to practise, simple actions to perform, which would be like His. Does it not, then, seem that your eldest brother would at least give you the opportunity of acquiring a family likeness?

4. But you will say His simplest actions were the actions of a God-man; mine are only the miserable actions of a poor worm of the earth.

Ah! remember that our Blessed Lord, like a dear eldest brother, has given us something which changes all those miserable human actions into deeds of almost infinite merit! He has given us His own transcending merits; and we have but to perform our simplest actions with the pure intention of doing the will of God, by this intention uniting them to the same actions of our eldest brother Jesus Christ, and they immediately become clothed, as it were, with nobility from His merits, and not only make us like Him here, but will obtain a reward from Him in heaven.

I think I have now said enough to show that Jesus Christ has really made Himself your eldest brother.

5. But the next question is, How does Jesus Christ treat His poor weak little brothers and sisters? And this is a question the answer to which would fill a very large book; and this little work of mine may possibly show you that it will take you all eternity in heaven to answer it fully, and even then you will not exhaust the subject. I will, therefore, only briefly say, He treats His little brothers and sisters as no other brother than the

eternal infinitely good God, son of the eternal infinitely good Father, could ever treat them.

6. But we may dwell a little upon the subject. In the first place, a good brother has much compassion for the weakness of his little brothers and sisters; and in the last chapter of the second part of this book I showed you how God's compassion surrounds us on all sides, and never tires of us during the whole course of our lives. Next, a good brother is willing to suffer in order to save his little brothers and sisters from harm, and the sufferings and death of Jesus show you that He has not failed us on this point.

Again, a good brother defends and protects his little brothers and sisters; and Jesus has done this by meriting for us the grace and assistance of God, on the road to heaven. But of this I shall have more to say hereafter. To sum up the whole matter: He is a very good brother, who, being the King of kings, purchases for his brothers and sisters a share in His own kingdom, provides them with almost superfluous assistance to help them to obtain it, and then stands by them and conducts them on the road, and is never satisfied until they have safely reached the goal. This is just what Jesus has done, is doing, and will continue to do for us His little brothers and sisters.

I think we may pause here a little.

7. Is there not a very practical lesson in all this? Does it not bring forcibly before us what is written upon my title page?—"I therefore beseech you, that you walk worthy of the vocation in which you

are called." The actions of children should be worthy of their parents. The children of a family which has for its head the Son of God made man should certainly strive to be, as far as possible, worthy of such an eldest brother. This should be especially the case when that brother became man with the special object of teaching His little brothers and sisters to become like Himself. You have seen elsewhere how He has bestowed upon you the gift of being able to lead innocent lives. You have seen how, by the present of His own merits, He gives nobility to the commonest actions of that innocent life. What then? It follows that, if you will, you are perfectly able to become very like your eldest brother. On the other hand, however, you have the power of becoming terribly unlike Him, and this fearful possibility becomes tenfold more horrifying to those who remember who is their father, who their mother, and who their eldest brother.

8. When I consider, my young friends, that you are all princes and princesses of the House of God, I feel almost afraid to mention the horrible monster I am about to name. And yet I will speak of it, that I may arm you against the possibility of your ever permitting it to come near to you. It is called wilful and deliberate sin.

I am sure that, after what you have learned about yourselves, you would be very much obliged to me if I could tell you of some infallible way of preventing the approach of this monster. Here, then, is a very simple method of doing so. Never let one day pass without saying from your hearts after your morning prayers: God my Father, and Jesus my eldest brother, bless me; and Mary, my dearest mother, protect me.

CHAPTER V.

Your Divine Guest.

1. In speaking of the various beautiful relations, which redeeming love has made to spring up between you and Almighty God, I purposely abstain, my dear young friends, from referring to that which brings them into each of your individual souls, because I wish in the next part to close, as it were, your picture, when I speak of Baptism.

I mention each of these relations, therefore, as a something put within the reach of man by redeeming love. And this is strictly true, because, as Jesus Christ died for the salvation of all, and as every one is called to salvation in one way or another, every human being is called to the possession of what Baptism brings to such as receive it.

Thus it is with your Eternal Father's gift; thus with the Blood that bought and paid for every human being; thus with the adoption of children of God, and the consequent brotherhood of Jesus Christ.

2. These relationships are beautiful indeed; and any one who could say that the knowledge and thought of them can do nothing to sanctify your lives, would show how little he understands what

has power to influence human actions. A man might as well be without eyes, if he uses them so little as not to perceive that even the clothes which they wear, and their employment of time influence his fellow-creatures, as to their conduct. Birth, position, and relationship, in fact, almost govern the world. They smooth men's manners, even if they fail to make them virtuous, And, on the other hand, it is, alas! too often the case that poor clothes and hard labour make those whose lot they are, forget the dignity of the Christian character.

3. Although it is a fact, this is not as it should be. These persons want to look into the "Mirror of Faith," which would show them that poverty and toil cannot alter the good old maxim: "Gentle is that gentle does." Aye, it would even show them that poverty and toil, far from degrading, are calculated to ennoble a man by making him more like to his eldest brother, Jesus Christ.

4. Wholesome, however, as are the influences which I have hitherto shown you in the "Mirror of Faith," they leave you, as it were, in your human weakness, at least to some extent. We have hardly yet spoken of any power entering into you, taking the reins of government into His own hands, and making your being rather His than yours. We have not yet spoken of One who so takes possession of you, that what seemed before a visible centre of every human infirmity, is made to become, instead, a sort of visible castle, from which God shows to the world the beauty of His own sanctity. Yet it is true that redeeming love has bestowed upon every

human being the power to become such as I have described.

5. Does not the expression, "receiving the Holy Ghost"—do not the words, "Temple of the Holy Ghost," belong to that language of faith, the idioms of which, as I said before, are familiar to every child of Holy Church, which contain so much, and are said so often without thought? Listen to the words of St. Paul: "Know you not, that your members are the temple of the Holy Ghost, who is in you, whom you have from God, and you are not your own? For you are bought with a great price. Glorify and bear God in your body" (1 Cor. vi. 19, 20).

See, my dear young friends, St. Paul might have mentioned the soul as the temple of the Holy Ghost; but he does not. He insists on the body as the temple, because in the body, more than in the soul, is that presence manifested to a visible world; and, as I showed before, there is a spiritual benefit gained by showing man that sanctity must rule the very lowest part of his nature.

6. In considering this beautiful truth, far from being astonished that God should dwell within you, a very opposite question presents itself to my mind; and I say, why should not the Holy Ghost become consciously your Guest? Why should He not make your body His temple? Were it not for redemption, such a thing would be indeed impossible, and the thought of it would be strange presumption and mere extravagance! But the wonderful manner of our redemption takes away all astonishment from the wonders which follow it.

God the Father made your body as well as your soul an object He cannot look at without seeing an image of His Divine Son. That Divine Son has united your body and soul so closely to Himself, that they will never be separated for eternity. Such has been redeeming love. What reason can there then be, after this, to prevent the Holy Ghost, the third Person of the Adorable Trinity, from being brought by this same love to make you His home? Surely none at all; and thus has redeeming love made man the temple of God, and the Holy Ghost man's guest.

7. The next question we must ask is this: When does the Holy Ghost dwell in us? He dwells in every Christian as long as, by innocence or by repentance, the Christian is in the grace and friendship of God. He dwells in the baptized child that has not yet come to the use of reason. When a Christian has the misfortune to commit a mortal sin, he drives the Holy Spirit away from him, and admits the devil in His place. This is another reason for being in dread of mortal sin. Your own sense would even tell you that God and sin cannot dwell together, and the Holy Ghost Himself has said by the mouth of the Wise Man: "Wisdom will not enter into a malicious soul, nor dwell in a body subject to sins, for the Holy Spirit of discipline will flee from the deceitful" (Wisdom, i. 4, 5.)

You see the Holy Ghost is here called the spirit of discipline, because, like a wise general, he keeps the whole man in order. I may here casually remark, that it is not much to be wondered at that people who have driven the Holy Ghost away from them, should talk of finding the body sinful! Poor body! As it has no reason of its own, it is badly off indeed when it has neither the soul's reason nor the Holy Ghost to guide it! And it must, indeed; be in woeful plight when it gets the devil in their place. With such a ruler, who can be surprised at anything people do? And the mere possibility of finding oneself in such a condition, ought, in itself, to make us dread the departure of the Holy Ghost. But that is no reason for accusing the body of being the cause of our sin.

8. We must next see how the Holy Ghost should be treated. One of the deepest instincts of the human heart, teaches us that any guest must be treated well. But yours, my dear young friends, is no ordinary guest. He is the Eternal God, the Holy Ghost, the third Person of the Blessed Trinity; and all that I can say upon the subject is, that He should, as far as possible, be treated according to His rank.

Knowing who He is, your own hearts will tell you, better than I can do, what reverence you should show Him. I have said before, that one of the reasons why children preserve God's image better than grown up persons, is because they are so simple. I do not mean simple in the sense of being foolish or ignorant, I mean that they possess that simplicity which is single-mindedness—the simplicity which teaches the infant to love its mother because she loves it—the simple ardour which makes children turn their hearts to God when once they have learned how good He is. Follow, then, this impulse; and, since you know that the Holy Ghost is your guest, be true to yourselves, and give to Him that reception which your hearts dictate.

Since you know that He is really within you, thank Him every morning for remaining with you, beg Him with love and confidence to take care of you, and never to allow you to drive Him away. Ask Him to speak to your heart, and to tell you what to do, that, having such a guide, you may make no mistakes in your daily course. Then, again, as you will plainly see, it will be necessary for you to examine your house, to see if it contains anything that could be displeasing to your Divine Guest, and to put such a thing away, by an act of sorrow if a fault, by a good resolution if it be an imperfect habit.

Just as in a material house we take care to dust and arrange the rooms every morning, doing so with especial attention, should the house contain an honoured visitant, so in our other house, ourselves, must everything be purified and set in order. The different chambers of this house are our different powers of soul and body, and all these rooms contain furniture which is very liable to get dusty and disordered.

Thus you have many thoughts in your understanding; your will is furnished with affections and dislikes; your body has its various senses. All these you have to examine and to set right, by contrition for what is wrong, by strengthening what is good. Then comes the time for you to ask the Holy Spirit to make Himself at home, and to beg Him to use each of these chambers as He pleases, and to offer yourself to serve Him in all things. Such is, I should imagine, the way your own heart would tell you to treat the Holy Ghost. But here a fact stares me in the face, and seems to upset all I have been saying.

9. The fact is, that very few persons do act in this manner; nay, most persons, I am sorry to say, think but little of the Holy Ghost at all!

Now, this sad error has its root in childhood, and is very much due to want of instruction. It is seldom that some time does not elapse between the child's coming to the use of reason, and his reception of the Sacraments of Penance and Holy Communion, and this time is a very important period, during which, as I have before said, he not only needs help to be good, but might grow a great deal in virtue and the love of God. The Holy Ghost descends into the little baby at its Baptism, and remains there whilst the baby knows nothing about Him; and why? Because He wishes to possess it beforehand, in order to seize the first glimpses of reason in the child and strengthen it in good.

This is all very well. But if the child is taught little or nothing about the Holy Spirit, it will take no notice of Him when reason does come. Then what will happen? There will be neglect of Him, and as soon as a child becomes a reasonable being, neglect becomes displeasing to God. Then probably the child will not correspond to His graces, and with the use of reason comes the necessity of correspondence, in order to gain by His presence. Then, to complete the mischief, the child, thinking nothing of the presence of the Holy Spirit, will not fear to displease Him, and will commit many venial sins which will freeze and harden its heart, so that the first temptation it meets with, will find it as cold and weak as possible.

10. Now, is not this not merely to prevent the Holy Ghost from doing good to the child, but even, in one sense, to make His presence almost a source of harm?—because He is there a guest, and not to treat Him well is to neglect Him, which is to treat Him very badly. This is, in fact, to turn the most precious time in life, in which all the ardour of childhood would help to turn young hearts into gardens for the growth of divine love, into a time in which those same hearts become barren wastes, in danger of being cursed as unfruitful by the Divine Husbandman.

I have said all this before, or something very like it, when speaking of mistakes in early education, but it cannot be dwelt upon too strongly; and I repeat it now, because I am persuaded that the want of knowledge of, and devotion to the Holy Spirit, is the beginning of ruin to many; and I put the matter plainly before you, that you may take it into your own hands, and may now, if you have not done so before, adopt a devotion which will enable you, at one stroke, to secure your temporal and your eternal happiness.

Suppose that a child should adopt this devotion, infused into its little heart by the Holy Spirit Himself, and that it should make it the first of all its devotions, what must be the effect? The thought of the Holy Spirit would make the little child avoid the very shadow of sin, and he would set about pleasing his Divine Guest with all the ardour and simplicity possible. Then the grand virtues which the Holy Ghost brings into the soul, and which are only awaiting the first corresponding act, would burst into a flame of love. And every act of love on the child's part would bring with it a new grace, so that he would daily grow holier and stronger, and at the time of youth he would be far on the road to heaven. I hope that this is so with some of you, my dear young friends; if not, I am sure that it will be so in a short time; for I take it for granted that, having had the subject now brought before you, you will henceforth begin to treat in a worthy manner your Divine Guest.

11. Let us, then, see what the Holy Spirit does within us. You remember the four emblems used to designate the four Evangelists, and which are so often seen upon altars and pulpits, and in other places about a church; the first is an eagle, the second a man, the third a lion, the fourth an ox, and all of them with wings. These emblems are taken from the beginning of the prophecy of Ezechiel, who describes them as four living creatures, and says of all the four, that—"Every one of them went straight forward; whither the impulse of the Spirit was to go, thither they went, and they turned not when they went" (Ezek. i. 14). Now, these four creatures represent four

different kinds of men, and the lesson they teach is this, and a very consoling one it is, namely, that whatever natural dispositions we may have, yet, if we, like these creatures, will only obey the Holy Ghost within us, He will guide us straight forward on the way to heaven, so that all we have to do is to take care never to turn aside from His inspirations.

Now, it is a grand thing to be thus, as it were, pushed along the road to heaven by the Holy Ghost, our guest and guide. Let us see what different kinds of creatures are thus pushed. The eagle is a bird which flies very high, and can look at the sun without blinking. It represents those who have powerful minds, and when these obey the spirit of God, and subject themselves to the yoke of faith, that spirit enables them to contemplate the greatest truths, such as the Trinity and the Incarnation, and it keeps them safe in all matters of science. But there are other eagles who have sharp intellects and yet will have nothing to do with the spirit of God; these fly off into absurdities such as I have before described to you, and may be said actually to reason away their own common sense.

The ox represents people who are simple and unlettered, and who yet, by the aid of the same Spirit, know, after all, as much from their Catechism, about the things of God, as the greatest philosophers do. Thus, the child who has learned his Catechism is quite as well aware that there are three persons in one God, that Jesus Christ became man, and that He is the dwelling-place of the Holy Ghost, as the most learned man on the face of the earth.

The lion, which is a very strong animal, represents men of strong passions and firm resolute purpose. Perhaps you will ask, Can the Holy Ghost guide straight such natures as these? Yes, my young friends, and it is of such as these that the greatest saints are made. Look at a case in point. The arch-heretic Martin Luther, and St. Ignatius of Loyola, came into the world about the same time. These men were somewhat similar in character, that is to say, they were both lions of resolution, and very possibly of passion too. Where was the great difference between them? Luther disobeyed and turned away from God's spirit, and was carried into every excess; while St. Ignatius, carried straight forward by God's spirit, became, by the society God made use of him to found, one of the greatest antagonists which either Luther or the devil ever had to contend with. Yes, if there be one thing about the saints of God which is more remarkable than another, it is the strength of character by which so many were distinguished.

But timid wavering souls, who are represented by the man, need not be afraid; for they too will be carried straight on the road to heaven, if they will obey the Spirit of God.

12. We have seen, then, my dear young friends, how the Holy Ghost guides men; all that has to be done is to listen to and obey His voice. But, in order to do this, the first thing is to know it. The Holy Ghost, who is the Spirit of Truth himself, tells us: "Believe not every spirit, but try the spirits if they be of God" (1 John iv. 1). See how the Holy

Spirit tells us that we must first of all be prudent and hesitate in this matter. So forcibly does the Church lay this duty on us, that she tells us to receive with a kind of incredulity every inspiration which is not proved good in itself, by being reconcilable with faith and reason. So those persons make a great mistake who think God's Church makes us credulous; for if Jesus Christ were even to appear to you, He would bid you take no notice of the apparition until you had tried it by your Catechism, and found that what He said was good.

But what the Holy Ghost says to us, very seldom requires any trial. He speaks to the heart, and bids us desist from doing something that is not good; He asks us to renounce some little gratification for the love of God; He bids us do a kind action or put away an angry feeling; He asks us not to go into dangerous company.

These are the kind of inspirations the Holy Ghost generally gives, and, oh! my dear young friends, will you not learn to obey Him? The Holy Ghost is very patient, and often bears being disobeyed in little matters in which He would urge us to please Him, and we still refuse; but what losers we are by such conduct! Surely love ought to oblige us to act very differently!

13. But you will make devotion to the Holy Spirit the devotion of your youth; and if you do, the effect will soon appear, for your Divine Guest will never suffer Himself to be outdone in generosity!

Think how this dear good God, who waits in the infant's breast for its first act of childish love, must cherish the heart which is wholly given to Him. Do this—give Him the freedom of your house, and you will find it richly endowed in return!

Your understanding will be filled with the light of His wisdom, your heart will be set on fire with His love! Yes, and even your body will become His obedient servant, so that your every movement will breathe forth the sanctity of Him whom you obey. Your countenance will, like a dial of the soul, become expressive of the control in which your passions are kept; even as that of him who yields to his inclinations, shows in his very looks that he does so, and the face of a holy person shows in it the outward signs of the peace and charity which are the fruits of the Holy Spirit who dwells with him; and be assured that, whatever then may be your natural dispositions, early obedience to the Spirit of God will make it comparatively easy for you to run straight along that road of God's commandments which leads to heaven.

CHAPTER VI.

God's Friends.

1. IN all the language of faith, there is not, I suppose, another expression half so familiar as that which expresses the relationship which exists between God and the soul in a state of grace. To be God's friend, to be separated from God by sin, to be reconciled to God, such are the words which echo from every pulpit, and are familiar at every Catholic fireside.

Yet, there is a remarkable difference between the weight these words carry with them to different hearts. Let these words sound in the ears of some, and immediately the thought that they have the power of being God's friends, turns the world into a Paradise, and makes all the trials of life disappear like shadows before the sun. And life would be to them a Paradise, but that they are recalled from their reverie by the remembrance that sin can rob them of this bliss on earth, and the very sound of the word, "separated from God by sin," makes them tremble from head to foot, as if they saw the gaping jaws of hell, in very deed, opening before their eyes.

How different the effect upon others of these very same words! To them the expression, "friends of God," is nothing more than pulpit talk, something which, of course, it is the duty of priests to say, and for them to listen to patiently; whilst "to be reconciled to God" is an affair they mean to attempt some day, a thing which it would be very well to have done at Easter or Christmas—something, in fine, which they intend to look to in earnest before they have to appear before their God; but something, however, which they have very little notion of doing at present.

Could it be believed that the same words could have such a very different effect on different persons? Scarcely, but it is too true.

2. Neither is it a matter of chance. It is the effect of a cause. Both of these classes of persons may have the same faith, they may be equally instructed; more wonderful still, the same person

may belong, first to the one class, and then to the other, and *vice versâ!* I have mentioned the cause before, but, as it is the first thing we have to learn about the friendship of God, I will repeat it. Separation from God, by one mortal sin, is not only enmity with Him, but it is death; and the insensibility I have described is the sleep of death. On the other hand, the friendship of God is life, and the sensibility I have described, the joy in possessing God, the fear of losing Him, is simply the first effect of it, and serves to preserve, as well as to mark, God's friendship.

What a reason have we not here to make us cherish and hold fast the blessed privilege redeeming love has bestowed upon us! What a warning have we not, in this insensibility, of the dread effects of that mortal sin which could deprive us of it!

3. Your Catechism tells you who is the friend of God. Every one is such whose soul is free from mortal sin, either by innocence or by repentance. This friendship of God is a relationship brought about and put within every one's reach by redeeming love. It accompanies those other relationships I have spoken of before; but yet it is in itself something too distinct and too beautiful to be passed over.

4. To mention the first effect of friendship, and to contemplate it as possible between God and man, is enough to stagger one. There can be no friendship without a sort of equality, although it may be the friendship itself which brings this equality about.

DIVINE CONDESCENSION.

Of course, in the friendship which God has formed between Himself and us, He has brought about the equality of intercourse, simply by infinite condescension on His part, and by exalting us almost infinitely.

You must not suppose, for a moment, that I speak here of any real equality, or of more than that equality which arises out of the fact that God deigns to stoop to treat us poor worms of the earth as His friends. If a mighty prince were to contract a friendship with a beggar, the condescension would not make the beggar anything different from what he was before; nevertheless, when that prince indulged in such a friendship, he would have for the time to forget all difference between him and his friend, for, if he did not do so, the relationship between them would fall short of friendship.

How does our dear good God treat His friends? In the first place He, as it were, tries to make us as much like Himself as possible, and then seems to forget the infinite distance which exists between Himself and us, treating us as if there were hardly any at all. To show how Almighty God has lowered Himself to us, would be but to repeat the history of the Incarnation, of which St. Paul says that it was nothing less than annihilating Himself to become like you and me. Hear his words: "Who, being in the form of God, thought it not robbery to be equal with God; but emptied Himself, taking the form of a servant, being made in the likeness of man, and in habit found as a man" (Phil. ii. 6, 7). Yes, thus it was that the Eternal God prepared Himself, as it were, to contract a friendship with us.

Then, what shall I say about the means He has taken to raise up His poor creature, at least so high as to force him, as it were, to a humble familiarity with His Divine Majesty? Has not the Eternal Father obliged Himself to see in us images of His only-begotten Son? Have we not, as I have already shown, become His adopted children? And have I not even ventured to show you, on His own authority, that Jesus Christ has made Himself your eldest brother, and that the Holy Ghost has made you His dwelling-place? What is all this but a beautiful attempt of divine love to raise you, as it were, to a level of familiarity sufficient to bring about that sort of equality which friendship requires?

Yet, which of us would venture, if faith did not bid us do so, to call ourselves, and believe ourselves in truth, to be the friends of God.

5. But there is something yet more astonishing than the truth that God has deigned to make man His friend, and that is the smallness of the requirements which are necessary upon our part to constitute and preserve this friendship. Faith teaches us that nothing but mortal sin can destroy it, and that though venial sin prepares the way for its destruction, no number of venial sins can, of themselves, put an end to it. Could human friendship, however strong, exist on such a basis as this? Venial sins are very, very often deliberate insults against God, and God alone knows how many of them may be committed without falling into mortal sin. Would you, my young friends, feel obliged to cherish a warm friendship for one of your companions who

had insulted you half a dozen times? Would you feel inclined to be amiable towards one who had given you a slap on the face, on the ground that he had not gone so far as to try to kill you?

6. Yet such is the desire of God to be friends with us, that nothing short of mortal sin will cause Him to withdraw His friendship. Surely it must be the compassion of our Heavenly Father, who knows how badly off we should be without His friendship, that makes Him put up with us so patiently. He warns us, indeed, of the final consequences of such outrageous conduct, but still He hopes, as long as He is there, His very love and patience will win us to better things. And should they not indeed have this effect? The very thought of the compassion which makes God, as it were, linger in the soul, in spite of so many evil deeds, as if He could hardly be persuaded to leave it, even by the presence of sin itself, should surely make venial sin doubly terrible in our eyes, and this tender patience should make our hearts burn with tenfold love for Him.

7. But, notwithstanding God's compassion, this friendship of which we have spoken can be cooled—terribly cooled. Yet, even in this case, the danger comes from the frightful coldness induced in the sinner's heart by sin more than from any decrease of tenderness on the part of God.

The Holy Ghost has uttered a warning which should be sufficient to make you form a resolution never to commit a deliberate venial sin as long as you live. Such a resolution is by no means an uncommon one; but I draw your attention to it because it is one of those practical things which mark the character of God's true servants. They make it principally out of love; but still the warning of the Holy Ghost should help to persuade you to make it. The warning is: "He that contemneth small things shall fall by little and little" (Eccles. xix. 1). The deliberate commission of venial sin is the high road to mortal sin. Neither can we wonder that it is so; for if we think of the ingratitude of the soul which is willing to treat God in this way, the thought disgusts us; no wonder, then, that it should disgust the All-holy God. Now, according to His own words, this is precisely the effect which it has upon Him. Hark! how He spoke and expressed His nausea with regard to a soul in this state: "I know thy works, that thou art neither cold nor hot, but because thou art lukewarm, and neither cold nor hot, I will begin to vomit thee out of my mouth" (Apoc iii. 15, 16). This must, then, be a very dreadful state, which makes Almighty God so sick of the soul, that He not only casts it off, but even prefers that it should actually not pretend to love Him at all. It is also a very helpless state, because people who live in it are neither warm enough to love God, nor cold enough to consider that they require conversion; so that there is little chance of their being changed. So true is this, that Almighty God sometimes leaves them to themselves, so that, through their subsequent fall into some great sin, they may at least become sensible of their misery, and in that way be converted. Surely that is indeed a terrible state which can require so severe a remedy.

But even if God's patience be content to bear with a long course of venial sin, what, on the sinner's part, is to prevent him from falling into mortal sin? Nothing at all. Any strength the Christian has in himself, to make him put aside temptation, is the strength of his love. Now, he cannot love God much, who not only deliberately insults Him, but even falls into so dreadful a state of indifference as not to care how often he does so, and to be unwilling to take any trouble to avoid venial sin. Why, not to care about offending God, is the very next thing to throwing away His love altogether, so that it is little wonder that such a soul should, on the very first provocation, actually cast away a love which it has learned to prize so little.

8. Thus you see how surely this tepidity leads to mortal sin. I do not, however, wish you to make the mistake of supposing that every venial sin makes a person tepid. No, it is only those cold, deliberate venial sins, which of themselves even prove a degree of indifference to God, which it is hard to distinguish from not loving Him at all, that do so.

Those numerous little faults of surprise and negligence, which frailty makes those commit who do truly love God, will never cause Him to withdraw from them. Aye, even sins that are apparently serious, if they be the effect of sudden passion in persons of fiery temperament, often serve to bring them nearer to God by the contrition and humility to which they give rise in the hearts of God's friends.

We have an instance of this in St. Peter, although his was a grievous mortal sin. Yet even before the descent of the Holy Ghost, who could help loving St. Peter, on account of his strong love for his Divine Master? Our Blessed Lord did love Peter dearly, and chose him to be the head of His Church. No one, however, can say that St. Peter's impetuous disposition did not lead him into serious blunders. Our Blessed Lord even called him " Satan " once, for trying to dissuade Him from going to Jerusalem before His Passion. " Get thee behind me, Satan" (Mark viii. 33). St. Peter ought to have known that His Divine Master knew His own business best, and what it was the Eternal Father willed Him to do. Again, St. Peter, in the garden, cut off a man's ear with a sword, in defence, indeed, of His Divine Master, but without having any authority to defend Him in that way; he, therefore, did wrong in doing so. Yet even when St. Peter paid the penalty of his self-confidence, by falling into the mortal sin of denying our Blessed Lord, our dear Lord cast upon him a loving look, and with that look converted him, so that as long as he lived he never ceased lamenting his crime.

9. This shows how indulgent Almighty God is to the frailties of His creatures; it shows how he cherishes that strong love which urges His children to please Him and to hate sin; and it should be a source of great confidence to us and an encouragement to love Him very ardently.

10. But the best thing we have to say about the friendship between God and His creatures is

yet to come. Requiring for its establishment, as I have already said, only the absence of mortal sin, it is nevertheless capable of an almost infinite increase of familiarity. Yes, this is the real end for which it was established, and consequently it is the great thing which we have to aim at, namely, to draw closer and closer the bonds of friendship between our soul and God. This is what is called aiming at perfection, and common sense teaches that it is the duty of every one, without exception, to make the most of the power which God has given them of being His friends. Not to do so would be, to say the least of it, foolish and ungrateful; and what has Almighty God Himself said upon the subject? "Be you therefore perfect, as also your Heavenly Father is perfect" (Matt. v. 48).

11. In the beginning of this chapter, I said something about equality, and you see that our dear good God would at least make us aim at carrying it as far as possible. But the process by which this friendship is rendered closer and closer, can only be carried on by means of help from above, and the graces received must be corresponded with. Thus, for instance, you make an act of love, you overcome a temptation, you mortify a passion, or you do something else pleasing to God. No sooner is this done, than you have won, not only another jewel for your eternal crown and other things attached to this good work, but also a new and beautiful grace from heaven, which, if you make good use of it, will bring you a step nearer to God, and so on, each grace making you

holier than before. Beside this, there are Sacramental graces; but of these I will not now speak. I have shown you how grace acts, and that is sufficient for our present purpose.

12. There are, however, two or three things, which naturally follow from what has been said, and which we will notice in conclusion. In the first place, you see how much depends on correspondence with grace. To correspond to one grace is to gain another grace, to neglect to correspond is to lose a grace, and at the same time to be guilty of making light of God's friendship and goodness. This proves that there is no such thing as standing still in God's service; we must advance, or we shall retrograde. It may seem wearisome to be always pushing forward, but if we do not make use of those graces which God's goodness showers upon us so thickly, we shall lose, not only them, but others which we should have gained by their assistance, and thus, instead of approaching nearer God, we drift away from Him. Again, we know enough of our weakness to be well aware that we should often be very badly off, if we were left without very special assistance from God. Now, that special assistance may be a grace depending upon correspondence to graces previously given to us.

13. What a misfortune will it, then, be to us, if we neglect present graces, and thus lose special assistance! Ah, my young friends, there is but one thing for us to do. We must do our very best, and leave the rest to our Lord's compassion.

But you will hardly need to be urged to do this.

You will, I have no doubt, feel too well what Holy David felt, when he said: "To me Thy friends, O God, are exceedingly honourable" (Ps. cxxxviii. 17).

Yes, you will feel yourselves too much honoured by your dear Lord in His giving you His friendship, not to do your best to correspond with it. Everything you have seen will tend to incite you to do so. First, the compassion which put the requirements of friendship so low, will only add to your love for Him who is so anxious to be your friend. Then, the horrible nature of that coldness which is so indifferent to God's friendship will make you shudder. After that, the necessity of not letting graces slip by will hurry you on.

14. Will you learn to correspond with grace, my dear young friends? There is one who knows how to teach you, because she, and she alone of God's pure human creatures, corresponded with every grace.

She corresponded indeed so well, that she became, not merely God's friend, but even God's mother!

Ask, then, this bright Queen of Heaven, always in the first place to keep you in God's friendship; and next, to teach you how to become, until the day of your death, more and more united to Him, who has made Himself your friend, in order to unite you to Himself in the closest possible friendship, which, begun in life, will last during a whole eternity.

CHAPTER VII.
Your Divine Food.

1. TREATING, as I have been, all through this part of my book, of relationships which are really contracted by the individual soul in that beautiful Sacrament, which will form the subject of the next part, I might, it would seem, without much apology, here treat of whatever I pleased. I shall not, however, for many reasons, branch out into co-relative subjects; for, although Baptism and everything to which it opens the door are the fruits of redeeming love, it would not be possible to touch upon all these points, and were it possible, the doing so would change the character of my work.

Another book, called "The Channels of Grace," might, however, very naturally follow the present one; indeed, there is room for a whole series, although many good books on the Sacraments, the Commandments, devotions, &c., already exist, and it is perhaps unnecessary to add to their number. My object is rather to leave such matters on one side, trusting that a sound knowledge of what Baptism implies, will lay a foundation that will make them more effectually fruitful, by preparing you to appreciate them.

Thus, I do not even intend to speak here of that special means which Jesus' love has provided for the reconciliation of those of His children who have unfortunately thrown away their baptismal robe. I will, however, tell you in passing, that this cleansing bath of Jesus' blood has another purpose, perhaps, as important as that of reconciling the sinner.

That purpose is the one for which I hope you will always have the happiness of using it—that of preserving God's friendship in the soul; the purpose of purifying God's friends from every stain of imperfection, and of continually washing them in Jesus' blood to fit them for a close communication with Him. For this purpose, indeed, this blood is always at your disposal, even without the Sacrament of Penance, whenever, by an act of true contrition, you apply it to your soul.

2. There is one Sacrament, however, of which I must say something, because it shows, beyond all other gifts purchased for us by our Lord, the extent of His love. It is that which casts the brightest light on your picture, showing you the sublime dignity to which redeeming love has raised you, and moreover frees me from the charge of exaggeration in anything I have hitherto said. This is, of course, the Blessed Eucharist. I shall, however, treat of it simply with a view to our object, without pretending to speak of it any further.

3. Jesus has, in the Blessed Sacrament, become the Christian's sacrifice, companion, and food. He has become your sacrifice, offering Himself daily, by the hands of a poor mortal, to His Eternal Father. For you He thanks God worthily for all His favours; for your sins He atones to His Eternal Father; and, finally, for you He begs every favour which you can need or ask of Him.

Yes, for all these ends of sacrifice He daily makes

to the Eternal Father an offering worthy of His acceptance, an offering infinite in value, namely, the unbloody offering of His own deified body and blood.

How eager should you be, my dear young friends, to assist at this divine sacrifice, in union with Jesus, to pay your debts to Almighty God, for here and here alone can you really pay them? Besides, who can tell the efficacy of one Mass, devoutly assisted at, towards procuring your salvation, and not only salvation, but perseverance and sanctification. Jesus died for the salvation of all men, and yet, through their own fault, His death will be of no avail to many.

4. Well, if some one were to tell you that our Blessed Lord had in dying a special determination to heap graces upon you on account of His death, and that He would render it almost impossible for you to resist their influence—supposing even you were simply told that He would take special care that His blood should not fail of reaching your particular soul, you would have reason to be full of joy. But what happens when you attend Mass devoutly? I will tell you. The very Sacrifice of the Cross, which was offered for the redemption of all on Calvary, is offered again on the altar, with this difference only, that it is offered for the special purpose of applying to the individual souls of those who assist at it the saving effects of Jesus' blood, without, however, excluding others. Thus, to assist at Mass, is, as it were, to acquire a first right to the blood of Jesus. I suppose many people do not think of this; for, if they did,

they would attach more importance to hearing Mass than they do. Yes, people should be much more eager to hear Mass than they are—for, God knows, they want every grace they can get, and can never know in this world to what extent their salvation may depend upon obeying God's inspiration to hear Mass whenever they are able. This is a hurried way of passing over so sublime a subject as the Holy Sacrifice of the Mass, but, as I said before, I can only allow myself to speak of these things in reference to my main object.

5. When Jesus then comes down upon our altars, and hides Himself under the appearance of bread and wine, He has another purpose in view besides sacrifice. He comes thus hidden in order to be the Christian's food.

He comes simply that you may receive Him. Here, indeed, is a proof of Redeeming Love. Did I not say, that the intention of Jesus in redeeming man was not only to atone for sin, but to repair all the evil brought on man by the fall? I told you how the Eternal Father gave us His only-begotten Son, as St. Paul says, "made of a woman, made under the law, that we may receive the adoption of sons" (Gal. iv. 4, 5), and when I inferred from that, the Eternal Father wished to oblige Himself to see in us images of Jesus, your very sense of unworthiness must have made you feel as if I were exaggerating.

When I called Jesus Christ your eldest brother, even though He was called so by greater than I, the words had a startling sound. And when I spoke to you of being temples of the Holy Ghost, perhaps you found it hard to realize the idea. But now what can you say? Jesus has made Himself bread, that you may be nourished with His own body and blood!

6. Does it not seem really as if our dear good God pursued us, as it were, in order to force us to love Him and to oblige us, whether we will or not, to become holy? Just as a gardener sometimes engrafts a delicious fruit-branch on the stem of a common crab-tree, by putting a little shoot under the back where the sap runs, so does it seem that our Lord would engraft Himself upon us, and correct the coarseness which sin has put into us, by infusing His own blood into our veins, so that after a time it should run through them instead of ours.

Do not think that I am exaggerating! You have in many of your prayer-books, for instance, the metrical translation of the beautiful "Anima Christi" of St. Ignatius, in which occurs the line, "Blood of Christ, fill all my veins"—a prayer you cannot use too often; and I am only putting into different words a doctrine coming down from the Fathers, and contained in every book on the Holy Communion, namely, the doctrine, that when you receive Jesus Christ, you do not change Him into yourselves, as you do other food, but you are changed into Him, so that you can say with St. Paul: "I live now, not I, but Christ liveth in me" (Gal. ii. 20).

7. Let us pause here awhile; for truly Christ, the food of Christians, is a thought, beyond all others,

calculated to inspire us with a high idea of the sanctity of body and soul to which we are called. You ought to regard yourselves as so many living tabernacles. Do you not even respect the very tabernacle which contains the Adorable Sacrament? You dare not approach to touch it, much less dare you open the door! That tabernacle is holy, because Jesus dwells there. Yet, on account of the poverty of the Church, it sometimes is only made of a piece of very common wood, painted and decorated with a little gilding to make it look at least respectable. Supposing it should be a costly work of art, still that makes it rather more suitable than more venerable. By receiving Jesus as your food, you become His tabernacle. You are far more costly than the most costly tabernacle, for the blood of Jesus Himself has been paid for you; you are beautiful works of art indeed, the design of which was formed in the mind of the Divine Artist Himself; formed as you are, not so much on your own account, as with a view to what was fit to be the assumed nature of the Son of God made man. Then, again, you are full of life, which no one but your Maker could give to the work of His hands. Thus, you see, that both in costliness and workmanship you far surpass any tabernacle man ever made to contain Jesus Christ Himself. What should you then think of yourselves, since it is your happy destiny to be, each one of you, the tabernacle of Jesus in the Blessed Sacrament. Surely such a thought must make you look upon yourself as something sacred, which you should respect as you would some holy statue or pious picture! God grant that you may do so! for a sacred thing you really are; and this I ask you to remember whenever you kneel before the altar, which is holy, because it is the dwelling-place of Jesus Christ.

8. Just as we have seen in treating of God's friends, perhaps one of the most astonishing things about God's way of leading fallen man to holiness, is the depth of lowliness to which He stoops, in the hope of raising up poor fallen creatures. As He has established a friendship between Himself and His children, and requires nothing on their part but freedom from mortal sin, so He makes freedom from mortal sin the only necessary condition for receiving Him in the Blessed Sacrament. What do we infer from this? Surely, His stooping so low can proceed but from one motive—extreme desire to enter the soul of each of us, that thus He may draw us to sanctity. Hence Jesus can have no greater enemies than those who, under the plea of man's unworthiness, try to prevent the weak from approaching Him. When our Blessed Lord pre-figured this divine banquet under the parable of the Marriage Feast, He did not represent the king as excluding people in this way. Far from it; for this parable rather exemplifies very perfectly the conduct of the Holy Church. For the Church, like the servants of the king, literally obeys His command who said: "Go out quickly, into the streets and lanes of the city, and bring in hither the poor, and the feeble, and the blind, and the lame;" and again, "Go out into the highways and the hedges, and compel them to come in, that my house may be filled" (Luke xiv. 21, 23).

Thus the Divine King obliges Christians, at least once a year, to approach this sacred banquet; and may we not hope that, after all the means He has provided for the purification of the soul in the Sacrament of Penance, He finds only a few comparatively like the unfortunate man who dared to approach the banquet without having on a wedding garment, who will deserve punishment for daring to come to receive this Divine food in a state of mortal sin?

9. But a question here presents itself. Why is it necessary that persons should be forced and compelled to eat of this divine food? Ought not Christians, on the contrary, to be eager for it? Truly they ought, and so those are who, by experience, have learned its delicious sweetness. So I have every hope that you, my dear young friends, will be.

A great many reasons have been given for this strange reluctance which many feel to receive the Bread of Life. Some persuade themselves that they abstain from humility. The greater number, however, feel the reluctance without attempting to explain it to themselves.

But the real cause might easily be discovered, if people would strive to find it out. Why might a collier, who had just come out of the pit, desire to avoid his best friend? Simply, perhaps, because he is too tired to wash himself, and would not like to be seen covered with grime! The fact is, a great many Christians are too fond of working for this world. They are too much occupied with making money, or doing other things which defile the soul, to be often cleansing themselves to receive our Blessed

Lord; and, indeed, they could not receive Him frequently without, not only getting rid of the stains which contact with the world leaves on them, but without giving up entirely many things they are too fond of—things which they know they ought not to love, and yet are unwilling to give up.

To feed continually on this heavenly food, they would have to cleanse their conscience and keep it clean; and, until they do this, they will either find some excuse or other to abstain from Holy Communion, or else do so without making any excuse at all. True, these people have the same call to sanctity that you have. They, like you, are called to be children of God, brethren of Jesus Christ, and temples of the Holy Ghost; but they forget their high calling. And when our Lord would unite them closely to Himself, as it were to oblige them to sanctity, they run away from Him.

Now you see, dear young friends, that our Lord is determined to make you holy, that not only has He surrounded you with the highest dignity, but also left you no other means of avoiding becoming His own tabernacle, than to run away from Him altogether.

10. Jesus is not even satisfied with being your food, because no one can be always feeding on Him, and many, from various causes, may be unable to do so as often as they would. What does our Lord do more? He remains a prisoner on our altars, there to receive our homage, and to hear our prayers. What a good God! Waiting even when He knows that, for many long hours, not a soul will come near Him! There the child can approach and talk to Him, even before

he has made his first Communion. He can ask Him to come into his heart, and fit it to become His living tabernacle.

11. Our Lord wants all to come to Him—loving children, loving youths, and maidens especially—for He is terribly neglected. Learn to love Him, then, dear young friends, and to come to Him, whenever you can, especially to the Holy Benediction, when He blesses His children; and ask Him to teach men to love Him more, to receive Him oftener; and, above all, to assist as often as possible at the Holy Sacrifice of the Mass.

CHAPTER VIII.
Heavenly Companions.

1. THERE is an old adage, which, like many of these familiar sayings, is remarkably true: "Tell me your company, and I will tell you what you are." Now, as the object of this book is precisely to impress upon you the knowledge of what you really are, I shall reverse the proverb, and, by describing to you your company, endeavour to give you a proper idea of yourselves.

Redeeming Love has bestowed upon man the means of holding converse with beings unseen; and, what is still more astonishing, it is not absolutely necessary, in order to be listened to by these beings, that man should be at the time a partaker in the benefit of redemption, by being in a state of grace, or even baptized, although this intercourse always tends to the grace of God. For the angels, being the friends of God, and already enjoying Him, wish that all His rational creatures should share in the same happiness; therefore, they listen to the unbaptized and the sinner, in order to bring them to Baptism and to grace.

2. With those who are the children of God, however, this heavenly companionship is close and familiar, as is natural, because on God's friends they look with love and solicitude, whose happiness it is to be established in God's friendship, without the danger of ever losing it again. It is this fellowship, existing between God's friends here and His friends in heaven, in which you profess faith when you say: "I believe in the communion of saints."

3. I have said before, that there are certain expressions which I called the language of faith, phrases "familiar as household words" to every Catholic. There are household practices, too, of a nature much akin to them, and one of these is, not merely to speak to Almighty God, but in all our wants to talk to angels and saints, just as we would to a friend standing by our side. Catholics do this without ever thinking how the saints hear them; even as they breathe without thinking of the air, without which they could not live, and which they are taking in at every inspiration. In fact, they act on their faith without even thinking of it.

However admirable this is, knowledge on every matter of faith is very desirable, and, therefore, I will tell you how the angels and saints hear us.

4. They see us in God. Of course, you know that the happiness of heaven consists in contemplating

God. Well, blessed be His holy name! God always has us all reflected in Himself, because He loves us so much, takes care of us so continually, and desires our welfare so ardently, that the saints cannot contemplate God without seeing us reflected, as it were, in Him.

Then, again, the saints are united to God so perfectly, in sentiment and love, that what God loves they love; and what God watches over with His providence, they are also interested in; and that welfare which he desires for all His poor wayfaring children, of course they desire also. So you see that, before any of you have said a word to one of them, they are all ready to hear you.

5. Our Blessed Lady, St. Joseph, the nine choirs of angels and every citizen of heaven is watching you with the intensest interest, and ardently desiring everything that is for your good. If this were not true, how could we understand those words of our Blessed Lord: "So I say to you, there is joy before the angels of God upon one sinner doing penance" (Luke xv. 10). The fact of the saints seeing you, and interesting themselves in you, once established, then comes the special interest taken in you by particular saints.

The first of these, of course, is the Immaculate Mother of God—her heart being, of all those of creatures, the one most like that of Jesus. Like Him, she desires with ardour the salvation of all men; but, above all must she love those who are God's friends, who hate sin and love God. Also does she love those much who strive to imitate the

P

special virtues which she loves, while they consecrate themselves to her service, and bestow on her those proofs of attachment which always mark Mary's dear children.

Then, again, there are the saints whose names you bear, and those for whom you have a devotion. They see all these things in God; and, when you speak to them, even in your inmost thoughts, they hear you, and present your petition immediately before the throne of God; and you may be sure there are no saints in heaven who will allow themselves to be outdone in love; for their charity, already so great on earth, is perfect in heaven. Thus you see that you can verify in yourselves the word of St. Paul: "Our conversation is in heaven" (Phil. iii. 20).

6. It is very easy to see what wonderful power this blessed society gives us, to obtain whatever we stand in need of from God. Why, it seems as if Almighty God had made us almost all-powerful before, when He gave us that beautiful promise: "Amen, Amen, I say to you, if you ask the Father anything in my name, He will give it to you (John xvi. 23), even without the aid of heaven's citizens. Still, you see, He would make the means of approaching His throne yet more easy, by allowing us to appeal to Him, backed, as it were, by the whole court of heaven.

7. But good company has other effects besides giving us in every friend a helper before the throne of God. One of the notable effects of friendship, is a communion of sentiment; and, in the case of good friends, encouragement in good. I will only

say a few words about this. Your association with the saints in this intimate way gives you this encouragement. With regard to the sentiments of the saints you are safe, for what made them saints can only tend to help you also to heaven; and as for the encouragement which familiarity with their lives gives you, perhaps it is, in a sense, a greater help to our weakness than the example of Jesus Christ Himself, or that of His Immaculate Mother; for these saints felt the effects of Adam's sin just as you and I do. Then, again, they fought and gained heaven in every lawful state of life—some of them in states not generally considered particularly adapted for the making of saints. Some of the saints were even very great sinners before their conversion, and had thus added the effects of their own sins to those of that of our first mother. We have examples of such amongst the canonized saints. What shall I say of those who are not canonized?

8. Have we not all known some one on earth who is now a saint in heaven? For myself, I recollect well, that when I knelt at God's altar to receive the sacred character of the priesthood, another knelt there with me, who, I have every reason to believe, is at this moment before God's throne; with that man I have held pleasant converse, aye, about the entrance of a soul into bliss. Which of you, my dear young friends, has not met with some innocent companion, whose soul seemed to have been specially formed for heaven rather than earth, who remained here for a short time, and was gathered ripe for blessedness? And what thoughts such things must

bring to us. They must occasionally startle us with the sight of the nearness of earth to heaven, and must urge us to fight valiantly for that crown which a little patience might make our own. Thus it is that the society of the blessed is on earth our aid and encouragement on the road to heaven.

9. But Redeeming Love has not been satisfied with this. To each of you has been appointed at the moment of his birth, for his special guardianship, a bright angel, who never leaves your side; not even sin can drive him away! There, close beside you, he watches over you, and enjoys God at the same time. How near then is heaven to each of us!

Whether this bright angel would have been appointed to guard you if Adam had not sinned, I am not going to say. One thing, however, I will say, that your likeness in nature to the Son of God made man must have had a great effect on his regard for you. Tradition even says, that when the angels fell, and by sin forfeited their thrones, it was because they refused to adore the human nature which it was revealed to them the Son of God would take, for you must remember that it is a nature in itself lower than that of the angels. Perhaps it was also revealed that, in consequence, they would have to become the guardians of creatures clothed in flesh and blood, like Jesus Christ. At any rate, you have a bright angel, one of the faithful ones, who treats you as a fellow-servant of God, and who deigns not only to guard your soul, but even to watch over the purity and innocence of your body also. On the other hand, it seems that not only has the devil gone to hell for his folly, but that, in punishment of his pride, Almighty God has allowed him only to approach His children to stir up within them the very lowest of those inclinations of that body which, not having any reason of its own, has to depend, for keeping them in order, upon the reason of the soul. Even here the evil spirit is doomed to disappointment, because you have an angel ever at your side to warn you of every unholy temptation; so that, unless you are willingly deaf to his voice, he will aid and enable you to make of that body a holy offering to God, a veritable image, in this at least, of the Incarnate God, or of His Immaculate Mother, which is the highest ambition of your angel guardian. If I had time, I could tell you beautiful histories relating to this; but you can read them in the lives of St. Agnes, St. Cecilia, and St. Lucy.

10. But not in this way alone does your guardian angel take care of you. One thing alone will satisfy this dear spirit, and that is, I need scarcely say, to present you triumphantly to our Blessed Lord as a trophy of His Precious Blood. Thus, when the soul the angel guards forsakes God, he abandons it not, but waits patiently until he gets a chance of being heard, and then speaks to the soul; and when he has brought it again to God he rejoices, and whatever may happen he never forsakes it, but remains to aid it in life and in death, and, whether it be saved or lost, appears with it before God's judgment seat.

I need not tell you how you pain this dear angel by committing sin. Neither need I exhort you to salute him every day, and often in the day to listen to Him when He speaks to your heart; for, after devotion to our Blessed Lady and St. Joseph, devotion to your angel guardian is one of the most powerful aids God has given you, to render you holy in life and safe in death.

11. But, before I close this chapter, my dear young friends, I must fulfil my promise of warning you against danger, by warning you to have nothing to do with certain people called spiritualists, who speak of another sort of commerce with the invisible. This spiritualism is only another instance how easily those who will not be guided by faith are cheated by the devil.

These people pretend to call up spirits to talk to them; but how can they tell whether they themselves, and those who consult with them, are not mere dupes of the devil, or deceived by cunningly-devised tricks?

They forget entirely the warning of our Lord: "Beware of false prophets" (Matt. vii. 15). They neglect to try spirits by the Catholic test of the Catechism; and so, those who tempt God, by having anything to do with them, deserve to be led away, by tricksters or devils, into what even a child might see promises nothing better than the destruction of every Christian dogma, and the reduction of all religion into an empty philanthropy, which, if it means anything, means that everybody is to be allowed to go astray after his own fashion. Your only duty, with regard to these spiritualists, is to have nothing whatever to do with them.

12. To conclude, then, you know what society you have. Walking this earth, you can talk to those in heaven, for they are most anxious to be the friends of those who here below are in the midst of the same risks which many of them ran themselves, and amongst which they worked out their salvation.

Do so, then, my dear young friends, and, by devotion and confidence, correspond to their friendship, because it will be no small pledge of being their companions in heaven, if you make proper use here below of the friendship of the saints and angels, and of that of our Blessed Lady, their glorious Queen.

CHAPTER IX.

The happy Choice.

1. BEFORE the people of God entered the land of promise, Moses, by God's order, sent twelve men to see what sort of land it was. These men "entered near the town of Hebron, and, going forward as far as the torrent of the cluster of grapes, they cut off a branch with its cluster of grapes, which two men carried upon a lever" (Numbers xiii. 24).

This is very much like what I have done for you, my dear young friends: I have put before you some of the beautiful relations which have risen up between you and Almighty God, by reason of Redeeming Love, in order, as it were, to show you the fertility and beauty of the land of promise, which is nothing else than the life of grace which is entered by Baptism. I have pulled some of its delicious fruit, in order, as it were, beforehand to let you see what a beautiful and happy land it is. I have done this with the less hesitation, because, although I have not yet called your attention to that holy Sacrament which puts you individually in possession of all that which I have described, and a great deal more, nevertheless you have all entered on that possession, even when you were infants, and knew nothing about the matter.

2. The fact of your Baptism, however, before the dawning of intelligence, does not in any way lessen your obligation to accept the responsibilities which devolved upon you as soon as you grew old enough to understand them. No, indeed, it rather confirmed your obligation, and in a sense made it more important than ever, that the very first conscious act of your understanding and will should be given to that God who, with a kind of divine impatience, had taken possession of you before you had a word to say in the matter.

But, putting this obligation entirely on one side, and without entering at all upon the question of how soon a child is obliged to make the deliberate choice of becoming a servant of Almighty God and renewing its baptismal obligations, this much is certain, that each child must early enter upon one of two roads: either it will love the way of God's commandments, and make progress in the path of salvation, or it will break the commandments, and forfeit, at least for a time, the rights and privileges of its Baptism. If it deliberately chooses to go away from God, may God help it, and in His mercy bring it back, for it has chosen a wrong path. If it should stray away without deliberate intention, what then?

3. It is a pity and a shame that some voice could not be found to give a warning to baptized children, that they might be saved from the misfortune of taking so miserable and so disastrous a step, by being taught the necessity of making a choice, and having opportunity given them to choose aright.

4. Pity for young people, whose ardour and impetuosity are so likely to lead them wrong, first gave me the idea of writing this book. Urged on by the desire to give you instruction, of which I feel that your are in need, I have persevered in carrying out my views, even against a certain amount of public opinion, because I feel that youth is pre-eminently the time for realizing the truths of religion, and being effectually influenced by them, because in youth the heart is yet tender, and innocent, and uncorrupted by the world.

The Holy Ghost has said: "Before man is life and death, that which he shall choose shall be given him" (Eccles. xv. 18). If this be true, as undoubtedly it is, for it is taken from the word of truth, at what time of life should this choice be made if not at its beginning? Will you be better able to make it after having thoughtlessly drifted down the stream, carried away by passion, and sunk in the mire of sin? Hardly! Because were you to make it then, every false step would be an occasion for tears! Besides, as each step would have taken you in a wrong direction, you would have to go back and begin again on the right road.

5. Yes, my young friends, at the beginning of life you are as one who stands at cross-roads, and has to deliberate which he shall take. The roads go in opposite directions: the one is the way of God's commandments, on which you are placed by Baptism, and which leads to heaven; the other is the road of sin and self-will, which goes directly towards hell.

6. On one point every one is agreed, namely, that unless death finds you on the road to heaven, your case will indeed be miserable. Of course, to be found on the road to heaven at that hour, is the fixed intention of almost every one! But would you know of what avail such an intention by itself will be to you? Of just as much, and no more than it has been to those who are now in hell.

The way to make such an intention profitable is to make a right choice now, and to use the proper means to keep to it; and by no means to imitate the folly of those who have first taken a wrong road, and have been glad to regain with infinite trouble the path of the commandments, quite wearied out with the ways of sin, and obliged to pay the penalty of lamenting the best part of their life as worse than thrown away.

7. The question, however, is not exactly whether you will be saved or lost, but whether you will take one step on the way of perdition, and not rather make rapid strides in the way of salvation! In other words, will you accept your Baptism with its privileges and obligations? or will you reject both?

Of course, the choice of rejecting your baptismal engagements is one you have not the shadow of a right to make. You owe everything to God, and are in justice bound to devote yourself to His service. It is, nevertheless, a choice which you have the terrible power of making. I put this question here, because, if any of you would deliberately make such an unworthy choice, it would be better for that one not to read what I am going to say about Baptism.

8. As it has not been my way as yet to hide anything from you, I am not going to do so now; therefore, I will, after calling your attention to what I have already written, tell you the plea on which men choose the wrong road, and then show you what keeps them upon it.

I am not afraid to explain things to you, but I fear one thing, and that is, an ignorance which makes mountains of mole-hills, and makes you judge from things you see, whilst you fail to understand their cause.

In the first place, I have shown you that as God, out of His pure benevolence, made you, body and soul, you must undoubtedly belong to Him.

In the second place, I have shown you how sin came in and made a terrible upset within you, putting your reason out of its place, blindfolding it, and letting loose all your passions, without any power to control them. Here, however, I also showed you that the good God had provided you with remedies which would save you from the destructive powers within you.

All this, I think, tended to persuade you to seek refuge in the arms of your Heavenly Father, from very fear of yourselves. Finally, I may say, I sent spies into the promised land of your Baptism, to bring forth for your admiration a few of the beautiful relations established between you and Almighty God by reason of Redeeming Love—relations to which every one is called, because every one is called to redemption, but which cannot be yours until they are signed and sealed in Baptism.

I have not the slightest doubt that what I have said has made you, more with the heart than with the mind, choose over and over again to give your whole being in eternal love to your dear good God.

9. Still I am not satisfied. It happened, when the spies returned from Hebron, that some of the people, magnifying in their own way the news brought back, fancied the Land of Promise to be full of giants who would kill them all. Something like this might happen in your case.

After all I have said about the happiness of serving God, and the misery of sin, there are a few strange facts which stare you in the face, and which look like giants ready with their clubs to smash to atoms all my arguments.

10. The first of these facts is, that, in spite of all that can be said of the misery of vice, a great many rush right into it.

The second is, that they seem to prefer remaining in it, to coming out again.

Lastly, they do this, although they know that they run the risk of going to hell for their pains.

11. Vice must be a pleasant thing, after all, since so many people choose it, is a thought which the

evil spirit will not be slow to suggest to you. We shall see, presently, that this is but a lie, and what else can we expect from the father of lies!

We may, however, look at the devil's way of persuading people to act upon his suggestions. He gets them to try the broad road for a little time, telling them they need not go far, and that God is so good that He will pardon them when they wish to come back. Ah! this is indeed a nice way to treat God on account of His goodness! If you act in this way, you are on the brink of a terrible descent. You will come back, will you? Almost every lost soul in hell, when they first took that road, intended also to come back! Do you know the proverb: "The way to hell is paved with good intentions"? Yes, from the child's first sin to the very gates of hell reaches this terrible pathway, and every single individual who enters upon it, has the intention of turning back, and yet glides deeper and deeper. Remember that, as your Catechism tells you, a divine power is needed to raise the sinner from sin—yes, even from the first sin.

12. Now, however, for the giants! What about them?

If it could be proved true, that any happiness is to be found in the ways of sin, there would, at least, be some show of reason for walking in them. But it is not so. Men walk in the way of sin because they are blind and foolish. If a blind man walks into a ditch, that does not prove it to be a delightful place, nor would it be proved to be delightful because any number of blind men might walk into it. To argue from what the blind do, is to be led by the blind, and our Lord says: " If the blind lead the blind, both shall fall into the ditch." Ignorance is one of the effects of the fall, and what can be more natural than that a number of blind, ignorant people should be deceived into entering a quagmire, urged by their own inclinations, or by the influence of evil companions? And, as I have said before, all young persons are not properly warned, and it is not surprising that some of them should, when they come to this marsh, plunge into it up to the neck. But you see, with " The Mirror of Faith " to put you on your guard, giant number one disappears altogether.

13. Now for giant number two. If the ways of sin are not pleasant, why do those who have begun to tread in them continue to do so?

There are two or three causes for this. You might ask a fly, stuck fast in a jar of treacle, why it does not come out? As I have shown you before, our passions are rather inclinations out of place than essentially bad things; and, by the disorder into which they are thrown, the understanding is misled into believing sin to be something agreeable and pleasant, and thus the deluded soul does not immediately perceive how unpleasant it is to be stuck fast even in sweets.

I say this, in order to be honest with you, because, to say the truth, the attraction of sin is so very small, that it would be almost true to say that it does not exist. For what attraction it does possess is so accompanied with disgust and dread, that it soon disappears. The poor fly in the treacle finds itself doomed to death, when it had hoped to find in abundance the good things of this life! Ask the man who is wallowing in the mire of sin, if his situation is so pleasant that he does not want to come out, what will he say? I had better try to make myself comfortable where I am, for, wretched as I am, I only fret and struggle and perplex myself to no purpose, when I try to get out; whereas, when I remain quiet, I am at least free from that extra trouble. Here faith tells you, that the man in mortal sin cannot raise himself to life. He is dead, and does not even see the possibility of living again. This is so literally true, that when he speaks of amending his life, he does not mean to leave the ways of sin, but only to escape punishment by calling on God some time before his death. This is why men put off repentance; this is why they act as if they only wanted to be fortunate enough to have sin here, and heaven hereafter. It is because they have no more idea of living than a dead man has. It is not because with life, and power to choose, they prefer the ways of sin to the way of God's commandments; a little knowledge of the world would soon show you this, my dear young friends. But, while it demolishes our giant, does it not tell you, perhaps more than anything else, what an awful misfortune sin is, which keeps men not only fast in a spiritual quagmire, but leaves them buried in it like miserable corpses?

14. But the compassion of Almighty God, who has given man a Sacrament to raise him from this

state, is another difficulty. Why do men rise and fall again, if the ways of sin are not pleasant?

A look at man's conduct is enough, not only to answer this question, but also to prove what I say.

In the first place, until God gives them grace to attempt better things, they seldom approach the Sacraments. Then, what makes them act as they do? They are so sick of sin, that they try again and again to get rid of it. But, what brings them into sin again? The habit of sin, which, like a horrid chain, they try to break and cannot. Sometimes they pull at it, sometimes they lie down in despair, then they pull again; and surely this is not much like being satisfied and pleased with a sinful life!

Now, as we have destroyed the giants, I think I have so far fitted you to choose, and to choose in earnest.

15. The case then stands thus: By every right of creation, redemption, and the most overflowing love, God claims your devotion. You cannot hold it back, without, in the first place, falling into the state of confusion and misery brought on by the fall. If you do so, you fall again under the terrible dominion of sin.

But, give your hearts to God, and at once you gain the approbation of your conscience—you feel that you are behaving honestly and well.

Then along with this you gain a complete deliverance from many dangers. Add to this, that you become the subject of the most wonderful dignity and glory, and, to crown all, you become the object of the tenderest caresses of your dear good God.

The two paths between which you have to choose are such, that whilst one of them is as nearly like a foretaste of hell as can be imagined to exist in this world, on which hope and mercy still shine, the other is as nearly a foretaste of heaven as can be found in this vale of tears, in which God can still be lost.

Hell is the loss of God for ever, and in it the soul will be delivered up to the power of the devil. Well, a life of sin is separation from God during life, the loss of every benefit of redeeming grace; while the soul is delivered up to all the miseries of fallen nature, and enslaved to the devil himself.

Such is a life of sin, and such, as far as it goes, is the first step on that miserable road, even if you take not into consideration your utter helplessness to retrace it of yourselves. Who in his senses could ever choose such a life? On the contrary, the life you have it in your power to choose now, is the possession here below of Him, the possession of whom for ever makes heaven what it is.

If you will, you may possess Him every moment of your life. By Him you may be restored to a far more glorious liberty, than that of which the fall deprived you. Together with this, you will have all the dignity which redeeming love has purchased for you, and may rest in that security of possessing God for ever, in glory hereafter, which nothing can give you but the possession of Him here by grace.

What a choice is yours, my dear young friends—a

choice between life, which the loss of God makes a forerunner of hell, and one which His possession makes the very antechamber of heaven.

16. Of course your choice was made long ago; nevertheless, the knowledge of these things may serve to strengthen it. If, however, you want to be strengthened not to take a single step in a wrong course, you must not go to the blind for counsel. There are plenty of hoary-headed penitents to tell you what a miserable mistake you would make by taking the wrong path; while, on the other hand, a multitude of God's children have proved by happy experience the truth of our Lord's words: "My yoke is sweet, and my burden light" (Matt. xi. 30), and who know that God's Commandments are nothing else but safeguards from destruction.

17. There is, yet, another consideration, which I think will go further with you than even self-interest. It is this. Should you be so fortunate as to regain the right path, after having lost your way, which, I will not disguise from you, might very possibly be the case, yet nothing can restore—no, not even penitential tears—the beautiful lustre of innocence which has been lost. Besides, what a blessed thing is it for you to give to God, who has loved you so much, the first and warmest beatings of your young hearts, which belong of right to Him.

With these reflections, I leave you for a short time, trusting, that after a little consideration of them, you will be ready and eager to enter upon the last and most important part of my subject—the Sacrament of Baptism.

PART FOURTH.

BAPTISM.

CHAPTER I.

Coming home to our Subject.

1. An artist, who wishes to get to perfection the fall of the drapery which he intends to transfer to the canvas, makes use of what is called a lay figure—a thing which is not like a human being at all, except in a few outlines which its object renders necessary, and in certain joints, by means of which it can be made to take every posture in which a living subject could be placed. While no one can deny the usefulness of such a machine, without which, indeed, a painter's studio would be incomplete, it would be extremely foolish to call it a model of the human figure: as well might one say so of a tailor's block.

2. But what, you may inquire, has the lay figure, of which I am speaking, to do with my subject? Just this, I have taken upon me an artist's task: I desire to draw the picture of a baptized child, and the necessity of the case requires me to have recourse to something like a lay figure, in order to produce it.

In this, you may see again the difference between the works of God, and those of men.

Wonderful as you are, my dear young friends, it

needed but the Word of God to create you, clothed with every excellence which Divine Wisdom and goodness thought proper to bestow. Perhaps, before you had been four-and-twenty hours an inhabitant of this world, the chains which bound you, in consequence of the sin of your first parents, together with all the essential effects of that misfortune, had been washed from your soul, and you stood in the full light of a more glorious destiny than that you had lost. Yes, such have been the dealings of creative love, and of all that comes from it in your regard, that, perhaps, as I said, before you were a day old, you possessed all, and far more than I can describe in this whole book. In this time, what has, in fact, happened to you? Before you existed at all, except in the mind of God, you had, if I may say so, ceased to be that which your Creator's love had intended you to be, and divine compassion had already intervened to prevent you from ever being, except through your own fault, the victim of that terrible fate which sin would have brought upon you. The "scene is changed," and, before you are conscious of your state of forlorn misery, you are made the object of a destiny so grand, that, in comparison with your redeemed privileges, the grandeur of original innocence fades away, and the beauty of the earthly paradise itself becomes undesirable, compared with the suffering life of warfare, which has taken its place, as the lot of the children of Adam under the leadership of your eldest brother, Jesus Christ.

3. Under such circumstances, how could I have described you exactly as you were before Baptism,

or as you are now? Had I told you of all the wonders of your body and of your soul, described, in short, your beautiful being, and then given you to understand that you were destined, before you came to the use of reason, to be deprived for ever of the possession of God, and that if you lived to acquire consciousness, it would only bring with it ignorance and passion, and assist you to work out for yourselves a place in hell—such a description would not have filled your hearts with love and gratitude; nevertheless, this would have been your lot, as a just punishment of original sin, but for redeeming love. Yet, before you had even the power of earning such a destiny, you were snatched from its jaws. Still, my first part would not have been an actual picture of you as you were before Baptism, unless it had been such as I have described.

4. On the other hand, had I depicted you as after Baptism, the beautiful things which belong to your creation would have been entirely lost sight of, on account of the brightness of your supernatural gifts and glories. Yes; beautiful as are the gifts of your nature, and positive as is your duty of gratitude for them, they would be entirely lost sight of in the presence of your supernatural gifts, just as the midday sun overpowers and hides the light of the stars.

Now, this would be a great misfortune, not only because gratitude for our Creator's gifts brings before us very delightful duties, but also, because, when these duties are passed over, all those which follow them necessarily lose in significance. For instance, it is impossible properly to understand the love of God which is manifested in Redemption, in Baptism, or in anything else, unless we know, in the first place, something about that wonderful love which drew us out of nothing, made us because He loved us, and which loves us exceedingly, because we are the work of His hands.

Thus, it is, that I am obliged, as it were, in this book, to separate for your inspection, what was in reality, either joined together, or very nearly so; just as you would shake out the different flowers of a beautiful bouquet, in order to examine each separately, so as not to suffer the beauty of the little violet to be eclipsed by that of the blushing rose.

5. I was obliged, then, to act somewhat as does the artist, when he uses a lay figure; I had to show the beauties of your created nature, by hanging them, as it were, upon a being which could not be exactly yourself, either before Baptism, or after it, simply, because, to describe you, overshadowed by the cloud of sin, would have made an untrue as well as a useless picture; whereas to describe you, as after Baptism, would have blinded you to the special beauties of your creation by the ways of a too refulgent light. Therefore, did I, in the first part, "God made you," ignore, as it were, the cloud which was destined to be taken away, and say little or nothing of that supernatural grace which was really yours at the very time you were listening to me. So, you see, I was compelled to suppose a kind of being, and put it, as it were, in your place, This lay figure having, however, done its work, it is

absolutely necessary that you should perceive the difference between it and yourselves.

6. With similar motives, I had also to do something of the same kind in the second and third parts, as well as in the first. Thus, in the second part, in showing what sin had done to you, I was obliged to anticipate the application of the remedies provided by your dear Redeemer to repair the mischief; for, had I not done so, I should have told you falsehood instead of truth, led you to despair, instead of saving you from disappointment, and turned a subject, which was rather cheerful than discouraging, into a melancholy treatise, which would have done you harm, not by telling you the truth, but by concealing from you the light which dispelled the darkness of a doom, from which you were, in fact, already free.

Then, as to the third part. Although I devoted it to the consideration of the beautiful relations originated in redeeming love; yet, in order to describe them, I had to pass through that gate of Baptism, in order, as it were, to delight your wondering eyes, with fruit stolen from the Promised Land, even before I had described your passage through its gates.

This, then, is what I have done, my dear young friends: I have made use of the artificial, the better to describe the real, just as the artist makes use of the lay figure, in order to paint nature more perfectly in the positions of the men and women he wishes to represent; and I repeat, that such a course was absolutely necessary, because when human creatures try to give an idea of that which the Creator in His Almighty power can effect by one little word, the artist must employ many strokes of his pencil, the writer many strokes of his pen, and, after all, the result will be no more than a feeble attempt at description.

CHAPTER II.

The Averted Doom.

1. IF, however, in describing you, it has been necessary to ramble, it is just as needful to know that we were rambling, and to come home from our rambles. This, we must do, at the very beginning of this fourth part, and I will, therefore, prepare you for the description of yourselves as you really were after Baptism, by intensifying your desires to reap all the benefit which that holy Sacrament bestows. I can see no better way of effecting this, than by showing you the terrible doom from which it saves you.

2. The question, What becomes of children who die without Baptism? is one upon which the Church has said nothing, except that they are incapable of possessing the enjoyment of the sight of God.

Where the Church has not spoken, I am not going to speak, except to tell you that it is almost universally believed, that far from being in a state of suffering, they enjoy a sort of happiness, but a happiness which is only rendered possible by their ignorance that they ever could have attained the bliss of heaven.

The bird who whistles merrily in his cage is tolerably happy, because he was made prisoner when very young, and never knew what liberty was. Thus it must be with children who die unbaptized. They can be very happy in that place, which God has provided for them, only because they know of no higher happiness. Nevertheless, when we compare their lot, with that of those who have received Baptism, and become bright saints in heaven, surely their deprivation is infinite; and you may well learn, from the difference, to value that Baptism which Jesus has bestowed on you.

3. The real case, however, which I am going to bring before you, is of quite another character from that of those who die before they come to the use of reason. We are going to answer for ourselves the question, What would be the probable doom of those who should come to the use of reason with original sin and all its effects still upon them? The answer, though a melancholy one, is well calculated to make you value your Baptism; therefore, I do not regret to have to tell it to you. The fact that you have the terrible power of throwing away the grace of your Baptism even makes me rejoice to point out to you the doom of the unbaptized.

4. To come to the use of reason with hardly any prospect but that of working out for oneself a place in hell is a miserable lot indeed. Yet that such is the lot from which God has actually freed you by Baptism, I will very easily prove to you. You must, however, remember that faith teaches you that God calls every one of His rational

creatures to salvation, so that no one will ever be lost except by deliberately refusing it. This truth saves you from taking anything I may say in a sense dishonourable to Almighty God.

On the other hand, it shows what a stupendous blessing is that which redemption has given to the human race through Baptism.

5. Let us to the point, then. No sooner does the unbaptized one come to the use of reason, than one of two things stares him in the face. Either he knows his doom, or he does not know it. If he knew his doom, and had not Baptism to fly to, to save him from it, what else could he do but despair?

If he does not know his doom, instead of despair, he can only have something as bad, namely, a false hope.

Of course, as a matter of fact, despair would drive a man to Baptism; but I am supposing, for a moment, that there were no Baptism, nor anything else in its place. The question is, then, would despair make a man satisfied with original sin? or would it not be more likely to set him to work out for himself a place in hell? Why, it would make earth a hell, to begin with, because it would make a man blaspheme like the very devils in hell. No; God never allowed man to be in this awful position; for, since the beginning of the world, man was not only told what was necessary for salvation, but, at the same time, he was put in the way of obtaining it. Thus, when Adam fell, the Redeemer was immediately promised, and faith in a Redeemer to come became immediately his means of salvation.

6. Let us suppose, now, the other alternative, namely, ignorance. God never allowed ignorance, that was not wilful, to prevent man from knowing his doom, and how to avert it. Yet, when ignorance of any kind blinded man to his dreadful destiny, did it prevent him from sinking more deeply into sin? No, one little word is enough to show what ignorance can do for the unbaptized. That little word is Paganism. The state of man at the time of the deluge tells us what unbaptized human nature came to through ignorance.

7. Unfortunately for themselves, but fortunately for us, if we will only learn wisdom by the experience of others, we need not go to the unbaptized to see the effects of despair and ignorance on human beings. It is a truth, familiar to you from your Catechism, and one that you cannot too well remember, that mortal sin, to a great extent, robs men of the effects of their Baptism, and reduces them quite sufficiently to the state of the unbaptized, to make them examples in this matter. Yes, there are those whose crimes have brought them to a state in which they begin to despair of their salvation, which is in reality a greater crime than all the rest. When people get to this state, what effect has it on their conduct? They are miserable indeed, but their misery does not keep them from sinning on. No, they rush forward in their horrible career, trying to drive away thought and add sin to sin, just to assuage their misery, until they plunge themselves headlong into hell. Such is frequently the conduct of men who impiously

deny God's mercy, and thereby commit the greatest of all sins. Such was, for example, the conduct of Judas, who hanged himself in despair.

This is a horrible thing to think of, dear young friends, and yet you may turn it to good account, because it is a picture of that despairing doom from which your Baptism has delivered you.

8. Many years ago, a large section of those who had forsaken the Church of God, and boasted that they rested their faith on a Scripture which their private rebellious judgment was destined to pull in pieces, gave startling proof of what their shallow arguments led to in their rejection of Baptism.

So you see that ignorance, far from serving in any way to remedy a doom from which Baptism alone can save man, has blinded thousands, even to the very necessity of remedy, for the fall itself.

The evil stopped not here, but men were robbed of that light which God gave them as an antidote to the blinded intellect. Ignorance has deprived many of them of the infused gift of faith; and has also caused even those who had received it in Baptism to cast it away as soon as it could be of use to them, and to take up instead of it those absurdities which I have before described to you as the natural effects of sin on the mind of man. How far, then, ignorance would improve the lot of unbaptized man, I leave it to yourselves to imagine.

Thus I have, I think, proved that the doom from which Baptism has saved you, is one which would leave you between two dreadful alternatives, namely, despair or ignorance, either of which would make the attainment of the use of reason lead to no prospect, save the fearful one of making for yourselves a place in hell by the committal of new and positive crimes.

9. One would think we had sufficiently considered this melancholy hypothesis (for, thank God, it is nothing else). There is, however, another source of mischief in the power of which the absence of Baptism would leave man, and of this I have as yet said nothing. This source of mischief lies in our passions, which the fall of man has left to rage within his breast, until, through Baptism, he gains power to rule them. On this subject I must say a few words, not only because it is necessary that I should make you understand what a blessing baptismal grace is, but because, by forfeiting that grace through mortal sin, you can still place yourselves, to a great extent, under the dominion of those passions.

10. The fact that numbers actually do fall into this unfortunate mistake will obviate the necessity of going far for examples of this slavery. It is quite natural that those who wish you well should be anxious to keep from you the knowledge of the vast amount of crime and misery which exists in this lower world. If, indeed, you will believe one who loves you, and who is not inclined to keep from you any kind of useful information, you will credit me when I say that you have no need to covet knowledge which could only sicken you, and excite pity for the unfortunate beings who, by forsaking God, have brought untold miseries upon themselves.

11. But there is something still more important for you, even, than ignorance of a passion-governed world, which ignorance, too, the press is making each day more and more impossible.

The greatest danger to you lies in this, that you may read the stories of the evil deeds which lie thickly around you, and may read them in a way which may endanger your soul. A corrupt press is doing the devil's work, by presenting them to you written in a style well calculated to effect this, and thus to poison you. The writers of such books draw a grand picture of the villain whose ungovernable passions urge him on, and they call his unworthy desires noble aspirations. The law of God is entirely set aside, or even possibly, blasphemous as is the thought, hinted at as a tyrannical invasion of man's rights; the cruelty which follows the slave of unruly passion, as the shadow follows the body, is entirely put of sight; and the crime-laden villain is called a hero. His stratagems, the fears which assail him, his hair-breadth escapes, the very warring of wild elements within his breast, are dressed out and painted for the sake of causing in the reader that excitement which is called "sensation;" so that what is bad enough in itself is rendered doubly dangerous, because it is calculated to leave the impression that there is something noble in villainy, whereas a villain is, in reality, but a subject for pity or contempt.

12. The important thing, my dear young friends, is to know how to read the lesson of passion aright. There is no necessity to look for sin; there is no

profit, or even amusement, to be derived from the search. If, however, you cannot avoid knowing something about it, learn a lesson from it, for even sin itself carries a lesson.

13. What has ever been the history of passion? Has it been the history of a pleasant way, chosen because it is delightful, and given up with reluctance, even though salvation was at stake when it was followed?

For such, indeed, the simpleton might take it, but no one else.

No, it is slavery—heart-tearing slavery. True it is, that the promise of pleasure leads the unwary into first giving the passions leave to rule; but no sooner has it put the chain round its victim, than the delusion flies. I have said something before about how this comes to pass. I will not, therefore, repeat it, but will teach you how to read the lesson given you upon this subject by a sinful world. When Judas complained that the alabaster box of ointment was not sold, and the money given to the poor, he said this because he was a thief.

Little did he think, when he first began to steal, that he was rearing within him the serpent of avarice. Perhaps the first time he counted his stolen coins he felt a sort of pleasure.

Even when he first uttered his complaint, he hardly realized whither his passion, already strong within him, would lead him—you know to what it did lead him, however. That passion drove him on to sell our Blessed Lord, and then, in despair, he threw away the money and hanged himself.

Judge by this rule the history of any criminal who has paid the price of his crimes upon the gibbet, and you will only find a repetition of the history of Judas—the rearing of the serpent within, the growth of the monster, the fears, the schemes, the stratagems, the gibbet.

What is rather extraordinary about many a history of crime is, that in spite of the attempt at concealment, which naturally follows, and which is necessary to avoid its punishment, the passion itself, or the excitement which accompanies it, generally becomes the very means of divulging it. Evil doers, like rats, hate the light. If they were their own masters, and their deeds were under their own control, they would always covet darkness; but, no, the tyrant passion gets too strong, and strikes them when prudence would say no, and thus their wickedness comes to light. A false idea of pleasure leads them on, but by what road? Look at it—remorse, fear, scheming, agitation, despair, ignominy, death.

14. Perhaps you will say that these are extreme instances of passion and its effects. So they are. Every slave of passion does not come to the gibbet, or hang himself like Judas, to save other people the trouble of doing it.

It is true, also, that every hill is not a mountain, and yet a mountain, after all, is only a very high hill; or, if you like it better, a hill is a small mountain.

Passions, indeed, are almost as various as the breasts wherein they rule. There are some persons who seem to have no passions at all, and yet, if they knew themselves, they would find that their passion is the love of ease, and that they do not disturb the peace of the world around, simply because it would be too much trouble; yet, if they let this passion rule them, they will not escape remorse of conscience for duties neglected; and sometimes they will find that their cherished passion will involve them in trouble, which they might otherwise have escaped. Here we have the two extremes, and between them are a host of passions; and if you study the history of every life in which passion rules, you will find in each hills of greater or less magnitude, and you will hear eternally at every step on passion's rugged path the tale of slavery and woe.

Go into the family with a drunken father—ask what has stripped the house of furniture? What makes the mother prematurely old? The answer you get will be, slavery to passion. Ask the mother what chained her to that man for life, although she knew that he was a drunkard? Her choice was the effect, not of reason, but of passion.

Go to the prison, and ask the prisoner what makes him spend his life there? You will get the same answer. He is the slave of passion. Go to the hospital, and see that wasted form decaying in the very prime of life: ask the cause? Passion, again. Question the care-worn man who, with agitated step and haggard look, hurries along his way as if he were eaten up with anxiety. Ask him how he slept last night? He slept not at all—passion disturbed his rest. If, accidentally, your eye should rest in the daily paper on the fearful tragedy, murder and suicide, and you ask what occasioned it, still the same answer! It is the tragic end of unbridled passion.

Such is the way to read aright the oft-repeated tale of human misery: read it always that way, for it is the only true one, and will do you little harm.

There is, however, no necessity to read it at all; you will see enough of it without taking that trouble; and the sight will, if you are wise, enable you to learn at the expense of others, instead of yourselves becoming unfortunate examples to them.

Such, then, is bondage to passion, even in those who, after Baptism, willingly become its slaves.

15. But Baptism, by reason of the graces it puts within your reach, enables you to become complete masters of your passions. The fate from which Baptism saves you, is that of having all these passions, without either light to know how false are their allurements, or grace to control them. First, without Baptism, you would be the victim of either despair or ignorance. This would be your start in the path of life; and, if it were not in itself sufficient to ensure your ruin, passion would surely come in and work out for you a terrible doom.

I have not told you all this to make you suppose, for one moment, that your dear good God would leave you in such a situation. In point of fact, He leaves no one thus, for Jesus Christ died for all. I have shown it to you, first, in order to make you value more the beautiful Sacrament of which I am about to speak; and, secondly, because it gave me an opportunity of teaching you some useful lessons well calculated to make you hold fast your Baptismal grace.

CHAPTER III.

Divine Haste.

1. SMALL as may be the pleasure of placing before your eyes prospects too dismal for our Heavenly Father to allow any of His creatures to be helplessly destined to look forward to them as their own, still the process of picturing them to the mind's eye may be, at least, a means of rendering more keen your appetite for that which I am now going to place before you.

Just as the cravings of hunger, in themselves far from pleasant, make the eyes of the hungry man enjoy the sight of the feast prepared for him, so must the contemplation of what you have been saved from serve to make you consider, with double pleasure, the glorious destiny to which you are called.

Such, my dear young friends, should be the effect of the last chapter upon those which are to follow; so that, gloomy as it was, far from passing it over, I would have you refer to it, from time to time, as people often take a bitter tonic to sharpen their appetite for wholesome food. Even the first remark I have to make about Baptism owes a great deal of its beauty to the way in which it stands out, as it were, in bold relief, rendered lovely by the deep shadow of your averted doom.

Let us say a word, then, of the touching haste which Almighty God seems to employ in snatching His dear children from the yoke of sin.

This it is which is especially brought out, by considering it immediately in conjunction with the dark cloud from which Baptism has delivered you, and makes that cloud only a means of showing the light more brightly.

2. You know that Baptism is a Sacrament, a solemn rite, well worthy of the deep meditation of a reasonable being; and, if you had not known it before, I am inclined to think what has been already said upon the subject has shown you so much, if it has done nothing more.

This must be apparent, when you take notice that all this talk includes very little besides Catechism.

Well, then, sublime as is this rite—grand as is this Sacrament—all that it bestows is given to whom?

To an unconscious infant, who knows nothing about it, more than to splutter and make wry faces when the salt is put into its mouth, and to cry because the water is cold which washes it from sin, and clothes it with the attributes of a child of God.

3. Such is the being on whom God looks down with complacency; not that complacency of compassion which came from seeing in it a spoiled and sin-stained image of His only-begotten Son, but the complacency wherewith He regards His own adopted child, washed and rendered all beautiful by the very blood of Jesus.

Such is the being whom Jesus, the Son of the

living God, begins to regard as the trophy of His Cross and Passion—the being whom He acknowledges as His adopted brother—the creature whom He enriches with all His own merits—for whom He provides, even in this life, a royal revenue of good things, and on whom He bestows an undisputed right to a throne in His own kingdom.

It is in the soul of this unconscious being that the Holy Ghost, the third person of the most Blessed Trinity, takes up His abode. Into it He infuses the sublime gifts of Faith, Hope and Charity, together with the seeds of His sevenfold gifts.

It matters not that the child is as yet incapable of corresponding to one grace. For years does the Eternal Father's love go unrequited; for years do the gifts of the ever-adorable Trinity remain unnoticed.

4. Why is this? That is the question. Ah! my dear young friends, it is, as it were, the haste of your good God to bestow His love upon you: in the first place, lest death or accident might come and rob you of the possession of a throne in heaven, before you have done anything to merit it; in the second place, to forestall the use of reason, that God may already reign in your soul, before you have sense to choose Him, and that He may, by His presence, cause the graces He infuses into you to strike deep root and grow, so that they may enter into your first conscious acts.

5. But let us see how anxious God is to gain the first of these objects, namely, the gift of heaven, for

one who is incapable of meriting it. It is only right that such a sacrament of Baptism should be accompanied by solemn ceremonies; yet these give way before the anxiety I have mentioned. The Church, who is, in all such things, God's living mouthpiece, and the exponent of His will, has bid the priest baptize the child, in any ordinary case of danger, without any ceremonies at all. She has done more.

In such a case, she has not restricted the power of baptizing to her ministers, but has extended that power to every man or woman, aye, even to the unbaptized infidel himself.

Such is the anxiety of God, that no child should die without receiving, through Baptism, a right to heaven by the personal application of the Blood of Jesus Christ to the unconscious soul.

6. Again, the Spirit of God, which dictates this anxiety, dictates also extreme caution. Thus it is that, while the Church declares that Baptism is a Sacrament which cannot, without sacrilege, be repeated, she orders it to be given conditionally, in every case where there can be a shadow of doubt as to whether it has been, in the first instance, validly administered.

7. Therefore, seeing how, in these latter days, Protestantism has shaken the very first principles of divine faith, so that even those who make the most pretensions to it have not the remotest idea what divine faith really means—what has the Church done? On account of the well-known carelessness of many, and the suspicion of carelessness in all whose principles

may allow them to deny the necessity of Baptism to-morrow, she has decreed that all those who are received into the Catholic Church should be baptized conditionally. Thus has she reserved a special prerogative of want of confidence in the case of the universal modern heresy, which she never sanctioned in that of Arius, Nestorius, Eutychius, or any of the heresies which existed before.

You see, then, that this anxiety, and this caution, simply show how ardently Almighty God desires to secure every one, who is born into this world, from being deprived of a personal share in the blood which He shed for all.

CHAPTER IV.

On the Threshold of the Church.

1. NOTWITHSTANDING the fact that the ceremonies of Baptism may be dispensed with by the Church, by reason of her anxiety for all to be regenerated in that holy Sacrament, these ceremonies are very beautiful.

Like all the ceremonies ordained by God through His Church, they are so full of meaning, that they form, as it were, the groundwork of the very best instruction on the nature of the Sacrament which they accompany.

I intend, therefore, in this chapter, and the two or three which follow it, to adopt them as the foundation of what I am going to say.

To begin, then. When the child is brought to

the Church, it is accompanied by one or two sponsors, as is the custom, that is, by a godfather and a godmother. There are two good reasons for this arrangement. In the first place, as Baptism is a contract, in which the infant not only receives something from Almighty God, but, at the same time, incurs obligations, it is absolutely necessary that it should have some one to answer questions which it is not able to answer itself. The second, and far more important, reason for having sponsors, is much the same, as that for which Almighty God Himself takes such early possession of the child. You may, in fact, see in this appointment another proof of God's care for you. I think I showed you before, that Almighty God has appointed, as a remedy against the effects of the fall, not only that you should have a supply of grace to strengthen your soul, but also that you should have, in the Catechism, the doctrine contained in the Gospel put before you, in words adapted to the weakest understanding, so as to be your guide through life. Well, then, as the Holy Ghost remains with you after Baptism, to supply you with grace, God would give you, in your godfather and godmother, guides to take care that you get all the benefit and help which the Gospel and the Catechism can give you. For this end, does God ordain that children should have sponsors; and, as far as they possibly can, it is a positive duty, on their part, to fulfil this obligation. To assist godfathers and godmothers in this matter, is one of my objects in writing this " Mirror of Faith." I trust that it may be a help to them in teaching little ones; while you, my young friends, who are capable of fully understanding it, can study it for yourselves, and repair, by what you learn from it, any defects that may have existed in your earlier religious education.

2. The first question which is asked, and which the sponsors answer in Baptism, is one which shows that it is a free gift, and not a thing which comes to us of right, although Almighty God is so desirous to bestow it. The infant comes to the door of the church, it is not admitted inside, and it comes there as a beggar, to ask something. The question is then put: "What dost thou ask of the Church of God?" Then comes the answer: "Faith." How is this? It is Baptism, is it not, that is asked for? But the answer is, "Faith." What can this mean?

Baptism is the door of the Church. The gift of divine faith, which is infused into your soul in Baptism, makes you a child of the Church, as well as a child of God. Baptism, while it makes God your Father, makes the Church your Mother. We must say a word about this.

3. You will hear people, who do not belong to God's Church, talk about the faith of their Baptism, meaning the opinion of the man who baptized them, or, more properly, that of the sect to which the material building in which they were baptized belonged.

Now, this man either thought enough of Baptism to administer it conscientiously, or he did not.

In case he did not administer it properly, the persons who speak in this way are not baptized at all, and, therefore, do not belong to any Church.

If he did baptize properly, he made the child a member of the Catholic Church, so that the Catholic Church is the Church of his Baptism. The Catholic Church is, in reality, the only Church of Baptism, as the Nicene Creed, which many Protestants very inconsistently say, has it: "One Church, one Baptism."

Thus, when the child comes to be baptized, it asks for faith, and gets faith when it is baptized.

The way, then, in which baptized children come afterwards to be Protestants, or something else, or, perhaps, nothing in particular, is this.

Their parents and their sponsors are, unfortunately, "blind leaders of the blind," united in unbelief; and the child loses its faith, either because it is left without instruction, or is taught doctrine, which is erroneous, before it is old enough to know the meaning of faith.

The talk about the faith of our Baptism, reminds me forcibly of the famous judgment of Solomon, in the case of the two women who claimed one child.

It happened, at the beginning of the reign of Solomon, just after Almighty God had bestowed on him his wonderful gift of wisdom, that two women came to him, who claimed one child. It seems that both the women lived in one house, and each had a child only a few days old. Now, it happened, that one of them, accidently or through carelessness, smothered her child in her sleep, and, finding that she had done so, she went and stole the other woman's child, and put the dead one in its place. But the instincts of a mother's love were too strong not to find out the deception; so that she came to Solomon to complain of it, and to seek redress. Of course, the other woman denied the charge, and claimed the living child.

What does Solomon do? In order to find out on which side were the maternal instincts, he calls for a sword, and proposes that the living child shall be cut in two, and half given to each. What we have to remark, is the different ways in which this proposition was received by the real and the pretended mother. Let us hear their answers: "But the woman whose child was alive, said to the king (for her bowels were moved upon her child), I beseech thee, my Lord, give her the child alive, and do not kill it," &c.: but the other said: "Let it be neither mine nor thine, but divivde it" (3 Kings iii. 26). Of course, Solomon immediately ordered the child to be given to its own mother.

Thus it is, with those who have the misfortune to be born of Protestant parents.

I speak not here of the parents—God forbid; but of that horrid lie, Protestantism, which hoodwinks them, and, through their guardianship, leads the children astray. It is Protestantism that claims as its own children, whom Baptism has given to the Church.

It is she who, speaking through her blinded ministers, imitates the woman whose own the child was not. What are her words? Let it be High Church, Low Church, Broad Church, Christian, Baptist, Quaker, Ranter, Methodist, Unitarian, aye, even infidel, or no Church. One thing alone it must not be: it must be no Papist! Aye, indeed: "Let it be neither mine nor thine, but divide it." It matters not whether it lives or dies, so long as it is not the acknowledged child of its mother. How very different is this answer from that of the child's real mother, who is content to let the one who has stolen it take it for the time, and quietly waits in the hope that mature common sense, like another Solomon, may give it back to her some day.

We have seen, now, why the answer to the question, "What dost thou ask of the Church of God?" is properly, "Faith."

4. Now come the question: "What does faith bring thee to?" and the answer: "Life everlasting."

Here is a truth. Faith brings to life everlasting, so truly, that the only way to get off the road to heaven, is by doing what our faith forbids, or by refusing to do that which it tells us: so that a living faith not only brings us to life everlasting, but even prevents one step on a road which could put our salvation in danger.

This truth is beautifully brought out in the little exhortation which immediately follows. Listen to it, my young friends. It is as follows: "If thou will enter into life, keep the commandments; thou shalt love the Lord thy God with all thy whole heart, with thy whole soul, and with thy whole mind, and thy neighbour as thyself."

Thus, you see, that the child is not only told how to secure its salvation, but the very commandment of love, which contains all the rest, is given to it on the spot.

5. In the next place, the priest breathes three times on the child, and says: "Begone out of him

(or her), unclean spirit, and give place to the Holy Ghost, the Paraclete." Here is warning, number one, for the devil to go out of the soul, to which he has not a shadow of right, although original sin has let him in.

As for the devil, we will not waste our time about him, for he will surely get sufficiently humbled soon, without my taking the trouble to throw stones at him. You see, we are beginning now to hear about the intention of the Holy Ghost, to make the unconscious child His home.

6. The priest then makes the sign of the cross, with his thumb, on the forehead and breast of the child, saying: "Receive the sign of the cross on thy forehead, and in thy heart; receive the faith of the heavenly commandments, and let such be thy manners, that thou mayest become the temple of God."

At each step that we are taking, my dear young friends, we are meeting with truths which may seem like old acquaintances, from what I have said before, and you see how closely I have kept to the simple truth of faith, when I told you about your Divine Guest. The child is to be the temple of God; and just as when a church is built, they put a cross on the top of it, and another on the high altar, so must it have a cross on its head, and another upon its heart, which is the high altar which God claims for Himself, as the centre and source of all the offerings which it will make to Him.

7. I must, however, say a word about the sign of the cross.

We cannot do better than go to the language of

faith, and say that the sign of the cross is "the sign of redemption," aye, and "the sign of salvation," too.

By the cross, were all mankind redeemed; by the sign of the cross, all are continually reminded that we are redeemed creatures; and, by this sign appearing on our forehead, will all the saved be known at the day of judgment.

Yes, this is why, in the Apocalypse, the long list of the signed is given, which is read in the lesson on All Saints' Day.

It is also a practice, which is to be continually followed, to make the sign of the cross, as a memorial and a means of driving away temptation, and at the beginning and end of every prayer.

And, when it is thus made, this sign is joined, as you well know, to an act of faith, in the first and greatest of revealed truths, namely, in the Blessed Trinity; at the same time, that the sign itself is another act of faith in the mystery of redemption. Thus, you see how the Church, guided by the Spirit of God, has joined together redemption by the cross, and faith, just to show that faith alone can bring salvation to redeemed souls.

You must make this sign often; and would to God that, when you make it, you might always remember what I have told you about the great dignity to which redemption has raised you. This should not be hard to do. You have only to recollect that every building, with a cross on the top of it, ought to be a house of God.

8. But, we must proceed. After the child has

been signed, the priest says two prayers, which you will find in the appendix. In the first of them, he prays that God will guard and protect the child, who has been marked with the cross of His Divine Son, and that, by this protection, he may walk in the way of the Commandments, and may thus deserve to attain that salvation, which is the proper end of Baptism. In the second prayer, you will be reminded of what I said to you about the blindness of the understanding; for the priest prays that God may take from the child all blindness of heart—that He will give it wisdom, as He has given it faith—that He will make it strong against the artifices of the devil—that He will enable it to suffer, without taking any notice of the assaults of all unruly passions, and that He will give it grace to follow faithfully, after the sweet prospects of a life, in the loving service of its dear good God.

After this, the priest puts into the mouth of the child, a little blessed salt; which is a symbol of wisdom, and signifies that, in Baptism, the Holy Ghost especially bestows this, the greatest of His gifts, namely, that wisdom which will always show the soul that the service of God is its great and only good.

Then, after bestowing on it, in God's name, that peace which belongs to God's children alone, he prays that, as God gives to him wisdom, as his first food, He will never allow him to be deprived of those spiritual blessings and graces, which are so well adapted to keep the soul strong and perfect in God's service, so that, by spending his whole life in serving his God, he may come to a great reward.

9. If ever the devil regrets his foolish pride in refusing, as tradition says he did, to adore the human nature of Christ, I think it must be every time that the exorcism is addressed to him, and he is expelled from the infant immediately after the prayer I have just spoken of. This prayer, as well as the second one I have before mentioned, is said with the priest's hand on the child's head.

To show you the ignominy and humiliation with which the devil is expelled from the child, I need but repeat to you the words of exorcism. They are as follows: "I exorcise you, O unclean spirit, in the name ✠ of the Father, and ✠ of the Son, and ✠ of the Holy Ghost (the priest making three crosses), for you must be gone from this servant of God, for He Himself, O cursed spirit, commands thee, who walked upon the sea and kept Peter from sinking. Therefore, accursed devil, remember thy sentence. Give honour to the living and true God, honour Jesus Christ His Son, and the Holy Ghost. Get thee away from this servant of God, whom God and our Lord Jesus Christ have deigned to call to His holy grace, and to blessing, and to the baptismal font. And thou dare not, O cursed demon, to violate this cross (here he signs the forehead), which we place on his forehead. Through Jesus Christ our Lord."

10. Then, again, the priest places his hand on the child's head, and says another prayer, in which he asks that God will enlighten the little one with the light of true knowledge, that He will cleanse and sanctify it, and make it worthy of its Baptism.

Now, we have come to the time, when the child is allowed to enter the door of the church, and I will pause for the present. But you will easily see how necessary it was for me to make you familiar beforehand, with things it would be impossible for me to explain fully in this place, and you will also perceive that every step in this beautiful ceremony brings out the truth of what I have already taught you. Meditate on this, and you will see in it a kind of epitome of what has gone before, and then we shall be ready for the next chapter.

CHAPTER V.

Within the Doors.

1. Up to the present time the applicant for Baptism has been outside the church, and then three questions have been asked and answered: the salt of wisdom has been given to it; it has been marked with the sign of the cross, and these beautiful prayers have been offered for it even before the outer door of the church has been opened for its admission. In order, however, to show how impossible it is outside the precincts of the church to have any real knowledge of the secrets of God's kingdom, the child must be admitted, in a sense, within her boundaries, even before it becomes a living member of her body. There its knowledge of the truths of faith and willing acceptance of them, through its sponsors, must be, as it were, tried; and there the child must enter into certain

agreements as to the performance of its part of the contract, before it receives the benefit of the Sacrament.

2. Yes, our good God has, indeed, deigned to give to Baptism the nature of a two-sided contract, thereby to add solemnity to the receiving of this great Sacrament. He has done so, also, to force us, if I may say so, to live a life worthy of our new privileges. Blessed be His holy name! You will see, when you examine the obligations He imposes, and the renunciations He requires, that they themselves, far from being burdens, are in reality only blessings disguised, under the appearance of commands. These commands are blessings hardly less noble in themselves than the gifts which they accompany.

To settle these matters, then, as it were, between God and the child, the Church, by the voice of her minister, invites it into the Church by the following words: "Enter into the Church of God, that thou mayst have part with Christ unto life everlasting." This is, indeed, a cheerful invitation. It is an invitation, in one breath, to enter the Church, to have a full share in the merits and blessings bought by Jesus Christ, and to have life everlasting as the end of all.

It is, in fact, an invitation to enter heaven through the merits of Christ, which are found in the Church, and shows better than any other words could do, that eternal life is the undoubted consequence of living as a true member of the Church of Christ in a state of grace.

3. It will serve to show you that I have been far from exaggeration when I spoke in the third part of this book of the relations brought about by redeeming love between your soul and God, when I tell you that there is still another relation, of which I have as yet said nothing. I spoke to you of being the children of God, of Jesus Christ being your eldest brother, of the Holy Ghost being your guest. I said nothing, however, of Jesus Christ being your head. I did not tell you that you were members of His mystical body. Nevertheless, this is true; and I am bound to tell it you now, or else you could not understand either this invitation, or some of the things I have yet to explain.

St. Paul tells us this plainly. Thus in one place he says: "Know you not that your bodies are the members of Christ?" (1 Cor. vi. 15). You see he takes it for granted that those to whom he wrote were aware of the fact; and again: "For as the body is one and hath many members, and all the members of the body, whereas they are many, yet are one body, so also is Christ—for in one spirit we are all baptized into one body" (1 Cor. xii. 12, 13).

How wonderfully expressive is that word: "so also is Christ"! See, my dear children, St. Paul hesitates not, but with that intense sense of reality which springs from a lively faith in the truth of what he says, without more ado, he gives the name Christ to this union of many bodies under one head.

It is this mystical union, which alone explains what would be otherwise inexplicable, namely, the close connection between entering the Church, having part with Christ, and life everlasting.

4. It explains, also, what follows, namely, that the priest, as it were, in anticipation of the union about to be accomplished, unites with the child, who, by the mouth of the sponsor, makes his profession of faith by reciting the Apostles' Creed.

This practice may have been the cause of the talk about the faith of our Baptism; yet it would be hard to tell how it could be twisted into a plea for remaining outside the Catholic Church, when we consider that this creed itself says: "I believe in the Holy Catholic Church." As a matter of fact, this special creed is used for the sake of convenience, as it is the shortest, and in reciting it the child engages to believe everything the Church teaches.

5. Thus, in this act, the child undertakes to perform the first of its obligations, namely, entire submission to the Church in believing all she teaches.

Is this, however, a burden? No. As I have shown you, it is an incalculable blessing, for whilst others are tossed about upon a sea of universal doubt, about God, about themselves, about everything; this very obligation bestows, on the simplest soul, the certain, unwavering knowledge of more than human philosophy could ever teach, namely, the knowledge of the sublimest mysteries of God; and, at the same time, it furnishes the best of all guides against absurd mistakes in the examination of the wonders of the material universe.

6. To continue, however. Immediately after the

profession of faith, the child, by means of its sponsors, in union with the priest, fulfils another of the most important of Christian duties, namely, that of prayer.

This is done by reciting that most sublime and beautiful of all prayers, which Jesus Christ Himself taught to His apostles.

And what prayer could be so appropriate for this occasion as that in which Jesus Christ taught us to address God as our Father, and to ask of Him, in a few words, everything that is either necessary or good for us to have.

7. When this prayer has been said, the child is made to approach near to the baptismal font; and here, again, another exorcism follows, as if it were impossible to drive the devil too far away from one, who is immediately to become God's own property; and, with regard to this, I shall simply give you the words of it:—

"I exorcise you, every unclean spirit, in the name ✠ of God, the Father Almighty, and in the name of Jesus Christ His Son ✠ our Lord and Judge, and by the virtue of the Holy Ghost, ✠ that you begone from this work of God's hands (N), which the Lord our God has vouchsafed to call to His Holy Temple, that it may become the Temple of the living God, and that the Holy Ghost may dwell in it, through the same Christ our Lord, who will come to judge the living and the dead, and the world by fire."

See, my dear young friends, how familiar this doctrine, that you are really the temples of the

Holy Ghost, is made by simply looking into these ceremonies.

8. Here follows a ceremony which is evidently taken from a passage of the Gospel, in which Jesus Christ cured a deaf and dumb man, by putting spittle into his ears, for the words used are the very same.

The priest wets his finger with spittle, and touches the right ear, using the word "Ephpheta," which our Lord used, and then, touching the left ear, he uses its Latin translation, which means, "Be thou opened;" after this he touches the nose, saying, "In an odour of sweetness," and then, again addressing the devil, he says: "But you, demon, vanish out of this, for the judgment of God approaches."

It is evident from this that the ears of the child are to be henceforth free from spiritual deafness, and open to receive the sacred truths of the Gospel, which will make the young Christian's life give out, before God and man, the good odour of sanctity.

9. We now come to a passage of great importance, in which, from the very necessity of the case, the child declares eternal warfare against the enemies of God. Of course, as it is to be His own child, it is but fair that God's enemies should be also those of the infant. Besides, its baptismal dignity forbids it to have anything to do with God's enemies, who would endeavour to draw it from His service.

You must know, also, that not only is your Heavenly Father honoured or dishonoured in His children, and Jesus Christ in His little brothers and sisters, but the Holy Spirit will not remain with those who admit the enemies of God into their hearts. You must always remember that you have been adopted into God's royal family, and it would not do for royal children to have any other than royal manners or royal company. But I need not tell you that: for I am certain you cannot wish to have anything to do with the devil, or with any of his works or pomps.

10. If the devil were the only enemy you had to fear, I should not much mind; but these pomps and works, which have been interpreted the flesh and the world, are enemies far more to be feared, although in a different way. The flesh has to be feared, not because it is bad in itself, but because it has no reason, and strong inclinations, which, if not kept in subjection, will cause it to become the victim of the malice of the devil.

Some people, on account of this unreasoning nature of our bodies, have called them all sorts of hard names, and have taken the words of St. Paul, about the law of the members, as the text for their sermon. What they say is quite true in one sense; for, if a person once gives his body leave to rule him, instead of ruling his body, he will be almost sure to break his neck, or at least get spiritually crippled for life.

11. Nevertheless, this truth is easily distorted, and many are inclined to distort it; just because, by making out that their body is unruly, they throw a cloak over their own wickedness in neglecting to rule it.

Now any idea about our body, however true in one way, which interferes with that gratitude we owe to God for this gift, must do as much harm as good, and almost implies contempt for a gift which God has bestowed.

Besides, St. Paul certainly says much more about the holiness of our body than he ever did about its unruliness.

As a matter of fact, God's children have ever been more remarkable for their entire independence and complete control over their bodies, than the degraded slaves of their bodies have ever been for their bondage.

12. Thus, you see that the flesh which we renounce when we renounce the works of the devil, is an enemy: the danger of whose attacks comes not from any malice in our bodies, as if they were reasonable beings, responsible for their own acts; but, from their powerful inclinations, being either excited by the devil, or, perhaps, as often by the absence of that reasonable guidance, without which He who made them never intended that they should be left.

It is evident that safety from injury, through the lower inclinations of the flesh, is a good deal the affair of proper management, and, therefore, requires knowledge on your part. As, therefore, you will be obliged to keep this control during your whole life, or else run the risk of losing the grace of your Baptism, I will take a little trouble to explain to you how it is to be done.

When an engineer sets a steam-engine in motion,

he employs a power, perhaps the most terrible that the world knows. Confine this power with any bands, however strong, and so tremendous is it, that the stronger the bands, the greater will be the explosion. He makes this engine with furnace and boiler, and everything complete—for what? Not surely to go at random, without any guidance: no, but to run on lines, and to be under the control of a driver, who knows his business well. Thus this terrible machine, of almost infinite destructive power, becomes one of the greatest benefits this nineteenth century knows. Yet, let a malicious man jump on the engine, throw down the driver, and heap coals on the fire, what will be the consequence? On, on it will go, with terrific speed, dragging after it the carriages and the doomed passengers, until probably it will run into some obstacle, and fearful loss of life, or, at any rate, horrible injuries, will surely ensue. The unfortunate man—the cause of all this—might say that the engine did the evil; but, in reality, the catastrophe was of his own causing, and the engine was a noble machine after all.

There could scarcely be a better figure of us, in this respect, than that engine. A divine engineer has made us, with every inclination fitted in its proper degree, and with its proper object. He has placed the commandments as lines for us to move on, but He never meant the engine to go without a guide. Before the fall, we had reason for this guide. Now we are better off, for we have reason strengthened by grace. We have Jesus by our side; we have His Sacraments, aye, His own body and blood, for food, to fit us for our task, and to render the engine obedient to us. We have the Holy Ghost to tell us what to do and where to drive.

What your baptismal vow bids you do, is only not to let the devil mount the engine—not foolishly to heap coal on the fire, so as to let the steam get beyond your power; and, above all, never to venture off the line.

And well, indeed, may you keep this vow; for, believe me, if you either let the devil become driver, or if you venture to go off the line, whatever hopes temptation may hold out, you may be perfectly sure you will not escape without serious injury; you will pay for your folly by many a tear wrung from a broken heart: for it is true as the Gospel, that in this matter sorrow, deep and sore, follow sin, as surely as a shadow of giant-length follows the body just before sunset.

Let us have another simile, as it will serve to put the matter more clearly before you. What more beautiful than a magnificent thorough-bred horse, full of spirit and life? Look at him, as he stands there, pawing the ground with impatience, and champing the bit. Look at the bit, and see how it is made. There are rather two bits, one small, and with the bridle fastened to a little ring, so as to pull only gently on the horse's mouth; the other larger, with two bars, to give a lever power to the bridle which is fastened to the end. Then look at the rider; he has a whip in his hand, and spurs at his heel. Now, what does all this mean? It means a noble animal, with one upon his back who has bit and bridle, switch and spur—not to use with cruelty, but to make him completely his master.

But what would you say of a man who mounted such a horse without saddle or bridle, armed only with a large stick? You would say that he was mad; and if he broke his neck, it would serve him right. No one denies that the unruly passions of the flesh do terrific havoc in the world.

13. It does not, however, mend matters in any way to accuse the flesh of not doing that which it never was intended by its Maker to do, namely, to rule itself. The evil is not in the flesh: it is in this, that people forget their baptismal vow; they let the devil set their passions to work, for he can do nothing, after all, without their consent; they themselves, by their love of self-indulgence, heap fuel on the fire; they will not let God's commandments direct their course; and so a universal destruction is the natural result of their headlong career.

The neglect of the self-denial commanded by the Gospel, the useful check-rein with its lower bit, the whip and spur so well calculated to give them command—which are nothing else than the self-chastisement recommended by St. Paul; these things they do not like, and hence they find the spirit of the animal which carries them admits of no control. They seek not the assistance of Jesus Christ to aid and strengthen them. They allow their hands to become too weak to hold the bridle, because they neglect to eat of the Bread of Life

They see not where they go, because they take no notice of the Holy Ghost, who would guide them.

Yes: for these and similar reasons do men find themselves hurried to destruction, or left lame and disabled by the road-side, because by malice, stupidity, or neglect, they have allowed themselves to be run away with by that body, which was made to be their servant, and not their master.

14. How different is the case of those who, like wise children, remain close to their Heavenly Father; who cling to the grace of Jesus, and obey the guidance of the Holy Ghost? To them neither the devil nor the flesh can do any harm. As for the devil, he torments them, indeed, by making them feel the sting of the flesh, for he hates them with an inveterate hatred. But to what purpose? In his rage, he increases their crown, by his very endeavours to ruin them, giving them opportunities of increasing in merit, and of proving their fidelity and love by the attempts he makes to shake their constancy. Thus does he help to fulfil in their regard that prediction of St. Paul: "To them that love God, all things work together unto good" (Rom. viii. 28).

15. You will, perhaps, very naturally, ask me for a few words of practical advice, how to regulate your conduct with regard to these things in after life.

It is true, that the very best thing you can do, is to keep close to Almighty God; as, by doing so, you will be safer than any advice I can give you will make you. Nevertheless, as the Holy Ghost

17. So far, you see, I have kept your heart, as it were, disengaged.

The question then arises, Is it ever possible to admit an object of affection into it without danger or sin?

You do not, I am sure, suppose that I am going to say that it is not.

One thing, however, you must remember, that the admission to special affection should not be the work of chance. No, indeed; your heart should be a citadel into which no one can enter uninvited. Ah! here is the mistake; and it is a mistake over which more bitter tears have been shed since the world began, than over any other.

This giving of the affections to a special object is a thing of vast importance. In the first place, it should be done with hesitation, and after consulting God; in the second, it should be done with God's blessing, and without vexing the Holy Ghost.

The world teaches a different lesson: but does the world always give the happiness it promises? No: it oftentimes, with all its hurry, fails to attain the object which it seeks.

18. There is a robe, my dear young friends, about which the world thinks and talks a great deal. It makes it the symbol of happiness.

Well, thank God, it is sometimes the precursor of happiness; but shall I tell you when this occurs? It is when the whiteness of the wedding-robe is a symbol of the unstrained baptismal-robe that preceded it.

We have now considered, my dear young friends,

so far as is necessary, Satan and his works, and I have taught you how you can turn both these enemies into helps to make up your eternal crown. But you have another enemy, whose nature is so horrid, as to be a mere destroyer, whom no power on earth can turn to good; a monster who ever injures where he cannot destroy; this enemy is the world—Satan's pomps—and to this subject I will devote the next chapter.

CHAPTER VI.

God's great Enemy.

1. MANY as are the blows, the broken heads, the terrible wounds which come of open fight with an open enemy, still war has one good effect at any rate. It nerves the soldier, makes him robust and active, keeps him always on the watch, and, in short, teaches him the art of fighting, from the very practice.

This is especially the case with God's true loyal children in their contests with the devil, not only when he attacks them himself, but also when he makes use of their unreasoning and unreasonable flesh, by exciting in them the assaults of its unworthy suggestions.

Their habitual determination to die rather than commit sin, saves them from being actually killed.

Not only do the attacks, continually sustained by them, keep them from forgetting how to fight; but those attacks give them continual opportunities of proving their fidelity. They do more than this: their temptations are continually increasing their merit and sanctity in this world; by them the very virtue against which the enemy is using his artifices is strengthened, and, at every assault, they win new crowns of glory.

2. There is, however, one enemy more to be feared, by the most valiant soldier, than those who make him take up arms. The neighbourhood of an unhealthy swamp, sending up a deadly effluvium, can reduce to mere skeletons the strongest soldiers, aye, the largest army; and the very strength, the very numbers of that army, only hasten the work of destruction by carrying infection the quicker. Under the effects of this miasma, the strong man, against whom the sword of the enemy was as nothing, becomes weak. The man whose powerful frame could not be exhausted, either by the night watch or the forced march, is seized on by grim death. Thus has perished many a mighty army, which had carried devastation, by fire and sword, into an enemy's country—armies whose very name was a prestige of victory. The powers of destruction of a foe like this are indeed fearful and universal, for, where it does not actually kill, it injures, weakens, and brings its victim to the very gates of death. Incapable of doing any good, it is a mere destroyer; sure, though invisible, in its work of mischief.

3. The great enemy of God, the only real and deadly enemy, I may say, that you have, is neither more nor less than a moral pestilence; deadly, searching, and invisible, as is the noxious gas of the stagnant swamp.

T

Such is its nature, that, even if you would, you cannot kill it, because it has no personal existence; it has, in fact, no body to be killed; for the same reason, you cannot curse it, because it has no individual soul, to feel the effects of your curse.

It can be seen, indeed; but, like the pestilence, it can only be seen in its victims; and these are surely objects of pity, and not of anger, even though the infection they carry with them makes their presence deadly, as in the case of other moral pests, such as heresy, in all its varied forms, which may be known by the three letters, "ism," with which their various names end. It is necessary to be careful how you speak against it, lest, by some mischance, the unfortunate victims it is destroying might mistake your anathemas and reproaches for invectives against themselves, its unfortunate dupes.

From these very causes, its existence is daily denied; and, when men admit that there is such an enemy of God as the world, they always, unless entirely reprobate in their lives, make that polite proviso of society: "Present company always excepted;" in other words, they never admit that they themselves are victims of its poison. Like many inmates of lunatic asylums, no one is so earnest as they are in protesting that they are not mad.

It is plain, however, that there could not be a greater mistake than that of denying the existence of this pestilent world.

To deny the existence of infection, is to run into the jaws of death, without even the precaution of having either antidote or disinfectant.

If there be a precaution at all against the world, or against being indoctrinated with its principles, it must arise from the knowledge of its existence.

4. The first question, then, we must answer for ourselves, is this : Does this moral pestilence, which is called the world, this soul destroyer, this enemy of God and man, exist?

Let us see. In the very first place, I meet the world in the Gospel, and there I find it, with its usual cool impertinence, telling our Blessed Lord what He is to do; and, true to itself, it dares to hold up to Him the example of its own followers, and bid Him, like them, show Himself off, thus : "For there is no man that doth anything in secret, and he himself seeketh to be known openly. If thou do these things, manifest thyself to the world" (John vii. 4).

5. There is a piece of impudence. See, now, how our Lord replies to it.

He tells those who spoke to Him thus, that they have the world's pestilence, although they do not seem to know it, for He says : "The world cannot hate you (its dupes), but me it hateth, because I give testimony of it, that the works thereof are evil" (John vii. 7). Now, we do not read that publicans and sinners hated our Blessed Lord: we read that our Lord was all kindness and mercy towards them, and was even blamed for associating with them. This world, then, which hates Him, who holds Himself up to us as an example of meekness, must be something very bad indeed.

This, however, is only one little word our Lord said about the world. We have not done yet. See what He says in the next chapter of the Scribes and Pharisees: "And He said to them: you are from beneath. You are of this world; I am not of this world. Therefore I said to you, that you shall die in your sins" (John vii. 23, 24). Now, one would think that it should strike us with horror, to see that there were men found, who could only see the Son of God made man, to hate Him with a more than diabolical hatred! Yet we find that this was the case. We find, also, that these men were not law breakers; no, they were sticklers for the law. These men, who hated Jesus Christ, and on whom the Saviour of mankind pronounced the sentence of damnation, were what the world would call respectable members of society. They were more: they were the very leaders of society—men who prided themselves on uprightness of conduct. One thing alone could be said of them, which contained their whole reproach: they were men of the world.

6. We have seen, now, that there is a world which God hates; for which meekness Himself had not one word of kindness to say, but only words of reproach and condemnation. To examine the whole of our Lord's conduct towards this world, and its hatred of Him, would take too long. As, however, we cannot know too well all that the Gospel says on this subject, before we go farther I will put down, without much comment, a few of the hard things which the Gospel and the epistles tell us on this subject.

7. "If the world hate you, know ye that it hath hated me before you" (John xv. 18). Behold a

consolation for the children of God! "If you had been of the world, the world would love its own; but, because you are not of the world, but I have chosen you out of the world, therefore the world hateth you. . . . But all these things they will do to you for my name's sake, because they know not Him that sent me" (John xv. 19, 21).

Thus, you see, the hatred of the world is, to God's children, a proof that they are on God's side; and our Lord here reveals, that the true source of the world's wickedness comes from the fact, that the world knows not God, and will have nothing to do with Him. But to proceed. In the next chapter but one our Lord says: "I pray for them; I pray not for the world" (John xvii. 9).

Poor world! It must be badly sick of the pestilence; it must be in a state of utter impenitence, for Jesus—the friend of penitent sinners, the Good Shepherd, who came to find that which was lost, who laid down His life for sinners, who rejoices over one penitent—not even to pray for it! If you wish to see how solicitous our Blessed Lord is to separate His children from the world, you may take your Bible and finish the chapter, for the subject runs through it all. We must, however, before we conclude, give a few examples of what the epistles have to say about this subject.

8. After telling the Corinthians, in the first chapter, that, to the world, Christ was either foolishness or a stumbling-block; in the third chapter, St. Paul says: "that the wisdom of this world is foolishness with God. For it is written, I will catch

all the wise in their own craftiness" (1 Cor. iii. 19).

St. James, too, with a disregard for the world which it would consider anything but polite, speaks with equal severity; he says, in very plain words: "Know you not, that the friendship of this world is the enemy of God? Whoever, therefore, will be a friend of this world, becometh an enemy of God" (James iv. 4).

It seems, however, that St. John, the disciple of love, had the strongest instincts on this point; for, not only did he take particular care, as we have seen, to put into his Gospel all our Lord said on the subject; but his epistles, also, remarkable as they are for the prominent place given to love, are no less so for the way in which, in them, the world is condemned.

See here: "Love not the world, nor the things that are in the world. If any man love the world, the charity of the Father is not in him. For all that is in the world, is the concupiscence of the eyes, the concupiscence of the flesh, and the pride of life: which is not of the Father, but is of the world" (1 John ii. 15, 16).

I am sorry not to quote all the sentences in which St. John condemns the world; but if you want to learn more you can read his epistles yourselves.

9. Now, all this has been said about a world which would fain deny its own existence. If it does not actually do this, every individual, who breathes its pestiferous atmosphere, always makes an exception of himself, especially if he wishes to put on the semblance of being religious; and, that this is one of

the special fashions of our day, we shall see, if we look into the actions of worldlings. Just as it is only possible to discover cholera by seeing its effects upon its victims—as you can only see the full spirit of heresy in the absurdities and excesses into which it leads those deluded by it—so the only way to discover the spirit of the world, is by the symptoms it produces. Thus, we shall often find it rather cunningly displayed in the conduct of those who believe they have nothing to do with it, or it with them.

We shall presently have to examine these symptoms, and I will draw my picture of the world from no lesser authority than that of St. John. He says, in words I lately quoted: "All that is in the world is the concupiscence of the flesh, the concupiscence of the eyes, and the pride of life." Join this to the other doctrine, that the world has nothing to do with God; mix these ingredients together, and you have a compound gas, capable of poisoning the whole human race; in other words, you have the world.

Now, that such a compound should arise out of the moral, or rather immoral, lives of godless men, is very natural; and that it should produce more or less evil effects, on those of God's children who happen to be thrown within its influence, is very likely too.

And, indeed, it does so. Our business, then, is to know the disease, and to provide ourselves with some strong antidote against its infection.

Now for our task. Which component part shall we take first? The cloak of hypocrisy and pride of life? or the scarcely concealed concupiscence of the flesh, which, for the sake of respectability, it tries to keep hidden? or the concupiscence of the eyes; or, in plain English, grasping covetousness, to which it gives polite names? or would it not be better to speak first of the utter irreligion which it hides under the pretence of acknowledging God?

Of itself, it matters little which we choose; as these things, which compose the spirit of the world, must have an origin; however, we will begin by searching out the causes of each, and how one may have the effect of producing another.

Much as people talk about the difference between theory and practice, no one can deny that the opinions which people hold have much to do with their lives; and, on the other hand, that their lives have a considerable effect on their opinions. Saints, for instance, measure both the things of this world and the next very differently from sinners. May it not be true, then, that the habitual thoughts of sinners, who have forsaken God themselves, create opinions which, floating in the atmosphere, poison it, and thus not only kill them, but endanger their unfortunate neighbours?—just as persons, bearing about with them the corruption of disease, often poison the atmosphere which they breathe.

This is not only probable, but actually true; for the Holy Ghost has said: "Evil communications corrupt good manners" (1 Cor. xv. 33).

Now, it is a familiar truth, that, as by sin man turns his back upon God, those who live habitually in a state of sin must, in time, become blind to His goodness, His dominion, His justice, His sanctity; they must lose sight of God and of the next world altogether. This is certain; because, as I told you, as man's will is obliged to love what appears to it to be good, he cannot think of the Infinite Good without loving Him; nor can he think of hell without fearing it, or of heaven without desiring it.

10. So you see, we have already discovered one of the ingredients of the world, or rather two of them. We have a fashionable opinion, created by the disordered will of sinners, that God is not worthy of their notice, and that the other world has nothing to do with them. Ah, but you will say, this is downright impiety! Well, so it is. So, also, is carbonic acid gas downright poison; but, for all that, you cannot be shut up for an hour in a densely crowded room, without swallowing a great deal of it, as the healthiest people in the world emit a certain quantity of it with every breath.

The impiety, then, of the world gets diluted by being mixed up with man's natural ideas of right and wrong, just as the carbonic acid in a crowded room becomes mixed with the atmosphere it deteriorates, and thus is not so much noticed: although, as carbonic acid often gives severe headaches, so this atmosphere of impiety seriously affects, not the impious, but people who would be terribly shocked, if you were to tell them they were full of its spirit.

11. Thus does the world become all the more dangerous, because its influence is unacknowledged. Beware, my dear young friends! for, notwithstanding its diluted form, the world is deadly impiety,

joined to an utter disregard of a future life. Thus it is not merely sin, but it has in it that which alone makes sin unpardonable—it is essentially impenitent. How, indeed, can it be otherwise?

In the first place, it acknowledges no guilt; in the second, it cannot be sorry for offending God, because it will have nothing to do with Him. As for its impenitence, does not our Lord denounce it in words which, if we consider them, are very terrible? *" I came not to call the just " (Matt. ix. 13). Now, He was speaking to the Pharisees—the worldlings of His day. Who, then, were they whom the Redeemer of all, came not to call? Surely the self-justified, who would not acknowledge their sins. He did not mean that He came not to save them, but that impenitence would prevent their salvation.

As for its impiety, it is surely terrible to reflect, that when Jesus walked this earth, it was not the sinners, but the Pharisees—the worldlings, respectable members of society, who hated Him at first sight, and who persecuted Him, even until they finished by plotting and bringing about His death. Have we any doubt, whether these men constituted the world? Surely, He Himself tells us they did, as I have shown you above. So much, then, for the world's impiety; now, let us look at its "pride of life."

12. Yes; the world is, above all things, "highly respectable." It is quite noisy about its deep sense of propriety. It is always imitating the proud

---

* This interpretation is that of St. John Chrysostom, hom. 31, of St. Hilarius, and others.

Pharisee, in pointing the finger of scorn at publicans and sinners. Therefore, if one of those it has miserably deluded, yield to the passions which its own maxims have fostered, so that they gain the mastery, its outcry is dreadful. The world preaches propriety, and hunts the poor victim to destruction, as the best way of holding up to view its deep sense of what is correct. ¦Oh, yes, what a pity! Blackballed by society. Now, what does all this mean?

Simply pride, unadulterated pride! Of course, the world does not like open sin. It must even pay so much respect to the beautiful law of God, as, for the sake of its own respectability, to keep sin out of sight, and even to show an outward dislike for it.

Even more than this: it must try to hide sin itself, because open sin would take away that pleasant delusion, about its righteousness, which can pass over any number of sins of omission, and perhaps not a few sins of thought and desire also. I cannot see why it should not, for he who is able, without flinching, to put God out of sight, will find no difficulty in passing over anything.

13. Now, we will consider the "concupiscence of the eyes."

Although the world has got rid of God, and of eternity, it cannot, nevertheless, exist without some object. It has an object, and that object is self.

Call it success in life, call it a noble ambition, call it a desire to get on, call it what you will, those who form the world have one mission, the attainment of the world's felicity, according to their own notions.

Self, self, self! This world, this world, this world! And very often, with all their efforts, they fail entirely, and only find disappointment and misery.

14. Oh, Christianity! where are you gone? You throw a halo about human nature, which makes even this world beautiful.

Yet, how has the world distorted those noble aspirations, after a better life, which give beauty to this one!

Throw into society a youth, who, in spite of the world, aspires after giving himself to God, and living for God and his fellow-men! Here is a test, which will try even those who imagine themselves to be good Christians, and will prove whether or not they are tainted with the spirit of the world. It has been somewhere said: "Touch a Christian, and you will find a savage." Perhaps this is the dictum of a misanthropist; but touch a Christian on this point, let God make a claim on a son or daughter—touch a Christian in this way, and you will very possibly find a worldling. Yet, God has a right to do as He pleases with His own. His claims are not weakened by the fact of your ignoring them; and, if you persist, you will gain nothing but sorrow.

But, you may say, a little resistance is excusable. A little delay and hesitation, before giving consent, are desirable, to prevent vocations from being inconsiderate, if not carried too far. After all, marriage is a holy state, ordained by God for the greater number.

We admit, that it is often a very holy state —especially, when aspirations after another world give a high ideal of Christian virtue in this one. It is a holy state, when God's children, after proper direction, and consulting God and those who guide them in His name, embrace it in deference to God's blessed will.

But, does the world uphold the high ideal of Christian marriage? No, indeed. And if, in its eagerness after temporal things, it would even respect its votaries, as reasonable beings, we might pardon it. But, instead of this, it sacrifices, to its favourite deity self-aggrandizement, reason, affection; in fact, everything which can render sacred the union of two immortal beings. So true is this, that, to speak of "marrying a title," "marrying so many thousand pounds," is only to mention, boldly and with sarcasm, that which is secretly the leading idea under which unions are contracted in that circle, which is pre-eminently the world's representative; and "the London season" is, in reality, an annual market, in which the devoted daughters of fashion are shown off, in a way which reminds one too strongly of the sale of irrational animals, to allow of even a momentary supposition that the world could be capable of comprehending the high ideal which renders marriage sacred.

But, this matter of settling in life, is only one form in which the world seeks self-exaltation; there are many other ways in which it does this. And, as the end proposed is evil, so are the contrivances for gaining that end mean and deceitful.

So we find it, from the highest class of society to the lowest. One class imitates another on its own scale. This is so true, that in every class the world in its impiety, its pride of life, and its concupiscence, answers to the description of St. John.

15. We will now say a word on the other component part of the world, namely, the "concupiscence of the flesh," which is, however, rather an effect of worldliness, than a premeditated cause of it. Impiety naturally puts an end to any idea of ruling the passions for God's sake. Pride of life only requires outward respectability. The concupiscence of the eyes, for a highly respectable reason, inflames all the passions to the very verge of open sin. Habitual self-indulgence puts aside all idea of self-denial; and thus, whilst pride of life gives things outwardly a look of propriety, it acts rather as a hot-house upon those lower passions, which seathe, like the confined fires of a volcano, under the covering of respectability, and sometimes, like them, burst forth, defying control, and revealing to a world, which is terribly shocked at the sight, scandals which it fain would hide, but cannot.

16. So now, my young friends, you know not only what prevents men from doing that which this "Mirror of Faith" would teach you to do, but you see that your greatest enemy is the world. You see that its impiety would forbid you to love the God who made you; that its two concupiscences would add flames to passions already sufficiently troublesome; and that, as for redeeming love and Baptism, it would forbid you to think of the

one, and would deprive you of the benefits of the other.

17. Is there an antidote against the world, which can make you invulnerable?—that is the question.

Yes, there is one, and only one. That is, the love of God; strong, positive, indissoluble, personal love of your dear good God. You must persevere in loving Him who made you, Him who redeemed you—shall I say it?—in spite of everything. You have seen how much impiety has to do with this world, and all its unbelief! The personal love of God strikes it directly, and at its root. He alone who serves God through love, knows worldliness by sight; and the sight but increases his hatred of it.

Oh, my dear young friends, if I could hope that this "Mirror of Faith" could have the effect of making your love strong enough to defy the world, I should be content. Pray, then, with me, that He who hates the world, and in whose good cause I hope I hate it too, may bless my work, and preserve you, like the children in the firery furnace, so that you may pass through life with your baptismal robe unscorched by the flames which rage in the world, and which will burn it, until they themselves are swallowed up in the fire of the last day.

CHAPTER VII.

Baptism.

1. Necessary as it was to pause, and consider the nature of the enemies to whom you declared eternal hatred before you were baptized, it is a relief to turn from the horrid monster of diluted and polite impiety, with its half revealed undercurrent of seathing corruption, of which we have been speaking, to continue our comment on the solemnities of Baptism.

You see, my dear young friends, that the nearer we approach to this sacred rite, this holy Sacrament, we gain, at each step, some additional proof of the consecration of your whole being to the God who, in it, adopts you for His own child.

In the preceding prayers and ceremonies, the coming consecration of the infant has been spoken of; but it is immediately after the pronouncing of the baptismal vows that the act is performed, which is the special mark of that consecration.

2. You know, that whatever is consecrated in the Church of God, is anointed with oil, which has been solemnly blessed by the bishop. This oil is so sacred, that no layman is allowed even to touch it. With this sacred oil is the church consecrated, which is dedicated to the worship of the Most High; the church which is the resting-place, wherein dwells Jesus in the Blessed Sacrament. With sacred oil are consecrated the hands of those priests who are,

as it were, the servants of God's children, because for them they offer the Holy Sacrifice of the Mass, for them they call down Jesus upon the altar, to them they give Jesus in Holy Communion, and on them they bestow His cleansing Blood in holy absolution.

With sacred oil, too, the altar is consecrated, as well as those things which specially belong to it.

What can it mean, then, when the infant is consecrated with this sacred oil, except that it is thereby made God's own special dwelling-place, His chosen temple, dedicated to His service?

Yes, and it is consecrated on the breast and between the shoulders, with these words: "I anoint thee with the oil of salvation in Christ Jesus our Lord, that thou mayst have eternal life."

There are two things in you which Almighty God wishes to show you belong to Him, namely, your works; which after Baptism He claims as specially His own, and your intentions, or the love for Him with which you do these works. The shoulders, which are consecrated, represent your works; for, when you labour, it is your shoulders that bear the greater strain, hence the figurative saying, "Put your shoulder to the wheel." Besides, it is your shoulders which must bear the sweet yoke of Christ.

Then, as to the breast which is consecrated, it covers the heart—that heart the love of which Jesus seeks—that heart from which proceeds the love which alone can give worth to our actions in His sight.

3. Here the priest changes his stole; putting aside the purple one, which denotes penance, and putting on the white stole of innocence and joy. This is done because he has now finished the exorcisms and ceremonies required by the child's previous state of original sin, and is preparing to perform the grand and glorious action which washes it from sin, and clothes it with innocence, and adorns it with all the glories of a child of God.

This changing of the stole should also remind us that after Baptism we must have nothing at all to do with sin, which would necessitate bitter tears; but must try to keep clothed with that beautiful innocence which is the source of the only true joy. After this, and as if to show again what that faith is which Baptism gives for an inheritance, the priest inquires, in three separate questions, what is the child's belief as to the Three Divine Persons, joining to each name that part of the creed which speaks of the concurrence of each in its creation, redemption, and sanctification.

4. And having done this, to show that the choice of Baptism is the free act of the sponsors, and must be afterwards ratified by the child, he asks the question: "Wilt thou be baptized?" which question is answered by the sponsors, who say "I will."

5. Now comes the solemn act; and in it water, by a special power given to it by Jesus Christ, is made the visible sign of an invisible grace, namely, the washing of the sin-polluted soul in the Sacred Blood of Jesus Christ.

Oh, that I could open your eyes, and let them

see, not in a poor attempt at a "Mirror of Faith," but in very deed, the purity, the beauty, the glory that shone upon each of you, my dear young friends, as the water flowed upon your forehead! With what complacency did the Eternal Father watch the ugly cloud of sin pass away, which before had hidden, as under a hideous mantle, the beauty of His work in you, and contemplate in you the image of another infant form, that of His only-begotten Son, born a little babe for you, that Son whom He heard long ago call Him with human lips by the name of Father, and who, by thus doing, gave you the right to do the same.

Yes; it is the Blood of Jesus, standing, as it were, in ruby drops upon your brow, which makes you so truly an object of His love. He sees there the merits of Jesus—His grace, and the inheritance which Jesus has chosen to share with His little brothers; and He looks upon His Divine Son and upon you, and straightway adopts you as His child.

What else could He do? Jesus has already made you partner in His Father's love. Yes, as St. Paul says: "You have received the spirit of adoption of sons, whereby you cry: Abba: Father. For the Spirit Himself giveth testimony to our spirit that we are the sons of God, and if sons, heirs, also, heirs, indeed, of God, and joint heirs with Christ" (Rom. viii. 15, 16, 17).

6. Oh, that you could see the delight with which Jesus caressed your soul, and exulted in all the precious graces and treasures with which He intended to adorn it in after life, rejoicing, even, in

the cruel sufferings with which He earned them! The very thought of these things makes me venturesome, and I am inclined to draw a picture, although but a poor human one, which may be to you a faint shadow of the feelings of your divine eldest brother on this occasion.

We will suppose a truly Christian family, in which the parents have brought up the children to look on all things in the light of faith, and where, consequently, the instincts of faith, which are a Christian family's special privilege, are strong and lively. The children, three or four, of ages from eight to fourteen, may be sitting round the breakfast table when their father announces to them that God has given them another brother.

What are their feelings? At first they are those of joy, but a cloud comes over them when they remember that he is not baptized. With sensations, partly loving and partly mournful, they ask to see him; and when they do so, they long to caress him, and yet refrain. With a kind of instinct they put off doing so until he is baptized—they urge that this must be done quickly—and scarcely, till after Baptism, do they own him for a brother, and bestow upon him their unceasing marks of love.

7. Let no one fancy that this picture is wholly imaginary. It is one which is sometimes seen; and would to God that families with these dear instincts of faith were more common. May we not think that their feelings, in some sort, faintly shadow forth the feelings of Jesus when He looks down upon the newly baptized child.

8. The Holy Ghost, too, who is the love of the Father and the Son, comes now to take possession at once of this soul, and sows within it the grand seeds of Faith, Hope, and Charity, and all his seven-fold gifts.

Here is no imagination; but the real presence of God Himself within the soul of the unconscious infant. There He will watch; there He will keep guard; there He will water the seeds He has sown, so that they may bear fruit at the first dawn of reason.

Imagine, again, with what complacency our dear Lady, Mary, the great Mother of God, regards her dear child. Does not the very blood, which still shines on Him, remind her of all she suffered at the foot of the cross, and how Jesus gave him to her there for her child?

How proudly, also, at your side stood that special angel chosen to be your guardian. Aye, and with what ardour did He not determine to do His very best to save you, seeing, as He did, the wonderful love with which the ever Blessed Trinity regarded you.

Yes, my dear young friends, you were at that moment an object of complacency to all the court of heaven; the whole of which seemed to be employed in regarding you, a poor unconscious babe, with admiration and wonder.

Oh, may God open your eyes, that you may see by such light as only faith can give, what you were like at that moment—what, as I have hopes, you are in God's sight even now!

9. But let us hasten to the end. Immediately after the child has been baptised, it is again anointed; not this time with the same oil as before, but with chrism. This time it is anointed on the top of the head, and a prayer is said to the Eternal Father, who has regenerated it by water and the Holy Ghost, and has pardoned its sins that He may anoint it with the chrism of salvation, in the name of Jesus Christ unto life everlasting.

This is praying that He who has begun the child's career with Baptism may finish it, by bringing it to heaven; and you must acknowledge that this is indeed a grand prayer. As for the anointing, I suppose it means that as the head is not only the chief part of a man, but also the highest, the whole being is henceforth consecrated to God.

10. Here follow two ceremonies, which are very significant, for they are intended to impress deeply upon us the obligations of Baptism. In the first the infant receives the typical white garment, and is told to carry it unstained before the judgment-seat of God; which simply means that he is to spend his whole life without committing one mortal sin.

Thanks to God's compassion there is still pardon afterwards, upon repentance, even if this is not done; but there is a glory in unstained innocence, which innocence regained by penance cannot have. Besides, as I have said before, nothing but misery can come of sin. Therefore, my dear young friends, hold fast your innocence, and believe me that to do so is to enjoy the greatest happiness that can be attained in this world; while, as to the next, such a course would earn for you a crown of glory peculiar to itself.

A lighted candle is next placed in the infant's hand, and it is told to keep the commandments ; so that when our Lord shall come it may be found with the light of good works burning in its hands.

11. After this, the child is dismissed, with the blessing of peace bestowed upon it, and a prayer that God may be always with it. A fit ending for so sublime a sacrament, and one not without its meaning.

I have taken much trouble to obtain one end, and I will now tell you what this end is. It is to save you from the misfortune of having to learn by experience, what that experience would certainly teach you, although too late—that sin and sorrow are inseparable companions; and that, if you fall into sin, you will lose a great deal, and gain nothing but sorrow and regret. Besides, consider the glory of your baptismal robe, and say whether it would not be an awful thing to stain it. You are a child of God. Would it not be terrible to make yourself His enemy?

Jesus has become your brother, and has washed you from sin in His Blood. Surely you will not trample that Blood under your feet, and crucify Him again? Or will you drive the Holy Spirit from you? But if you do so what will you gain thereby? You will become the slave of the devil, who only wants to draw you to hell! You will become the slave of passions which, like wild beasts, will tear you in pieces; and, after being disgraced and rendered miserable, you will be fortunate if, with sighs and tears, you get back the innocence you have lost.

No, my young friends, go in peace, and the Lord be with you. Keep close to the good God, from whom you have received so many gifts of nature and grace. Be not only His children, but be loving children who remain always near your Heavenly Father; let it be your whole business to please Him; and then He, who began your career with Baptism, will protect and love you with a Father's love and care in life, and will finish the work by admitting you into heaven when you die.

CHAPTER VIII.
Your Finished Picture.

1. It takes many strokes of the pencil, or of the brush, to make a picture; and its beauty consists mainly in the perfection with which the lights and shades are blended. So, my dear young friends, to make your portrait perfect, it was necessary to show the lights and shadows, or it would not have represented you such as you are in the sight of God, or such as faith reveals you to yourselves.

Your picture, then, has its shades as well as its lights; and to have made it otherwise would have been merely to execute a work of imagination, and not a likeness. It would even have destroyed the effect of the light; for, as every one knows, these are brought out by shadow. And in the present instance redemption, the brightest light which shines upon you, is seen in its chiefest glory beside the shadow of the fall.

Of course this picture is very imperfect—indeed, it is one to which human pen could never do justice; and I tell you this in order that you may not confound its imperfections with the completeness of the original; yet, as far as it goes, I hope that my picture is faithful.

We can seldom tell what a painting will be like from the first rough sketch, and it often requires the last finishing touches to bring it out as a connected whole.

2. Let us try to give these touches, and make the portrait I have been drawing, at least an approach to that which you can see for yourselves in the real "Mirror of Faith."

First of all, then, we have seen that at one time you were simply nothing. From the fact that out of this nothingness you have been made something by the power of the great God, arises a relation of the deepest love and dependence on Him to whose power and goodness you owe your very being.

We saw, also, that from this there arose a surpassing love, on the part of Almighty God, for that wonderful little creature which owed its existence to Him. You have seen the human figure of this more than parental relationship, in the unceasing love and confidence which exist between parent and child, on account of the partial way in which, under God, the parent gave existence to the child. God, alone, knows how far this paternal relationship, which has so much to do with your picture, acted as the cause of all the rest.

3. Then we examined the nature of your being; first, your body, which we found to be wonderful in itself, and doubly so in its senses. We saw that

this body is not in itself reasonable, but simply, and in so far blamelessly, animal, but intended to be governed by a soul, which it assists on the one hand; while, on the other, the soul, with its wonderful powers, acts on the body, and is responsible for its good or bad behaviour.

4. We saw, again, that the soul, with its reason and will, gives you the blessed power of knowing and loving God; while, through it, the body obtains the honour, privilege, and merit of being raised to the dignity of being God's servant. You saw, moreover, that God gave to your soul the gift of immortality; so that the soul, and, finally through it, the body also, will continue for all eternity to enjoy the knowledge and love of God. God thus made you His debtor by all these gifts; and, by giving you the power of consciousness, by which you can know and love Him, He has made you owe more than you can ever repay; and thus you have become, as it were, bankrupt without remedy. What, then, was the grand conclusion this first part of "The Mirror of Faith" forced upon you? It was this: that the least you could do, to be honest, was to devote yourself, body and soul—whole being—to the love and service of the dear good God who gave these blessings to you.

5. Then we came to the cloud of sin, which overshadowed your nature; and saw, in the first place, from the example of our first parents, what a wretched state those fall into who venture to disobey God. Then you saw, with a mixture of amusement and sorrow, the strange upset that happened

in your nature, when the passions took a kind of revenge against reason for allowing itself to be deceived by the devil.

You learned how the passions rebelled so as to blindfold reason in punishment for its sin.

To relieve the picture, I showed you how God has given remedies to restore tranquillity, and enable us to subdue our passions and keep them in check; and that by becoming His friends by Baptism, and remaining so by a Christian life, we can have those remedies always at hand.

We saw, too, how people, who forsake this way, bring on themselves, by their own faults, all the penalties of the fall, and run the risk of becoming blind enough to believe any absurdity, and be the sport of their own unruly passions.

You have seen all this; and what was the conclusion this shadowy part of your picture forced upon you? You had before seen that you belonged entirely to God; you next agreed that it would be not only very wicked, but most dangerous, to stir one step away from His love and service, lest by that step you might fall into a deep slough, from which you would never be able to escape, unless God's dear compassion should lift you out.

6. After this, we went, as it were, into the promised land, the door of which is Baptism, and examined, with overflowing hearts, the mysteries of redeeming love, and considered all the grand relations which these mysteries brought about between God and man. We saw that His restoration, although leaving man's life subject to suffering and

labour, not only restored Him to His former dignity, but added such immense glory to His state, that it seemed as if redeeming love was going to light up your picture, and make you, as it really does, something almost divine. Of course the effect of such an occupation as then was ours, was to reveal to you a whole kingdom of graces, which almost put your gifts of nature out of sight, and made your hearts overflow with tenfold love.

It has another effect, also, of scarcely less value, in a sin-degraded world. It throws a halo of dignity and grandeur over you, which makes your being, with all its powers, shine again with a divine honour and sanctity; so that it would force you, as it were, to a life of holiness, out of very reverence for the state to which God, in the generosity of His mercy, has raised you.

7. Then we came to Baptism, and showed the gloomy fate from which it has saved you; and, in order to make you appreciate the gift the more, we examined the ceremonies of this solemn sacrament, and said some words of explanation as to the way of treating the devil, and the flesh which you renounced at that time, so as to make their solicitations turn to your good instead of to your injury.

We next examined the nature of your most formidable enemy, the world—that dreadful mischiefmaker, whose concealed impiety tends to destroy all that God has effected in you by redemption and Baptism.

Lastly, we came to the baptismal font, and I showed your full likeness, life-size and glorious, as well as I was able to represent you, as you then stood in the sight of God; and as I hope, with the blessed care of God the Holy Ghost, and with the help of Jesus' grace you are at this moment, and always will be, walking the earth with baptismal robe unstained, the Holy Spirit always in your heart, with the grace of Jesus Christ earnestly sought, plentifully enjoyed, and always flowing in streams upon you.

Oh, would to God that it may be ever thus! What a joy; what a heaven on earth would your life be. Always to have the Eternal Father gazing with joy and love on His child, shining with the love of Jesus! Always to have Jesus at your side, often in your heart! To be the perpetual dwelling-place of the Holy Ghost! Never to grieve the dear angel at your side, who was so proud as He received you from the baptismal font! To be ever the specially beloved child of the great Mother of God! To be the companion of the saints, holding sweet converse with them! What is this? Is it heaven on earth? No. But it is the nearest approach to it this world can give, and it may be your own lot if you choose. It is nothing else but the life on earth of every one who carries to the end his baptismal robe unstained by sin.

8. I fancy that I hear you ask eagerly two questions:—Can I lead a life worthy of such happiness? and how am I to provide against my weakness?

The answer to these questions might occupy two more books; yet one word can, as far as it is necessary, reply to each.

As for the first, the answer is the Ten Commandments. These commandments, well kept, produce a life not unworthy of the eye of God, because they are simply the representation to man of that moral law which is founded on God's own sanctity. You know that the Ten Commandments are enough to admit you into heaven; surely, therefore, they are enough to fit you to walk with God on earth.

Then, as to your power of keeping them, this is simple enough. Keep close to God, by fervently trying to please Him; and, above all things, make eager use of those sweet channels of grace which are ever at hand to aid you. Become not tepid; for I have shown you that tepidity is the path which leads to sin and destruction. Be fervent; meditate, sometimes, on the mysteries of God's love for you, and never neglect the sacraments. If you take care to do this, you will find it very easy to lead a life in some degree worthy of your Baptism.

It was in order to aid you in the task of preserving your baptismal robe unstained that I undertook to write this little book. Imperfect though it be, I offer it to you, dear young friends, and beg you to accept it; for at least, as far as it goes, it will tend to save you from being deluded by a wicked world, and I hope, also, to inspire you with a great love for your dear good God.

CHAPTER IX.

Grown-up Children and Parents.

1. THE inclination to become a child with children, is one of those beautiful arrangements of Providence, for the benefit of the human race, which, in spite of all that sin has done to hide the marks of God's hand in nature, still remains to reveal the Divine Almighty Power by whom all things were made.

Who has not been amused to see the sage professor throw off his gown, and prepare to join with all the ardour of youth in the games of his pupils. Aye, and the assumed idea that he is making a concession, hides in his secret soul a real satisfaction in recalling the remembrance of boyhood's days.

Perhaps the most remarkable manifestation of this propensity, is the almost magical effect, the presence of a baby or of a child of two or three years, has on a company of grown-up men and women. No matter how serious may have been their previous thoughts and conversation, the appearance of this little object on the scene, is sufficient to put the sagest of them, with rapid transition, into a state of babyhood.

A look or smile from the infant, or a word of prattle from the child, that can just talk, finishes the work, so that, no sooner is the spell of childhood cast in this manner, than it would be hard to tell, by their words or actions, the infant from his imitators.

This propensity, however, which even the world itself can but partially smother, is especially remarkable in its effects upon that gentle being whose office it is to tend childhood's earliest years. Yes; the noblest instincts of woman are such as create a sympathy between her and childhood; and these instincts leave them not, as some suppose, when consecrated to God, but spread and intensify their influence a hundredfold.

These instincts, I say, are so deeply imprinted in the woman's being, that if she would, she could not stamp them out, while it is admirable to see what an amount of resources they supply for the keeping up of that patient affection required during the child's long and helpless dependence upon its mother.

2. The inclination to become a child with children is a beautiful thing. Let us see, then, what was the object of God in implanting it in our nature.

It provides the child with loving care, so long as it is helpless; and with loving teachers who guide its first steps. Through this, each of those who tend it, becomes, as it were, a baby while it is a baby, a prattling child so long as it is such, and, by stooping to its childhood, they gradually train it up to walk, to talk, to act with the steadiness of older years. Think you not, that you and I, my dear friends, might, hand in hand, do something of this kind in a spiritual sense, in order to teach the rising generation to walk steadily along the path of virtue?

3. St. Paul said of himself: "I became all things to all men, that I might save all" (1 Cor. ix. 22).

Might we not become children with children, in order to save children, by guiding their steps on perhaps the most important passage of life? There is, indeed, a question as to how this is to be done, though none about the blessing of being able to do it. Nor is there any about the misfortune that springs from children being left to find their own way across that chasm which exists between the inexperienced innocence of childhood, and the path of strong virtue which lies beyond. You know, as well as I do, the blessing it would be if that chasm could be bridged over. You know that inexperience often renders children liable to be deluded by the devil, and by the false charms of unknown and dangerous paths. I am convinced that we thoroughly sympathize on this subject.

4. This "Mirror of Faith" is not intended for young children. They could not be expected to read it spontaneously. My "Mirror" is intended for the young, it is true; but for the young who are old enough to wish to contemplate themselves in it, and, in doing so, to become daily nearer to perfection.

But cannot my elder friends—parents, guardians, sponsors, all who have the care of little ones—read, digest and improve for themselves upon this little sketch, which I have given rather as a suggestion than anything more? And can they not throw the result into easy oral lessons, which will not tire, but rather delight a young child?

It can but do him good to be told how the good God made him, and to be taught to thank Him for the gifts of life and powers. And as children pass through many stages, before they have to fight the real battle, they cannot be better armed than by a thorough knowledge of the position in which Baptism places them; and why should they not gradually learn to understand, and take pleasure in a work which is devoted to their own best interests?

Might not a class of literature spring up which should fill the gap between the mere tale and the dry lesson-book? Perhaps my notions on this point are exaggerated, owing to my strong love of children. Yet, you must admit the possibility of a course of literature too serious, perhaps, for young children to take up like story-books without a little pressure from their elders, yet possessing sufficient interest to make, at least, the older children cherish them as companions and friends, and not be inclined to cast them aside when once they have got hold of them. To you, then, dear friends, I recommend the "Mirror of Faith," as a suggestion, an attempt in this direction.

You know well, for the reasons I gave in the first chapter, that there is a new want at this moment, which may well set us all at work to supply it. Let us then, to use a common saying, take the bull by the horns, and enter the field in which the secularists and sectarians have already taken their stand.

5. And as to my first proposal, that we should become children as a means of learning to teach children, has not our Lord Himself told us that we must become children if we would enter the kingdom of heaven? These are His words: "Unless you become as little children, you shall not enter into the kingdom of heaven" (Matt. xviii. 2).

It will be well then, indeed, for you and me, my dear friends, if we learn in some things to be childlike. With what warmth and singleness of heart does not a child return the love which is lavished upon it! God alone knows what He has done for each of us. Will it not be well for us, then, to learn to love Him like children?

The "Mirror of Faith" might do no harm to any of us, reminding us, as it does, of God's loving dealings with us. While, therefore, you read it for the sake of children, may it do you good, by assisting you to become childlike yourselves!

6. And now for a word on my choice of a subject. Some may say, Why did you not write on this? Why not on that? Why did you not choose the Sacred Heart? Why not the rosary? Well, in the first place, many good things have already been written upon both these subjects. In the next, some years passed in the exercise of my priestly functions have forced upon me the conviction, that one of the wants of the age is self-respect, and that this could not be better taught than by dwelling upon Baptism.

Again, our state of transition after persecution, and our necessarily overworked priesthood, makes any effort to add to the number of books which contain solid Christian knowledge peculiarly desirable. Think not for a moment, that this course argues any want of sympathy with devotions. He who sees to the tilling of land, is quite as good a friend to agriculture, as he who sows the seed in it.

Our Baptism is the foundation of our Christian life; and you will agree with me in the opinion, that those who look at themselves in the " Mirror of Faith," will not be less, but rather more given to devotion, more fervent in it, and more devout in the reception of the holy Sacraments, than they would otherwise be. Thus, I have chosen this subject in the hope that it will promote every devotion.

7. If, as I believe, the subject of the proper up-bringing of children, is one in treating of which I can count upon the sympathies of all devout Christians, what shall I say to parents?

Blanche of Castile, the mother of St. Louis, in her heroic desire to see her son dead at her feet, rather than that he should commit a mortal sin, is a true type of the really Christian mother; and thank God she is not the exception to a rule, but rather the sample of a class not at all uncommon amongst God's children.

To every such mother, the problem I would solve, is one of deep interest. The spiritual welfare of her children is involved in the case.

Hide it not from yourselves, Christian mothers! The time has gone bye, in which the lack of literature, had at least this benefit, that it enabled you to screen your children effectually from the too early knowledge of the world's wickedness.

The decree has gone forth, that all must learn to read; a heap of literary trash, and worse than trash, is in the market.

We wish not to stay the times. We would only give wisdom to the young readers. It is useless to talk in platitudes of the fatal effects of Godless education. We must man the breach; we must make use of the very same weapons for God and His little ones, which the devil himself employs to attack and destroy them. If any of you have the literary mania, seize the pen, apply it to produce good reading for the young; and in the place of better weapons, till you have them, to you, fathers and mothers of God's children, to you I hand over the "Mirror of Faith."

THE END.

APPENDIX.

THE CEREMONIES OF HOLY BAPTISM,
ACCORDING TO THE ROMAN RITUAL.

The Priest, vested in surplice and purple stole, addresses the child as follows :—

SACERDOS. N., Quid petis ab Ecclesia Dei ?

PRIEST. N., What dost thou ask of the Church of God ?

SPONSOR. Fidem.

SPONSOR. Faith.

SAC. Fides quid tibi præstat ?

PRIEST. What doth faith bring thee to ?

SPON. Vitam æternam.

SPONSOR. Life everlasting.

SAC. Si igitur vis ad vitam ingredi, serva mandata. Diliges Dominum Deum tuum ex toto corde tuo, ex tota anima tua, et ex tota mente tua, et proximum tuum sicut teipsum.

PRIEST. If, then, thou desirest to enter into life, keep the commandments. Thou shalt love the Lord thy God, with thy whole heart, with thy whole soul, and with thy whole mind; and thy neighbour as thyself.

Here he breathes thrice upon the face of the child, and says once :—

Exi ab eo (vel ab ea), immunde spiritus, et da locum Spiritui Sancto Paraclito.

Go out of him (or her), thou unclean spirit, and give place unto the Holy Ghost, the Paraclete.

APPENDIX.

Here he makes the sign of the cross, with his thumb, on the forehead and on the breast of the child, saying:—

Accipe signum crucis tam in fronte ✠, quam, in corde ✠, sume fidem cœlestium præceptorum, et talis esto moribus, ut templum Dei jam esse possis.

Receive the sign of the cross both upon thy forehead ✠, and upon thy heart ✠; take unto thee the faith of the heavenly precepts, and in thy manners be such that thou mayest now be the temple of God.

OREMUS.

LET US PRAY.

Preces nostras quæsumus, Domine clementer exaudi, et hunc electum tuum (vel hanc electam tuam), N., Crucis Dominicæ impressione signatum, perpetua virtute custodi: ut magnitudinis gloriæ tuæ rudimenta servans, per custodiam mandatorum tuorum ad regenerationis gloriam pervenire mereatur. Per Christum Dominum nostrum.

R. Amen.

We beseech Thee, O Lord, mercifully hear our prayers; and by Thy continual guardianship keep this Thine elect, N., signed with the sign of the Lord's cross, that, preserving the rudiments of the greatness of Thy glory, he may deserve, by the keeping of Thy commands, to attain the glory of regeneration. Through Christ our Lord.

R. Amen.

Then he lays his hand on the child's head, and says:—

OREMUS.

LET US PRAY.

Omnipotens, sempiterne Deus, Pater Domini Nostri Jesu Christi, respicere dignare super hunc faumlum tuum, N.,

Almighty eternal God, Father of our Lord Jesus Christ, vouchsafe to look upon this Thy servant, N., whom Thou hast been

quem ad rudimenta fidei vocare dignatus es; omnem cæcitatem cordis ab eo expelle; disrumpe omnes laqueos Satanæ, quibus fuerat colligatus aperi ei, Domine januam pietatis tuæ ut signo sapientiæ tuæ imbutus, omnium cupiditatum fœtoribus careat, et ad suavem odorem præceptorum tuorum lætus tibi in Ecclesia tua deserviat, et proficiat de die in diem. Per eumdem Christum Dominum nostrum.

R. Amen.

pleased to call to the rudiments of the faith; expel from him all blindness of heart; break all the bonds of Satan wherewith he was tied; open unto him, O Lord, the gate of Thy bounty, that, being imbued with the seal of Thy wisdom, he may be free from all wicked desires; and by the sweet odour of thy precepts, may joyfully serve Thee in Thy Church, and go forward from day to day. Through the same Christ our Lord.

R. Amen.

Then the Priest blesses the salt, which, after it has been once blessed, may serve the same purpose again.

Oremus.

Exorcizo te, creatura salis, in nomini, Dei Patris ✠ Omnipotentis, et in charitate Domini nostri Jesu ✠ Christi, et in virtute Spiritus ✠ Sancti. Exorcizo te per Deum vivum ✠, per Deum verum ✠, per Deum sanctum ✠, per Deum ✠, qui te ad tutelam humani generis procreavit, et populo, venienti ad credulitatem

Let us Pray.

I exorcise thee, creature of salt, in the name of God the Father ✠ Almighty, and in the charity of our Lord Jesus ✠Christ, and in the power of the Holy ✠ Ghost. I exorcise thee by the living God ✠, by the true God ✠, by the holy God ✠, by God ✠ who hath created thee for the preservation of mankind, and hath appointed thee to be con-

per servos suos consecrari præcepit: ut in nomine Sanctæ Trinitatis efficiaris salutare Sacramentum ad effugandum inimicum. Proinde rogamus te, Domine, Deus noster, ut hanc creaturam salis sanctificando sanctifices ✠, et benedicendo benedicas ✠, ut sit omnibus accipientibus perfecta medicina, permanens in visceribus eorum, in nomine ejusdem Domini nostri Jesu Christi, qui venturus est judicare vivos et mortuos, et sæculum per ignem.	secrated by His servants for the people coming unto the faith, that, in the name of the Holy Trinity, thou mayest be made a salutary sacrament to drive away the enemy. Wherefore, we beseech Thee, O Lord our God, that sanctifying ✠ Thou mayest sanctify this creature of salt, and blessing ✠ Thou mayest bless it, that it may become unto all who receive it a perfect medicine, abiding in their bowels, in the name of the same our Lord Jesus Christ, who shall come to judge the living and the dead, and the world by fire.
R. Amen.	R. Amen.

Then he puts a small quantity of the salt into the mouth of the child, saying:—

N., Accipe sal sapientiæ; propitiatio sit tibi in vitam æternam.	N., Receive the salt of wisdom; let it be to thee a propitiation unto life everlasting.
R. Amen.	R. Amen.
Sacerdos. Pax tecum.	Priest. Peace be with thee
R. Et cum spiritu tuo.	R. And with thy spirit.

Oremus.

Deus patrum nostrorum, Deus universæ Conditor veritatis te supplices exoramus, ut hunc famulum tuum N, respicere digneris propitius, et hoc primum pabulum salis gustantem, non diutius, esurire permittas, quo minus cibo expleatur cœlesti, quatenus sit semper spiritu fervens, spe gaudens, tuo semper nomine serviens. Perduc eum, Domine, quæsumus, ad novæ regenerationis lavacrum ut cum fidelibus tuis promissionum tuarum æterna præmia consequi mereatur. Per Christum Dominum nostrum.

R. Amen.

Exorcizo te, immunde spiritus, in nomine Patris ✠, et Filii ✠, et Spiritus ✠ Sancti, ut exeas et recedas ab hoc famulo Dei, N. Ipse enim tibi imperat, maledicte, damnate, qui, pedibus super mare ambulavit, et Petro mergenti dexteram porrexit.

Let us Pray.

O God of our fathers, O God, the Author of all breath, we humbly beseech Thee, graciously vouchsafe to look upon this Thy servant, N., and, tasting this first nutriment of salt, suffer him no longer to hunger for want of being filled with heavenly meat, so that he may be always fervent in spirit, rejoicing in hope, always serving Thy name. Bring him, O Lord, we beseech Thee, to the laver of the new regeneration, that, with Thy faithful, he may deserve to attain the everlasting rewards of Thy promises. Through Christ our Lord.

R. Amen.

I exorcise thee, unclean spirit, in the name of the Father ✠, and of the Son ✠, and of the Holy ✠ Ghost, that thou go out and depart from this servant of God, N. For He commands thee, accursed one, who walked upon the sea, and stretched out His right hand to Peter when sinking.

Ergo, maledicte diabole, recognosce sententiam tuam, et da honorem Deo vivo et vero, da honorem Jesu Christo Filio ejus, et Spiritui Sancto, et recede ab hoc famulo Dei, N., quia istum sibi Deus, et Dominus noster Jesus Christus ad suam sanctam gratiam, et benedictionem, fontemque Baptismatis vocare dignatus est.

Therefore, accursed devil, acknowledge thy sentence, and give honour to the living and true God; give honour to Jesus Christ His Son, and to the Holy Ghost, and depart from this servant of God, N., because our God and Lord Jesus Christ hath vouchsafed to call him to His holy grace and benediction, and to the font of Baptism.

Here he makes the sign of the cross, with his thumb, on the child's forehead, saying:—

Et hoc signum sanctæ crucis ✠ quod nos fronti ejus damus, tu, maledicte diabole, nunquam audeas violare. Per eumdem Christum Dominum nostrum.
R. Amen.

And this sign of the holy cross ✠ which we make upon his forehead do thou, accursed devil, never dare to violate. Through the same Christ our Lord.
R. Amen.

Then he lays his hand on the child's head, and says:—

OREMUS.

Æternam, ac justissimam pietatem tuam deprecor, Domine Sancte, Pater Omnipotens, æternæ Deus, auctor luminis et veritatis, super hunc famulum tuum, N., ut digneris illum illumi-

LET US PRAY.

I beseech Thy eternal and most just goodness, O Holy Lord, Father Almighty, eternal God, Author of light and truth, in behalf of this Thy servant, N., that Thou wouldest vouchsafe to

nare lumine intelligentiæ tuæ; munda eum, et sanctifica; da ei scientiam veram, ut dignus gratia Baptismi tui effectus, teneat firmam spem, consilium rectum, doctrinam sanctam. Per Christum Dominum nostrum.

enlighten him with the light of Thy wisdom, cleanse him, and sanctify him, give unto him true knowledge, that, being made worthy of the grace of Thy Baptism, he may keep firm hope, right counsel, and holy doctrine. Through Christ our Lord.

R. Amen.

R. Amen.

After this, the Priest lays the end of his stole, upon the child, and admits him into the Church, saying:—

N., Ingredere in templum Dei, ut habeas partem cum Christo in vitam æternam.

N., enter into the temple of God, that thou mayest have part with Christ, unto life everlasting.

R. Amen.

R. Amen.

When they have entered the Church, the Priest, as he proceeds to the font, joins the sponsors in reciting, in a clear voice, first the Apostles' Creed, and then the Lord's Prayer. When these are concluded, still, outside the baptistery, he commences the second exorcism, saying:—

Exorcizo te, omnis spiritus immunde, in nomine Dei Patris omnipotentis ✠, et in nomine Jesu Christi, Filii ejus, ✠ Domini et judicis nostri, et in virtute Spiritus ✠ Sancti, ut discedas ab hoc plasmate Dei N., quod Dominus noster ad templum sanctum suum

I exorcise thee, every unclean spirit, in the name of God the Father ✠ Almighty, and in the name of Jesus Christ His Son ✠, our Lord and Judge, and in the power of the Holy ✠ Ghost, that thou depart from this creature of God, N., which our Lord hath

vocare dignatus est, ut fiat templum Dei vivi, et Spiritus Sanctus habitet in eo. Per eumdem Christum Dominum nostrum, qui venturus est judicare vivos et mortuos, et sæculum per ignem.

vouchsafed to call unto His holy temple, that it may be made the temple of the living God, and that the Holy Ghost may dwell therein. By the same Christ our Lord, who shall come to judge the living and the dead, and the world by fire.

R. Amen.

R. Amen.

After this, the Priest wets his right thumb with spittle, and makes with it the sign of the cross, first on the right ear, then on the left, saying:—

Ephpheta ✠, quod est ✠, adaperire:

Ephpheta ✠, that is to say ✠, be opened:

and, touching the nostrils, adds:—

in odorem suavitatis.

for a Saviour of sweetness.

Tu autem effugare, diabole; appropinquabit enim Judicium Dei.

But thou, Satan, begone, for the judgment of God is at hand.

Then he interrogates the child, by name, saying:—

N., Abrenuntias Satanæ?

N., Dost thou renounce Satan?

R. Abrenuntio.

R. I do renounce him.

Sacerdos. Et omnibus operibus ejus?

Priest. And all his works?

R. Abrenuntio.

R. I do renounce them.

Sacerdos. Et omnibus pompis ejus?

Priest. And all his pomps?

R. Abrenuntio.

R. I do renounce them.

Then the Priest dips his thumb in the oil of the Catechumens, and anoints the child on the breast, and between the shoulders, in the form of a cross, saying:—

Ego te linio oleo salutis, in Christo Jesu ✠ Domino nostro, ut habeas vitam æternam.

R. Amen.

I annoint thee ✠ with the oil of salvation, in Christ Jesus ✠ our Lord, that thou mayest have life everlasting.

R. Amen.

Then, having wiped his fingers with cotton wool, the Priest changes his purple stole for a white one. Then he addresses the child, by name, saying:—

N., Credis in Deum Patrem omnipotentem, Creatorem cœli et terræ?

R. Credo.

N., Dost thou believe in God the Father Almighty, Creator of heaven and earth?

R. I do believe.

Credis in Jesus Christum, Filium ejus unicum, Dominum nostrum, natum et passum?

R. Credo.

Dost thou believe in Jesus Christ, His only Son, our Lord, who was born into this world, and who suffered for us?

R. I do believe.

Credis in Spiritum Sanctum, sanctam Ecclesiam Catholicam, sanctorum communionem, remissionem peccatorum, carnis resurrectionem, et vitam æternam?

R. Credo.

Dost thou believe in the Holy Ghost, the Holy Catholic Church, the communion of Saints, the forgiveness of sins, the resurrection of the body, and life everlasting?

R. I do believe.

N., Vis baptizari?

R. Volo.

N., Wilt thou be baptized?

R. I will.

APPENDIX.

Then the godmother holding the child, and the godfather (if there be one) placing his hand on it, the Priest takes the baptismal water in a vessel or shell, and pours it thrice on the child's head, in the form of a cross; at the same time uttering, once only, the following words:—

N., Ego te baptizo in nomine ✠ Patris, et Filii ✠, et Spiritus ✠ Sancti.

N., I baptize thee in the name of the Father, ✠ and of the Son ✠, and of the Holy ✠ Ghost.

This done, the Priest dips his thumb in the holy chrism, and anoints the child, on the top of the head, in the form of a cross, saying :—

Deus omnipotens, Pater Domini nostri Jesu Christi, qui te regeneravit ex aqua et Spiritu Sancto, quique dedit tibi remissionem omnium peccatorum, ipse te ✠ liniat chrismate salutis in eodem Christo Jesu Domino nostro in vitam æternam.

God Almighty, the Father of our Lord Jesus Christ, who hath regenerated thee by water and the Holy Ghost, and who hath given unto thee remission of all thy sins, may He ✠ Himself anoint thee with the chrism of salvation, in the same Christ Jesus our Lord, unto eternal life.

R. Amen.

R. Amen.

Sacerdos. Pax tibi.

Priest. Peace be to thee.

R. Et cum spiritu tuo.

R. And with thy spirit.

Then he wipes his thumb on the cotton wool, and puts on the child, a white linen cloth, or a white garment, saying :—

N., Accipe vestem candidam, quam immaculatam perferas ante tribunal Domini nostri Jesu

N., Receive this white garment, and see thou carry it without stain before the judgment-seat

Christi, ut habeas vitam æternam.

R. Amen.

of our Lord Jesus Christ, that thou mayest have eternal life.

R. Amen.

Then he gives to the person holding the child, or to the godfather, a lighted candle, saying :—

N., Accipe lampadem ardentem, et irreprehensibilis custodi baptismum tuum : serva Dei mandata, ut cum Dominus venerit ad nuptias, possis occurrere ei una cum omnibus sanctis in aula cœlesti, habeasque vitam æternam et vivas in sæcula sæculorum.

R. Amen.

N., Receive this burning light, and keep thy Baptism so as to be without blame : keep the commandments of God, that when the Lord shall come to the nuptials, thou mayest meet Him in the company of all the Saints in the Heavenly Court, and have eternal life, and live for ever and ever.

R. Amen.

Lastly, he says :—

N., Vade in pace, et Dominus sit tecum.
R. Amen.

N., Go in peace, and the Lord be with thee.
R. Amen.

FINIS.

www.ingramcontent.com/pod-product-compliance
Lightning Source LLC
Chambersburg PA
CBHW030316240426
43673CB00040B/1182